DELICAT

Crochet

SHARON HERNES SILVERMAN

STACKPOLE
BOOKS

Guilford, Connecticut

Published by Stackpole Books
An imprint of The Rowman & Littlefield Publishing Group, Inc.
4501 Forbes Blvd., Ste. 200
Lanham, MD 20706
www.stackpolebooks.com

Distributed by NATIONAL BOOK NETWORK
800-462-6420

Supplemental crochet charts by Kj Hay and Karen Manthey
Photographs by Daniel Shanken (model photography) and Alan Wycheck
(technique photos)
Standard yarn weight system chart and skill level symbols used courtesy of
the Craft Yarn Council of America (CYCA), www.yarnstandards.com

We have made every effort to ensure the accuracy and completeness of
these instructions. We cannot, however, be responsible for human error,
typographical mistakes, or variations in individual work.

British Library Cataloguing in Publication Information available

Library of Congress Cataloging-in-Publication Data available

Names: Silverman, Sharon Hernes, author.
Title: Delicate crochet : 23 light and pretty designs for shawls, tops and
    more / Sharon Hernes Silverman.
Description: First edition. | Guilford, Connecticut : Stackpole Books, [2018]
    | Includes bibliographical references and index.
Identifiers: LCCN 2018040812 (print) | LCCN 2018041233 (ebook)
| ISBN 9780811719889 (paperback) | ISBN 9780811768191 (ebook)
Subjects: LCSH: Crocheting—Patterns.
Classification: LCC TT825 (ebook) | LCC TT825 .S54424 2018 (print) | DDC
    746.43/4—dc23
LC record available at https://lccn.loc.gov/2018040812

♾™ The paper used in this publication meets the minimum requirements
of American National Standard for Information Sciences—Permanence of
Paper for Printed Library Materials, ANSI/NISO Z39.48-1992.

Printed in the United States of America

Contents

Introduction

Welcome to *Delicate Crochet*! Twenty-three patterns from eleven top designers highlight crochet at its sumptuous, drapey best, using yarn no heavier than lightweight #3. Whether you're looking for a lacy, elegant style or something a bit more daring, the garments and accessories in this book provide a wide variety of projects to choose from.

Delicate Crochet is for people who are already comfortable with basic crochet stitches (chain, single crochet, double crochet). Review the instructions in the back of the book if you need a refresher. Skill levels from Easy through Experienced are represented in these pages—there really is something for every crocheter. And if you are ready to expand your skills, this book can help you do so. Instructions for special stitches or techniques are included with the patterns and are covered in the Techniques section. Step-by-step photographs supplement the text where appropriate. In addition, symbol charts and schematics are provided. These focus on specific parts of the patterns that benefit from visual representation, and are included to make the patterns easier to understand. See the Techniques section for instructions on how to read charts.

Several of the projects are done in Tunisian crochet. All of the Tunisian basics are explained in the back of the book. If you are new to Tunisian crochet and want more detailed instructions about the technique, you might find *Tunisian Crochet: The Look of Knitting with the Ease of Crocheting* (Stackpole Books, 2009) helpful.

Blocking your work can elevate it from "Okay" to "Oh, wow!" Instructions for blocking are in the Techniques section.

Take care to read the "Special Stitches" section of a pattern carefully before you start crocheting. A V-stitch can mean one thing to one designer, for example, and a different thing to another designer. It is important to understand the meaning in the context of your desired project.

Reference material, including a list of abbreviations, suggested books, supplier information for yarn and hooks, and crochet associations, appears at the end of the book. There is also a Visual Index in which you can see all of the projects at a glance.

Happy crocheting!

PROJECTS

Berrywine Wrap

Designed by Sharon Silverman

The yarn transitions gently from pale pink rosé to deep bordeaux in this lightweight wrap with just a hint of sparkle.

SKILL LEVEL

EASY

MEASUREMENTS

51 in. (129.5 cm) by 17 in. (43 cm)

MATERIALS

Fine

Nako Arya Ebruli Sim, distributed by Plymouth Yarn Co. Inc. (76% premium acrylic, 10% alpaca, 10% wool, 4% metallic polyester; 3.5 oz./100 g; 547 yd./500 m)
» Electric Pink (6401F): 1 skein
» U.S. size J-10 (6 mm) crochet hook
» Tapestry needle
» Blocking pins
» Blocking board or towel

GAUGE

13 sts and 7 rows in dc = 4 in. (10.2 cm), blocked.
For gauge swatch, ch 27. Last 3 chs count as first dc on Row 1.
Row 1: Dc in fourth ch from hook and in each ch across.
Row 2: Ch 3 (counts as dc), turn. Sk st at base of chs. Dc in each st across.
Rep Row 2 until swatch measures at least 4½ in. (11.4 cm).

SPECIAL STITCHES

Double crochet 4 together (dc4tog): [Yo, insert hook where indicated, yo, pull up lp, yo, pull through 2 lps] 4 times, yo, pull through all 5 lps.

PATTERN NOTES

» Wrap is worked from the top down.
» On Row 4, there are three groups of dc4tog all the way across. The first and third groups are worked over four stitches (the hook is inserted into a different stitch each time). The center group is worked into a ch-3 loop (the hook is inserted into that loop each time).
» To make the shawl narrower or wider, subtract or add a multiple of 12 from or to the beginning ch.

Pattern

Ch 170.

Row 1: Sc in second ch from hook. [Ch 5, sk 3 chs, sc in next ch] across.

Row 2: Ch 6, turn. Sc in ch-5 lp. [Ch 2, dc 7 in next ch-5 lp, ch 2, sc in next ch-5 lp, ch 5, sc in next ch-5 lp] across until 2 ch-5 lps remain. Ch 2, 7 dc in next ch-5 lp, ch 2, sc in next ch-5 lp, ch 2, tr in final sc.

Row 3: Ch 1, turn. Sc in tr. [Ch 2, dc in each of next 4 dc, ch 3, dc in same double as last dc made, dc in each of next 3 dc, ch 2, sc in ch-5 lp] across, working final sc into ch-6 lp from beg of previous row.

Row 4: Ch 5, turn. [Dc4tog over next 4 dc, ch 5, dc4tog into ch-3 lp, ch 5, dc4tog over next 4 dc, ch 1] across, omitting final ch-1. Tr in sc.

Row 5: Ch 1, turn. Sc in tr. [Ch 5, sc in ch-5 lp, ch 5, sc in ch-5 lp, ch 5, sc under ch-1] across, working last sc into ch-5 sp from beg of previous row.

Rows 6–29: Rep Rows 2–5 six times.

Rows 30–31: Rep Rows 2 and 3. Fasten off.

FINISHING

With tapestry needle, weave in ends. Steam block or wet block to size and shape.

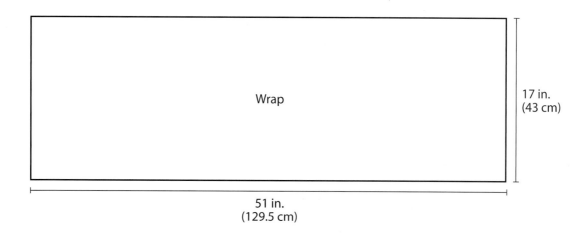

Wrap

17 in.
(43 cm)

51 in.
(129.5 cm)

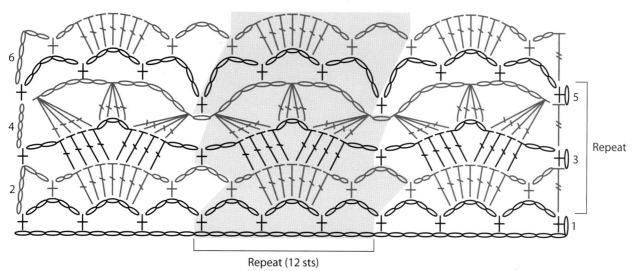

6

5

4   Repeat

3

2

1

Repeat (12 sts)

Reduced Sample of Pattern

Key

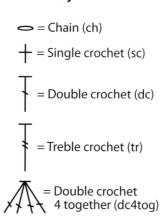

⬯ = Chain (ch)

+ = Single crochet (sc)

⊤ = Double crochet (dc)

⊤ = Treble crochet (tr)

⋀ = Double crochet
4 together (dc4tog)

Blox Shawl

Designed by Sharon Silverman

The shells and floating blocks in this lightweight shawl show off the subtle color variegations in this luscious cotton yarn.

SKILL LEVEL

INTERMEDIATE

MEASUREMENTS
16 in. (40.5 cm) by 78 in. (198 cm)

MATERIALS

2 Blue Heron Yarns Egyptian Mercerized Cotton
(100% cotton; 8 oz./227 g; 1000 yd./914 m)
Fine
» Strawberry: 1 skein

» U.S. size F-5 (3.75 mm) crochet hook
» Tapestry needle
» Blocking pins
» Blocking board or towel

GAUGE
16 sts and 10 rows in dc = 4 in. (10.2 cm), blocked.
For gauge swatch, ch 28. Last 3 chs count as first dc on Row 1.
Row 1: Dc in fourth ch from hook and in each ch across.
Row 2: Ch 3 (counts as dc), turn. Sk st at base of chs. Dc in
    each st across.
Rep Row 2 until swatch measures at least 4½ in. (11.4 cm).

PATTERN NOTE
» To make the shawl narrower or wider, subtract or add
    a multiple of 12 from or to the beginning ch.

How to Work Floating Blocks

1. Ch 6.

2. Sc in second ch from hook and in next 4 chs. Total 5 sc.

4. Anchor floating block to previous row with a sc in next sc, turn, sc in each sc across floating block (total 5 sc), (3 dc, ch1, 3 dc) into ch-sp in center of dc fan.

3. [Ch 1, turn, sc in each sc across floating block] twice.

Pattern

Ch 352. Last 3 chs count as first dc on Row 1.

Row 1: Work 2 dc into fourth ch from hook. *Ch 3, sk 5 sts, sc in next st, ch 3, sk 5 sts, (3 dc, ch 1, 3 dc) into next st. Repeat from * until 12 sts remain. Ch 3, sk 5 sts, sc in next st, ch 3, sk 5 sts, 3 dc into final st.

Row 2: Ch 3 (counts as dc), turn. Work 2 dc into st at base of chs. *Ch 3, sc in next sc, ch 3, (3 dc, ch 1, 3 dc) into ch-sp in center of dc fan. Repeat from * across until 1 sc remains. Ch 3, sc in next sc, ch 3, 3 dc into top of turning chs.

Row 3 (begin floating blocks): Ch 3 (counts as dc), turn. Work 2 dc into st at base of chs. *Ch 6, sc in second ch from hook and in next 4 chs (total 5 sc). [Ch 1, turn, sc in each sc across floating block (total 5 sc)] twice, anchor floating block to previous row with a sc in next sc, turn, sc in each sc across floating block (total 5 sc), (3 dc, ch 1, 3 dc) into ch-sp in center of dc fan. Repeat from * across until 1 sc remains. Ch 6, sc in second ch from hook and in next 4 chs (total 5 sc). [Ch 1, turn, sc in each sc across

floating block (total 5 sc)] twice, anchor floating block to previous row with a sc in next sc, turn, sc in each sc across floating block (total 5 sc), work 3 dc into top of turning ch.

Row 4: Ch 3 (counts as dc), turn. Work 2 dc into st at base of chs. *Ch 3, sc into top corner of floating block, ch 3, (3 dc, ch 1, 3 dc) into ch-sp in center of dc fan. Repeat from * across until 1 floating block remains. Ch 3, sc into top corner of floating block, ch 3, work 3 dc into top of turning ch.

Rows 5–28: Rep Rows 2–4 eight times.

Row 29: Rep Row 2. Fasten off.

FINISHING

With tapestry needle, weave in ends. Steam block or wet block to size and shape.

16 in.
(40.5 cm)

78 in.
(198 cm)

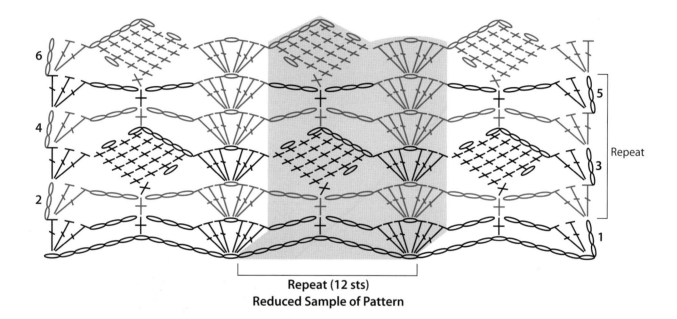

Repeat

Repeat (12 sts)
Reduced Sample of Pattern

Key

⬭ = Chain (ch)

✚ = Single crochet (sc)

⊤ = Double crochet (dc)

Cyndi Floral Lace Skirt

Designed by Vicky Chan

F eminine floral lace and contrasting lacy stripes bring eye-catching impact to this chic and stylish drawstring skirt with optional lining. The straight skirt is polished off with a slightly flared flounce.

SKILL LEVEL

INTERMEDIATE

MEASUREMENTS

	HIPS	LENGTH
X-Small	33¼ in. (85 cm)	17 in. (43 cm)
Small	35¾ in. (91 cm)	17 in. (43 cm)
Medium	38 in. (97 cm)	19 in. (48 cm)
Large	42¾ in. (109 cm)	19 in. (48 cm)
1X	47½ in. (121 cm)	21 in. (53 cm)
2X	52¼ in. (133 cm)	21 in. (53 cm)

Instructions are for size XS, with sizes S, M, L, 1X, and 2X in parentheses.

Choose size according to your hip measurements. For fitted pencil skirt style, allow up to 2 in. (5 cm) negative ease. For an A-line silhouette, allow 1 to 2 in. (2.5 to 5 cm) positive ease.

MATERIALS

Super Fine

Aunt Lydia's Fashion Crochet Thread Size 3 (100% mercerized cotton; 1.76 oz./50 g; 150 yd./137 m)
» Coffee (0365): 4 (4, 5, 6, 7, 8) balls

» U.S. size E-4 (3.5 mm) crochet hook and steel hook size 3 mm
» Tapestry needle
» Optional for lining: Lightweight knit fabric (58 in./148 cm wide), ¾ yd./0.7 m; sewing thread in matching color; fabric marker

GAUGE

21 fdc/dc and 11.5 rows with smaller hook = 4 in. (10.2 cm) blocked.
(Swatch is worked back and forth; skirt is worked in rounds.)
For gauge swatch, ch 4. Last 3 chs count as first fdc on Row 1.
Row 1: Fdc 29 (see Special Stitches below). Total 30 sts.
Row 2: Ch 3 (counts as dc here and throughout), turn. Sk st at base of chs. Dc in each st across, ending with final dc in top of turning ch. Total 30 dc.
Rep Row 2 until swatch measures at least 4½ in. (11.4 cm).

SPECIAL STITCHES

Double crochet 4 together (dc4tog): [Yo, insert hook in next st, yo, pull up lp, yo, pull through 2 lps] 4 times, yo, pull through all 5 lps.

2 double crochet cluster (2dcCL): [Yo, insert hook in same st, yo, pull up lp, yo, pull through 2 lps] twice, yo, pull through all 3 lps.

3 double crochet cluster (3dcCL): [Yo, insert hook in same st, yo, pull up lp, yo, pull through 2 lps] 3 times, yo, pull through all 4 lps.

4 double crochet cluster (4dcCL): [Yo, insert hook in same st, yo, pull up lp, yo, pull through 2 lps] 4 times, yo, pull through all 5 lps.

Foundation double crochet (fdc): Ch 4 (counts as fdc, with beg ch as foundation ch). Yo, insert hook under the 2 lps of fourth ch from hook, yo, pull up lp, ch 1 (this will be the entry point—the foundation ch—for the next st; pinch it with your thumb and finger to make it easier to find), [yo, pull through 2 lps] twice to finish the fdc; you now have a total of 2 fdc. *Yo, insert hook under the 2 lps of foundation ch just made, yo, pull up lp, ch 1 (the entry point for the next st), [yo, pull through 2 lps] twice. Rep from * until you reach the target number of fdc.

Half double crochet picot (hdc-picot): Ch 3, hdc in third ch from hook.

PATTERN NOTES

» Skirt is worked seamlessly in rounds top down from the waistband starting on Round 2. Do not turn when working in rounds; you are always working on the RS.

» Adjust the length by changing the number of floral bands before beginning the flounce.

» Rounds 9–12, 13–16, 21–24, and 25–28 each make a floral band.

Pattern

WAISTBAND

With smaller hook, leaving 8-in. (20 cm) yarn tail for sewing, ch 4. Last 3 chs count as first fdc on Row 1.

Row 1 (WS): Fdc 143 (151, 167, 183, 207, 223). Total 144 (152, 168, 184, 208, 224) sts.

Rnd 2 (RS): Ch 1 (does not count as a st here and throughout), turn. Sc in each fdc, ending with sc in top of final ch-3. Sl st in beg sc to join at center back, being careful not to twist round.

Rnd 3: Ch 3 (counts as dc here and throughout), sk sc at base of chs, dc in next sc. *Ch 1, sk next sc, dc in each of next 3 sc. Rep from * around until 2 sts remain. Ch 1, sk next sc, dc in final sc. Sl st in top of beg ch-3 to join. Total 36 (38, 42, 46, 52, 56) groups of 3 dc separated by ch-1. (The beg ch-3, first dc, and last dc of the round count as a 3-dc group.)

Rnd 4: Ch 1, sc in same st, sc in next dc. *Sc in next ch-1 sp, sc in each of next 3 dc. Rep from * around until 2 sts remain. Sc in next ch-1 sp, sc in final dc. Sl st in beg sc to join.

Rnd 5: Ch 3, sk sc at base of chs, dc in each sc around. Sl st in top of beg ch-3 to join.

Rnd 6 (inc): Ch 1, sc in same st, sc in each of next 4 (3, 5, 8, 5, 6) dc. *2 sc in each of next 2 dc, sc in each of next 10 (9, 12, 9, 11, 9) dc. Rep from * 10 (12, 10, 14, 14, 18) times until 7 (5, 8, 10, 7, 8) sts remain. 2 sc in each of next 2 dc, sc in each of next 5 (3, 6, 8, 5, 6) dc. Sl st in beg sc to join. Total 24 (28, 24, 32, 32, 40) inc, yielding total of 168 (180, 192, 216, 240, 264) sc to accommodate 14 (15, 16, 18, 20, 22) floral reps.

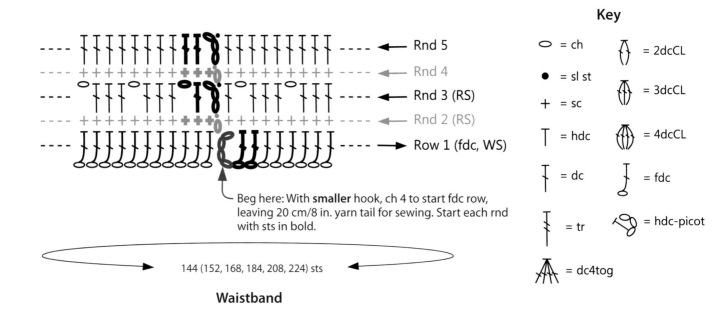

← Rnd 5
← Rnd 4
← Rnd 3 (RS)
← Rnd 2 (RS)
→ Row 1 (fdc, WS)

Key

○ = ch

● = sl st

+ = sc

T = hdc

† = dc

‡ = tr

⋔ = dc4tog

⫫ = 2dcCL

⫸ = 3dcCL

⫸ = 4dcCL

Ɉ = fdc

= hdc-picot

Beg here: With **smaller** hook, ch 4 to start fdc row, leaving 20 cm/8 in. yarn tail for sewing. Start each rnd with sts in bold.

144 (152, 168, 184, 208, 224) sts

Waistband

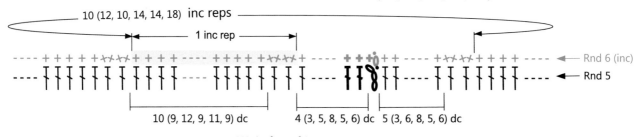

total of 168 (180, 192, 216, 240, 264) sc after inc

10 (12, 10, 14, 14, 18) inc reps

1 inc rep

← Rnd 6 (inc)
← Rnd 5

10 (9, 12, 9, 11, 9) dc   4 (3, 5, 8, 5, 6) dc   5 (3, 6, 8, 5, 6) dc

Waistband Increase

BODY OF SKIRT

Switch to larger hook.

Rnd 7: Ch 3, 2 dc in same st, ch 1. *Sk next 3 sc, 3 dc in next sc, ch 1. Rep from * around. Sl st in top of beg ch-3 to join. Total 42 (45, 48, 54, 60, 66) groups of 3 dc separated by ch-1.

Rnd 8: Sl st in next dc. Ch 4 (counts as dc, ch-1 here and throughout), *2dcCL in next ch-1 sp, ch 1**, sk next dc, dc in next dc, ch 1. Rep from * around, ending last rep at **. Sl st in third ch of beg ch-4 to join.

Rnd 9: Ch 1, sc in same st. *Ch 5, sk next 2dcCL, sc in next dc. Rep from * around until one 2dcCL remains. Ch 2, dc in beg sc to join, forming sp (counts as ch-5 sp here and throughout). Total 42 (45, 48, 54, 60, 66) ch-5 sps.

Rnd 10: Ch 3, 3 dc in sp just made. *Ch 2, sc in next ch-5 sp, ch 5, sc in next ch-5 sp, ch 2**, 7 dc in next ch-5 sp. Rep from * around, ending last rep at **. 3 dc in same sp as beg. Sl st in top of beg ch-3 to join. Total 14 (15, 16, 18, 20, 22) floral reps established.

Rnd 11: Ch 6 (counts as dc, ch-3), dc in same st, dc in each of next 3 dc. *Ch 2, sc in next ch-5 sp, ch 2, dc in each of next 3 dc**, [dc, ch 3, dc] in next dc, dc in each of next 3 dc. Rep from * around, ending last rep at **. Sl st in third ch of beg ch-6 to join.

Rnd 12: Sl st in next ch of same ch-6. Ch 2, 3dcCL in sp of same ch-6. *Ch 5, dc4tog over next 4 dc, ch 2**, dc4tog over next 4 dc, ch 5, 4dcCL in next ch-3 sp. Rep from * around, ending last rep at **. Dc4tog over next 3 dc and top of third ch of same ch-6 as beg. Ch 2, dc in first 3dcCL to join, forming sp.

Rnd 13: Ch 1, sc in sp just made, ch 5, sc in next 3dcCL. *[Ch 5, sc in next ch-5 sp] twice, ch 5, sc in next 4dcCL. Rep from * around until 2 dc4tog remain. Ch 5, sc in next ch-5 sp, ch 2, dc in beg sc to join.

Rnds 14–16: Rep Rnds 10–12.

Rnd 17: Ch 1, sc in sp just made. *Ch 3, sc in next ch-5 sp, ch 3, dc in next ch-2 sp, ch 3**, sc in next ch-5 sp. Rep from * around, ending last rep at **. Sl st in beg sc of this rnd to join.

Rnd 18: Sl st in next 2 chs. Ch 4, *dc in next sc, ch 1, dc in next ch-3 sp, ch 1, dc in next dc, ch 1, dc in next ch-3 sp, ch 1, dc in next sc, ch 1**, dc in next ch-3 sp, ch 1. Rep from * around, ending last rep at **. Sl st in third ch of beg ch-4 of this rnd to join. Total 84 (90, 96, 108, 120, 132) ch-1 sps.

Rnd 19: Sl st in next ch of same ch-4, sl st in next dc. Ch 3, 2 dc in same st, ch 1. *Sk next dc, 3 dc in next dc, ch 1. Rep from * around. Sl st in top of beg ch-3 of this rnd to join. Total 42 (45, 48, 54, 60, 66) groups of 3 dc separated by ch-1.

Rnds 20–25: Rep Rnds 8–13.

Rnds 26–28: Rep Rnds 10–12.

Rep [Rnd 13 then Rnds 10–12] for 0 (0, 1, 1, 2, 2) times, or as many times as desired. Each additional 4-row rep will lengthen skirt by 2 in. (5 cm).

Rep Rnds 17–19 then Rnds 8–9. Do not fasten off.

FLOUNCE

Rnd 1: Ch 3, 3 dc in sp just made. *Ch 3, sc in next ch-5 sp, ch 5, sc in next ch-5 sp, ch 3**, 7 dc in next ch-5 sp. Rep from * around, ending last rep at **. 3 dc in same sp as beg. Sl st in top of beg ch-3 of this rnd to join.

Rnd 2: Ch 7 (counts as dc, ch-4), dc in same st, dc in each of next 3 dc. *Ch 3, sc in next ch-5 sp, ch 3, dc in each of next 3 dc**, (dc, ch 4, dc) in next dc, dc in each of next 3 dc. Rep from * around, ending last rep at **. Sl st in third ch of beg ch-7 of this rnd to join.

Rnd 3: Sl st in next ch of same ch-7. Ch 2, 3dcCL in sp of same ch-7 (counts as 4dcCL). *Ch 6, dc4tog over next 4 dc, ch

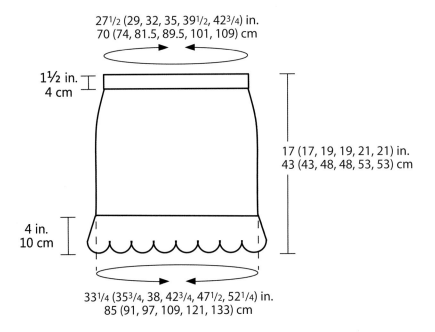

27½ (29, 32, 35, 39½, 42¾) in.
70 (74, 81.5, 89.5, 101, 109) cm

1½ in.
4 cm

17 (17, 19, 19, 21, 21) in.
43 (43, 48, 48, 53, 53) cm

4 in.
10 cm

33¼ (35¾, 38, 42¾, 47½, 52¼) in.
85 (91, 97, 109, 121, 133) cm

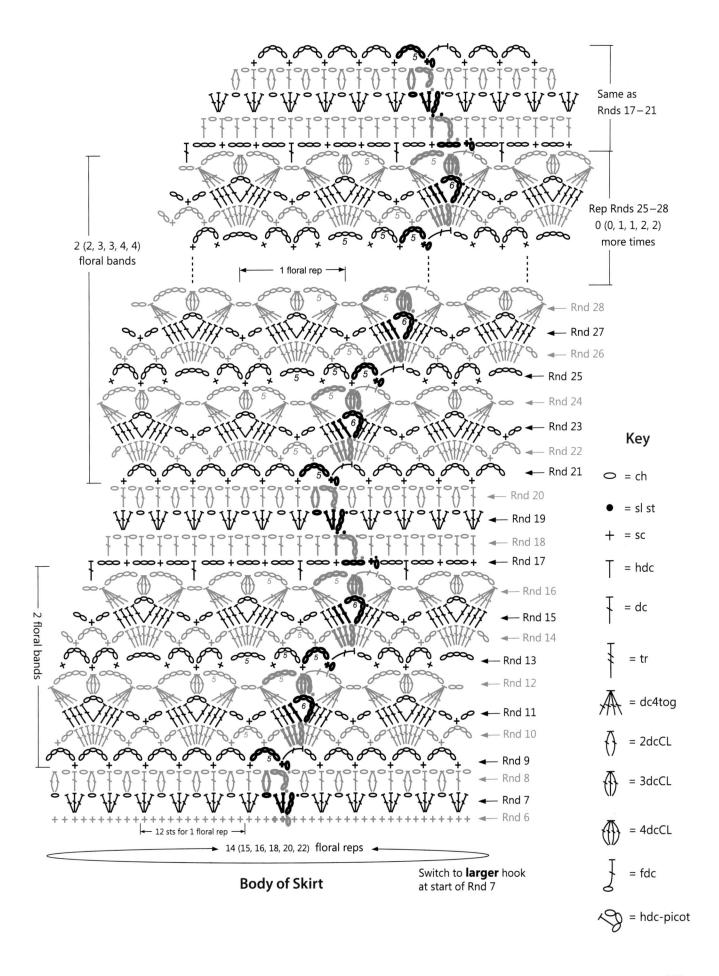

Same as
Rnds 17–21

2 (2, 3, 3, 4, 4)
floral bands

Rep Rnds 25–28
0 (0, 1, 1, 2, 2)
more times

1 floral rep

← Rnd 28
← Rnd 27
← Rnd 26
← Rnd 25
← Rnd 24
← Rnd 23
← Rnd 22
← Rnd 21
← Rnd 20
← Rnd 19
← Rnd 18
← Rnd 17
← Rnd 16
← Rnd 15
← Rnd 14
← Rnd 13
← Rnd 12
← Rnd 11
← Rnd 10
← Rnd 9
← Rnd 8
← Rnd 7
← Rnd 6

2 floral bands

12 sts for 1 floral rep

14 (15, 16, 18, 20, 22) floral reps

Body of Skirt

Switch to **larger** hook
at start of Rnd 7

Key

◯ = ch

● = sl st

+ = sc

⊤ = hdc

† = dc

‡ = tr

⋔ = dc4tog

⬦ = 2dcCL

⬦ = 3dcCL

⬦ = 4dcCL

⌡ = fdc

⟲ = hdc-picot

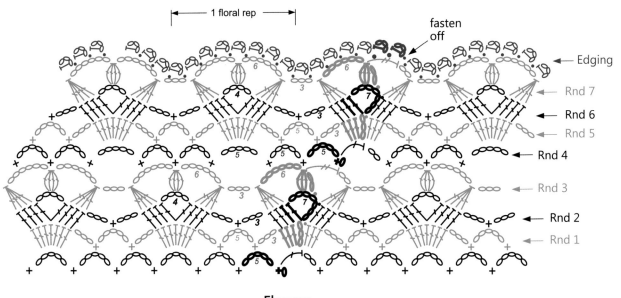

14 (15, 16, 18, 20, 22) floral reps

1 floral rep

fasten off

Edging
Rnd 7
Rnd 6
Rnd 5
Rnd 4
Rnd 3
Rnd 2
Rnd 1

Flounce

Key

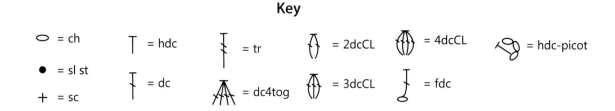

◯ = ch

● = sl st

+ = sc

⊤ = hdc

⊤ = dc

⧸ = tr

⋀ = dc4tog

⬙ = 2dcCL

⬙ = 3dcCL

⬙ = 4dcCL

⬙ = fdc

⬗ = hdc-picot

3**, dc4tog over next 4 dc, ch 6, 4dcCL in next ch-4 sp. Rep from * around, ending last rep at **. Dc4tog over next 3 dc and top of third ch of same ch-7 as beg. Ch 2, tr in first 3dcCL to join, forming sp.

Rnd 4: Ch 1, sc in sp just made, ch 5, sc in next 3dcCL. *[Ch 5, sc in next ch-6 sp] twice, ch 5, sc in next 4dcCL. Rep from * around until 2 dc4tog remain. Ch 5, sc in next ch-6 sp, ch 2, dc in beg sc to join.

Rnds 5–7: Rep Rnds 1–3.

Edging: [Hdc-picot, sl st] twice in first sp. *[Hdc-picot, sl st] 3 times in next ch-6 sp, [hdc-picot, sl st] twice in next ch-3 sp**, [hdc-picot, sl st] 3 times in next ch-6 sp. Rep from * around, ending last rep at **. Hdc-picot, sl st in same sp as beg. Sl st in first ch of beg hdc-picot to join. Fasten off.

FINISHING

Using a tapestry needle and yarn tail, sew ends of waistband Row 1 together. Weave in all ends. Steam block or wet block to finished measurements.

DRAWSTRING

With larger hook and 2 strands of yarn held together, ch until length equals your waist measurement plus extra 30 in. (76 cm) or desired length. Sl st in second ch from hook and in each ch to end. Fasten off. Weave in ends. Thread drawstring through ch-1 sps of waistband Round 3, beginning and ending at either side of center front.

Lining (Optional)

Wash to preshrink lining fabric as necessary.

Fold fabric in half widthwise with RS together. Place skirt on top of fabric. Trace around skirt with fabric marker, marking hemline at top of flounce or to desired length above hem of skirt. Add ⅜ in. (1 cm) of allowance all around. Add ¾ in. (2 cm) extra for hem. Cut through both layers of fabric along allowance edges.

With RS together, machine-stitch lining together along side seams. Trim side seam allowance to ¼ in. (0.7 cm). Sew trimmed edges together with zigzag stitch. Turn under waist edge ½ in. (1.5 cm) to RS and zigzag stitch in place. Turn up hem ⅜ in. (1 cm) to WS. Turn up additional ¾ in. (2 cm) and stitch in place.

With RS of lining facing WS of skirt, position the lining just below the waistband so it encases the drawstring but does not stick up above the waistband. Whipstitch in place by hand.

Damask Rose Wrap

Designed by Katya Novikova

The ornamental border with stitch symbols appears at the top of the page.

Thіs triangular wrap is worked in a delicate flower stitch from the top down. And just like the warm sun makes rosebuds burst into bloom, a good blocking will open up the lace pattern.

SKILL LEVEL

INTERMEDIATE

MEASUREMENTS

71 in. (180 cm) by 27 in. (68 cm)

MATERIALS

Lace

Malabrigo Silkpaca (70% alpaca, 30% silk; 1.76 oz./50 g; 420 yd./384 m)
 » Damask (130): 2 skeins

 » U.S. size C-2 (2.75 mm) crochet hook
 » Stitch marker
 » Tapestry needle
 » Blocking pins
 » Blocking board or towel

GAUGE

23 sts and 12.5 rows in dc = 4 in. (10.2 cm), unblocked.
For gauge swatch, ch 25. Last 3 chs count as first dc on Row 1.
Row 1: Dc into fourth ch from hook and in each ch across.
 Total 23 dc.
Row 2: Ch 3 (counts as dc), turn. Sk st at base of chs. Dc in
 each st across, ending with final dc in top of turning ch.
 Total 23 dc.
Rep Row 2 until swatch measures at least 4½ in. (11.4 cm).

SPECIAL STITCHES

V-stitch (V-st): (Dc, ch 3, dc) in same stitch.
Shell: 8 dc in ch-sp.
Cluster (CL): Ch 3, [yo, insert hook in the dc just made, yo, pull
 up lp, yo, pull through 2 lps] twice, yo, pull through all 3 lps.
Flower: 2 dc in each of the next 2 sts, dc in next st, ch 2, sk 2
 sts, dc in next st, 2 dc in each of the next 2 sts.
Picot: Ch 4, sl st in first ch made.

PATTERN NOTE

 » Ch-3 and tr counts as V-st. Ch-7 and dc in the corners
 counts as V-st.

Pattern

Row 1 (RS): Ch 4. Work 7 dc in fourth ch from hook. Total 1 shell.

Row 2: Ch 3 (counts as dc here and throughout), turn. Dc in same dc (at base of chs), 2 dc in next dc, dc in next dc, ch 2, sk 2 dc, dc in next dc, 2 dc in each of next 2 dc. Total 1 flower.

NOTE: *Place marker in center ch-2 sp to mark center of flower. Move it up to the corresponding st on subsequent rows. On rows with a central shell, place the marker between the fourth and fifth sts of the shell. On other rows, place marker in central ch-2 or ch-3 sp.*

Row 3: Ch 7 (with next dc, counts as V-st here and throughout), turn. Dc in first dc, CL, sk 3 dc, [dc, ch 2, dc, ch 2, dc] in next dc, CL, V-st in marked sp, MM to center of V-st, CL, [dc, ch 2, dc, ch 2, dc] in next dc, CL, sk 3 dc, [dc, ch 3, tr] in last dc. Total 3 V-sts.

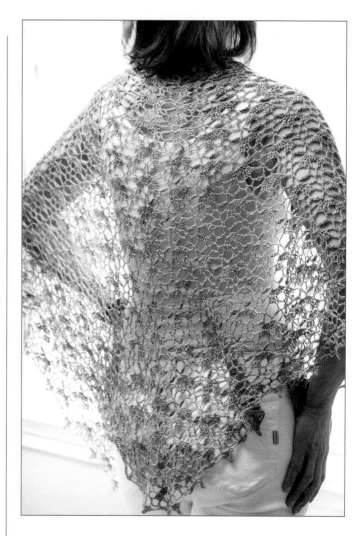

NOTE: *Be sure to work the CL into the dc just made, not into stitches from the previous row. The CL starts with ch-3. See photo at bottom left.*

Row 4: Ch 3, turn. 7 dc in ch-sp, ch 2, [dc in next ch-2 sp, ch 2] twice, shell in marked sp, MM to between fourth and fifth dc of shell, ch 2, [dc in next ch-2 sp, ch 2] twice, 7 dc in last ch-sp, dc in fourth ch of beginning ch 7. Total 3 shells.

Row 5: Ch 3, turn. Dc in same dc, 2 dc in next dc, dc in next dc, ch 2, sk 2 dc, dc in next dc, 2 dc in each of next 2 dc. *Ch 2, sk ch-2 sp, dc in next ch-2 sp, ch 2, sk ch-2 sp, 2 dc in each of next 2 dc, dc in next dc, ch 2, MM, sk 2 dc, dc in next dc, 2 dc in each of next 2 dc. Rep from * across (Note: No marker moved in repeat). Total 3 flowers.

Row 6: Ch 7, turn. Dc in first dc, CL, sk 2 dc, dc in next dc, ch 2, dc in ch-2 sp, ch 2, sk dc, dc in next dc, CL, sk ch-2 sp, V-st in next dc, CL, sk 3 dc, [dc, ch 2, dc, ch 2, dc] in next dc, CL, V-st in marked sp, MM, CL, sk dc, [dc, ch 2, dc, ch 2, dc] in next dc, CL, sk ch-2 sp, V-st in next dc, CL, sk 3 dc, dc in next dc, ch 2, dc in ch-2 sp, ch 2, sk dc, dc in next dc, CL, [dc, ch 3, tr] in last dc. Total 5 V-sts.

71 in.
(180 cm)

27 in.
(68 cm)

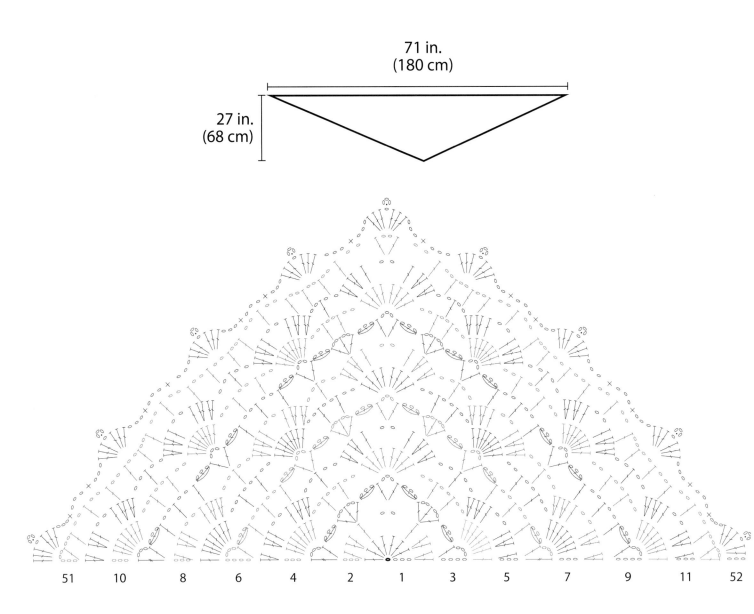

51   10   8   6   4   2   1   3   5   7   9   11   52

Repeat Rows 9–11 thirteen
times, then continue edging
with Row 51.

Key

O = ch

✕ = sc

⊦ = dc

= CL

= V-stitch

= shell

= picot

NOTE: *Continue to move marker to center of each row as you go.*

Row 7: Ch 3, turn. 7 dc in V-st. *Ch 2, dc in ch-2 sp, ch 2, dc in next ch-2 sp, ch 2, shell in next V-st. Rep from * twice. Ch 2, dc in ch-2 sp, ch 2, dc in next ch-2 sp, ch 2, 7 dc in last V-st, dc in fourth ch of beginning ch-7. Total 5 shells.

Row 8: Ch 3, turn. Dc in same dc, 2 dc in next dc, dc in next dc, ch 2, sk 2 dc, dc in next dc, 2 dc in each of next 2 dc. *Ch 2, sk ch-2 sp, dc in next ch-2 sp, ch 2, 2 dc in each of next 2 dc, dc in next dc, ch 2, sk 2 dc, dc in next dc, 2 dc in each of next 2 dc. Rep from * across. Total 5 flowers.

Row 9: Ch 7, turn. Dc in first dc, CL, sk 2 dc. *Dc in next dc, ch 2, dc in ch-2 sp, ch 2, sk dc, dc in next dc, CL, sk 3 dc, V-st in next dc, CL, sk 3 dc. Rep from * to the central flower.

NOTE: *After the sk 3 dc from instruction just completed, you will have 2 dc before center of garment. Work the next part of the instructions in the second dc from the center.*

[Dc, ch 2, dc, ch 2, dc] in next dc, CL, V-st in marked sp, CL, sk dc, [dc, ch 2, dc, ch 2, dc] in next dc, **CL, sk ch-2 sp, V-st in next dc, CL, sk 3 dc, dc in next dc, ch 2, dc in ch-2 sp, ch 2, sk dc, dc in next dc. Rep from ** until 3 dc remain. CL, sk 2 dc, [dc, ch 3, tr] in last dc. Total 7 V-sts.

Row 10: Ch 3, turn. 7 dc in ch-2 sp. *Ch 2, dc in ch-2 sp, ch 2, dc in next ch-2 sp, ch 2, shell in next V-st. Rep from * across, working final dc of shell into the fourth ch of beg ch-7. Total 7 shells.

Row 11: Ch 3, turn. Dc in same dc, 2 dc in next dc, dc in next dc, ch 2, sk 2 dc, dc in next dc, 2 dc in each of next 2 dc. *Ch 2, sk ch-2 sp, dc in next ch-2 sp, ch 2, sk dc, 2 dc in each of next 2 dc, dc in next dc, ch 2, sk 2 dc, dc in next dc, 2 dc in each of next 2 dc. Rep from * across. Total 7 flowers.

Rows 12–50: Rep Rows 9–11 thirteen times. Do not fasten off. There will be 17 flower rows total, with 33 flowers on Row 50.

Row 51 (begin edging): Ch 5 (counts as dc + ch 2), turn. Dc in same dc, ch 2, sk dc. *Dc in next dc, ch 2, dc in ch-2 sp, ch 2, sk 2 dc, dc in next dc, [ch 2, dc in next ch-2 sp] twice, ch 2, sk 2 dc. Rep from * to central flower. Dc in next dc, ch 2, sk 2 dc, [dc, ch 2, dc] in marked sp. **Ch 2, sk 2 dc, dc in next dc, [ch 2, dc in next ch-2 sp] twice, ch 2, sk 2 dc, dc in next dc, ch 2, dc in ch-sp. Rep from ** until 5 dc remain. Ch 2, sk 2 dc, dc in next dc, ch 2, sk dc, (dc, ch 2, dc) in final st. Total 168 dc.

Row 52: Ch 3, turn. 2 dc in ch-2 sp, picot, 3 dc in same ch-2 sp. *Ch 3, sk ch-2 sp, sc in next ch-2 sp, ch 3, sc in next ch-2 sp, ch 3, sk ch-2 sp, 3 dc in next ch-2 sp, picot, 3 dc in same ch-2 sp. Rep from * until 2 ch-2 sps remain before marker. Ch 3, sk ch-2 sp, sc in next ch-2 sp, ch 3, 3 dc in

next ch-2 sp, picot, 3 dc in same ch-2 sp, ch 3. **Sc in next ch-2 sp, ch 3, sk ch-2 sp, 3 dc in next ch-2 sp, picot, 3 dc in same ch-2 sp, ch 3, sk ch-2 sp, sc in next ch-2 sp, ch 3. Rep from ** until 3 ch-2 sps remain, sc in next ch-2 sp, ch 3, sk ch-2 sp, 3 dc in next ch-2 sp, picot, 2 dc in same ch-2 sp, dc in third ch of beginning ch 5. Total 35 picots. Fasten off.

FINISHING

Using tapestry needle, weave in ends.

Wet block the garment, pinning it gently to the correct size without overstretching. Pin the picots in place to show them off to their best advantage. Let the wrap dry completely before unpinning it from the board or towel.

Diamond Dreams Scarf

Designed by Judith Butterworth

*F*ashioned in a light and lovely merino wool, this deceptively easy scarf will have people thinking you're a crochet wizard! Diamond Dreams adds a feminine touch to anything in your wardrobe.

SKILL LEVEL

EASY

MEASUREMENTS

Before blocking: 9 in. (23 cm) by 56 in. (142 cm)
After blocking: 14 in. (36 cm) by 70 in. (178 cm)

MATERIALS

Lace

Debbie Bliss Rialto Lace (100% merino wool; 1.76 oz./50 g; 426 yd./390 m)
» Coral (26): 1 ball

» U.S. size G-6 (4 mm) crochet hook
» Stitch markers (3)
» Tapestry needle
» Blocking pins
» Blocking board or towel

GAUGE

5 pattern repeats and 11 rows = 4 in. (10.2 cm), unblocked.
(Each repeat is counted from the center of one LV-st to the center of the next LV-st).
For gauge swatch, ch 32. Work in pattern through Row 14.

SPECIAL STITCHES

Large V-Stitch (LV-st): (Tr, ch 5, tr) in same st
V-stitch (V-st): (Dc, ch 3, dc) in same st

PATTERN NOTES

» Practice working with the laceweight yarn until your stitches have an even tension. Be careful not to pull your stitches too tight.
» Each row is worked the short way (shoulder-to-hem). The borders are worked along both short sides.
» To make the size of the shawl down your back from neck to hem smaller or larger, subtract or add a multiple of 6 from the beginning ch. To make the wingspan

of your project smaller or larger, add or subtract a multiple of 2 rows.
» When instructions say to work "in LV-st," work under the ch-5 between the 2 trs of the LV-st. When instructions say to work "in V-st," work under the ch-3 between the 2 dcs of the V-st.

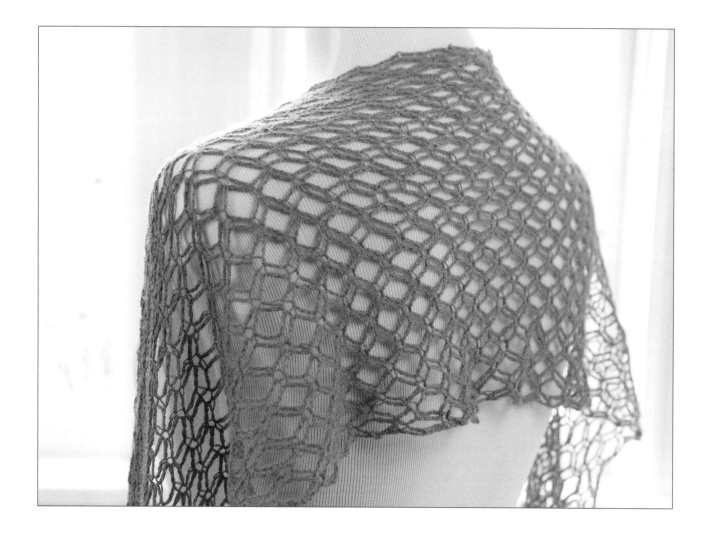

Pattern

Ch 68. Place marker in last ch made to identify the placement for the final st on Row 2.

Row 1 (WS): Tr in fifth ch from hook, ch 5, tr in same ch, sk 2 chs. *Sc in next ch, sk 2 chs, LV-st in next ch, sk 2 chs. Rep from * until 3 chs remain. Tr in last ch. Total 11 LV-sts.

Row 2 (RS): Ch 4, turn. Place marker under ch-4 lp to identify the placement for the final st on Row 3. Sc in LV-st. *LV-st in sc, sc in LV-st. Rep from * across. Tr in marked ch. Total 10 LV-sts. Place marker somewhere in the middle of the row to indicate the RS.

Row 3: Ch 4, turn. Move marker to under ch-4 lp to identify the placement for the final st on Row 4. LV-st in sc. *Sc in LV-st, LV-st in sc. Rep from * across. Tr in marked ch-lp. Total 11 LV-sts.

NOTE: *Move marker to under the beg ch-4 on each row. Work the final st on the following row into the marked ch-4 sp.*

Rows 4–117: Repeat Rows 2 and 3 fifty-seven times. Do not fasten off.

FIRST BORDER

Row 1 (RS): Ch 1, turn. Sc in tr, *ch 5, sc in LV-st. Rep from * across through last LV-st. Ch 3, dc in ch-lp. Total 11 ch-5 lps and 1 ch-3 lp.

Row 2: Ch 1, turn. Sc in ch-3 lp. *Ch 5, sc in ch-5 lp. Rep from * across. Total 11 ch-5 lps.

Row 3: Ch 7, turn. Sc in ch-5 lp. *Ch 7, sc in ch 5-lp. Rep from * across. Total 11 ch-7 lps.

Row 4: Ch 7, turn. V-st in ch-7 lp, ch 3. *Dc in sc, ch 3, V-st in ch-7 lp, ch 3. Rep from * across. Dc under turning chs. Total 11 V-sts.

Row 5: Ch 7, turn. V-st in V-st, ch 7. *Sc in dc, ch 7, V-st in V-st, ch 7. Rep from * across. Sc under turning chs. Fasten off.

SECOND BORDER

Row 1: With RS facing, join yarn with sc in tr at end of Row 1 from the shawl body. *Ch 5, sc in the same ch where the trs of the LV-st were worked on Row 1 of the shawl body. Rep from * across through last LV-st. Ch 3, dc in first ch of foundation. Total 11 ch-5 lps and 1 ch-3 lp.

Rows 2–5: Repeat Rows 2–5 of First Border. Fasten off.

FINISHING

With tapestry needle, weave in ends.

Wet block the garment, pinning it gently to the correct size without overstretching. Pin the loops on the borders in place to show them off to their best advantage. Let the scarf dry completely before unpinning it from the board or towel.

14 in.
(36 cm)

70 in.
(178 cm)

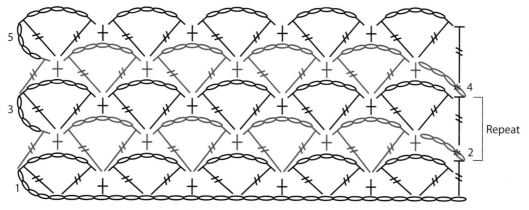

Reduced Sample of Pattern

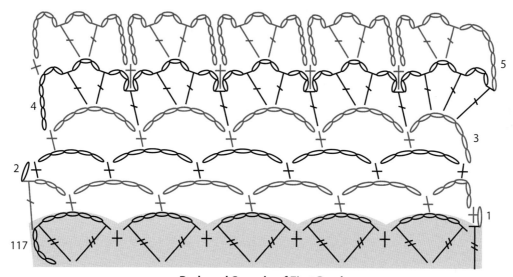

Reduced Sample of First Border

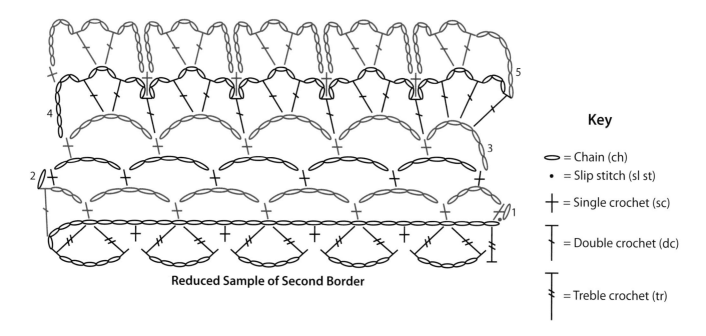

Reduced Sample of Second Border

Key

◯ = Chain (ch)

• = Slip stitch (sl st)

+ = Single crochet (sc)

┬ = Double crochet (dc)

┬ = Treble crochet (tr)

Elegant Trios Beaded Necklace

Designed by Amy Solovay

This elegant necklace makes a unique fashion statement for dressy occasions, yet is comfortable enough for everyday wear. Organic cotton yarn and gold-plated beads combine in a project with lasting value and visual appeal.

SKILL LEVEL

INTERMEDIATE

MEASUREMENTS

14¼ in. (36.2 cm) long plus toggle; 1-in. (2.5 cm) drop

MATERIALS

Super Fine

Plymouth Bio Sesia (100% organic cotton; 1.76 oz./50 g; 198 yd./180 m)
» Lemon (0099): 1 ball

- » U.S. size C-2 (2.5 mm) crochet hook
- » Cousin Corporation of America 3 mm round Gold Elegance beads (14 karat gold plated; 3 packages/76 beads)
- » Cousin Corporation of America Gold Elegance round toggle closure (14 karat gold plated)
- » Big-eye beading needle
- » Tapestry needle with a small enough eye to fit through toggle attachments

GAUGE

24 sts and 8 rows in tr = 4 in. (10.2 cm), blocked.
For gauge swatch, ch 30. Last 4 chs count as first tr on Row 1.
Row 1: Tr into fifth ch from hook and in each ch across. Total 27 tr.
Row 2: Ch 4 (counts as tr), turn. Sk st at base of chs. Tr in each st across, ending with final tr in top of turning ch. Total 27 tr.
Repeat Row 2 until swatch measures at least 4½ in. (11.4 cm).

SPECIAL STITCHES

Beaded chain (bch): Slide bead close to hook, ch 1 to enclose bead.

Beaded loop (bl): Slide 3 beads close to hook, ch 1 to close loop.

PATTERN NOTES

- » Beads and clasps are strung onto yarn and pulled into place on Row 1. The work is turned for Row 2. More beads are pulled into place on this row, then the yarn is fastened off. New yarn is used for Row 3. Beads are strung onto it, then pulled into place as the row is crocheted. Row 3 is worked into the opposite side of Row 1 than Row 2 is worked.
- » Beads on Rows 1 and 3 show on back of the work, which will be the right side (the public side) of the necklace when the project is complete.
- » Make a longer necklace by adding a multiple of 9 sts. Each additional repeat requires 6 additional beads as follows:

    Add 3 beads to the first group of 39 beads strung prior to starting Row 1.
    Add 1 bead to the second group of 12 beads strung prior to Row 1.
    Add 2 beads to the third group of 24 beads to be strung prior to Row 3.

To string beads, use a big-eye beading needle. Be careful: Both ends are quite sharp. Rather than holding the beads and trying to manipulate the needle into the hole, pour some beads onto a table or into a shallow dish and pick them up with the end of the needle. When you are done with the needle, return it to its original packaging so nobody gets poked.

1. Put the yarn through the large eye of the beading needle.

2. Use the end of the needle to pick up several beads.

3. Slide the beads past the needle onto the yarn.

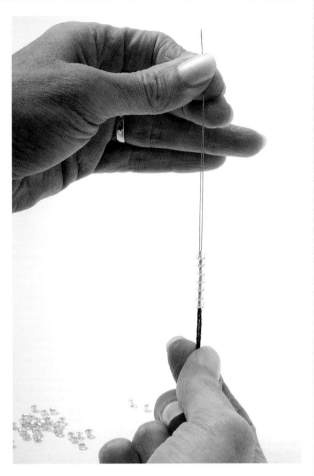

4. Push the beads down the yarn away from the needle, spreading them out as you go.

5. Remove yarn from needle.

Pattern

With big-eye beading needle, string 39 beads onto yarn.
String bar side of toggle onto yarn. String 12 beads onto
yarn. String loop side of toggle onto yarn.

Row 1 (WS): Leaving a 6 in. (15.2 cm) tail, attach yarn to hook
with slip knot. Slide toggle close to hook, ch 1 to enclose
toggle. Ch 6. *Tr in sixth ch from hook, ch 1, work 1 bch,
ch 7. Rep from * 11 times. End row by working a tr in the
sixth ch from hook, ch 1, slide toggle close to hook, ch 1
to enclose toggle.

Row 2: Turn. Position ch-6 lps facing up so you can work into
them, making sure necklace is not twisted. *Sc in ch-6 sp,
ch 3, sc in same sp, ch 2, blp, ch 1, sc in same sp, ch 3, sc
in same sp. Sl st in next ch, ch 4, sk next bch and following
ch, sl st in top of next tr. Rep from * across until 1 ch-6 sp
remains. Sc in ch-6 sp, ch 3, sc in same sp, ch 2, blp, ch 1,
sc in same sp, ch 3, sc in same sp. Sl st in bottom of next tr.
Fasten off, leaving a 4-in. (10.2 cm) tail.

With big-eye beading needle, string 24 beads onto yarn.

Row 3: Position necklace with Row 1 down, WS facing you.
Join yarn in top of first tr (at bar end of toggle), ch 5. *Sl st
in st before bch, slide 2 beads close to hook, sk bch, sl st in
next st. Rep from * across, working final sl st into st before
loop end of toggle. Fasten off, leaving a 4-in. (10.2 cm) tail.

FINISHING

Weave in ends with tapestry needle, stitching through toggle
attachments to reinforce them. Wet block to finished measurements.

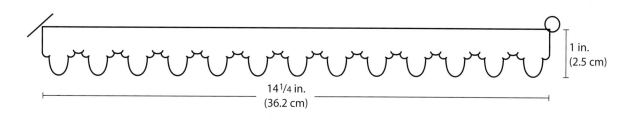

14 1/4 in.
(36.2 cm)

1 in.
(2.5 cm)

Section of Pattern

Row 3

Row 1

Row 2

Section of Pattern

Row 2

Row 1

Row 1

Key

$\underline{\text{O}}$ = Bar end of toggle

8 = Loop end of toggle

$\bigcirc$ = Chain (ch)

= Beaded chain stitch (bch)

= Beaded loop (blp)

O O = Slide 2 beads close to hook

• = Slip stitch (sl st)

X = Single crochet (sc)

⊤ = Treble crochet (tr)

= Indicates skipped repeats

Filet Crochet Pullover

Designed by Marty Miller

Four simple rectangles, worked in a variation of a filet stitch pattern then crocheted together, make this versatile pullover. Wear it over a blouse, sweater, or camisole to give your wardrobe some pizzazz!

SKILL LEVEL

EASY

MEASUREMENTS

Allowing for 4–6 in. (10.2–15.25 cm) of ease

	CHEST	LENGTH
X-Small	32 in. (81.5 cm)	20 in. (51 cm)
Small	36 in. (91.5 cm)	20 in. (51 cm)
Medium	40 in. (101.5 cm)	23 in. (58.5 cm)
Large	44 in. (112 cm)	23 in. (58.5 cm)

Instructions are for size XS, with sizes S, M, and L in parentheses.

MATERIALS

Plymouth Yarn Cleo (100% mercerized pima cotton; 1.75 oz./50 g; 125 yd./114 m)

Light

» Bijou Blue (164): 6 (6, 7, 8) skeins

» U.S. size H-8 (5 mm) crochet hook
» Stitch markers (4)
» Tapestry needle
» Straight pins
» Blocking pins
» Blocking board or towel

GAUGE

16 sts and 10 rows in pattern stitch = 4 in. (10.2 cm), blocked.
Row 1 of gauge swatch can start with either foundation single crochet or a traditional chain foundation.
For fsc method:
Row 1: Work 26 fsc. Total 26 sc.

For traditional foundation chain method:
Ch 27.
Row 1: Sc in second ch from hook and in each ch across. Total 26 sc.

For both methods:
Row 2: Ch 1, turn. Sc in each of first 2 sc, *ch 2, sk 2 sc, sc in each of next 2 sc. Repeat from * across. Total 14 sc.
Row 3: Ch 3 (counts as dc here and throughout), turn. Sk first sc, dc in next sc. *Ch 2, dc in each of next 2 sc. Repeat from * across. Total 14 dc.
Row 4: Ch 1, turn. Sc in each of first 2 dc. *Ch 2, sc in each of next 2 dc. Rep from * to end.
Repeat Rows 3 and 4 until swatch measures at least 6 in. (15.2 cm). End with Row 4.

SPECIAL STITCHES

Foundation single crochet (fsc): Ch 2 (does not count as fsc). Insert hook into first ch made, yo, pull up lp, ch 1 (this is the next foundation ch, and will be the entry point for the next st—pinch it with your thumb and finger to make it easier to find), yo, pull through 2 loops to finish the single crochet. *Insert the hook into fch just made, yo, pull up lp, ch 1 (the foundation ch and entry point for the next st), yo, pull through 2 loops on hook to finish the fsc. Repeat from * until you reach the target number of fsc.
Single crochet 2 together (sc2tog): Insert hook where indicated, yo, pull up lp, insert hook into next st, yo, pull up lp, yo, pull through all 3 lps.

PATTERN NOTES

» Most crochet patterns start with a long chain, then a row of stitches worked into those chains. Foundation crochet stitches combine these two steps. This reduces the possibility of missing a stitch or twisting the chain, makes tension more consistent throughout the garment, provides a nice finished bottom, and offers some stretch. It takes a little practice to isolate

the target entry point for each stitch and to have all of the stitches on the row come out even. However, once you master foundation stitches, you may find that you prefer them to the traditional long chain!

This pattern includes both methods for the start of each panel. Whichever method you choose, the pattern instructions are the same starting on Row 2.

» Because the four sections of the sweater are joined by crocheting them together around the end stitches, each section measures slightly larger before assembly than after.

» Ch 3 at the beginning of a row counts as a dc.
» Garment is worked in a multiple of 4 stitches + 2. To make the garment wider or narrower, add or subtract a multiple of 4. Make the same adjustment on the corresponding panel (front/back or side/side). To make the garment shorter or longer, add or subtract multiples of 2 rows (Rows 3 and 4) on all four panels.
» Adjust the armhole depth by working more or fewer rows on the side panels. The top of each side panel is at the bottom of the underarm.

Pattern

FRONT/BACK PANEL (make 2)
Fsc method:
Row 1: Work 54 (58, 62, 66) fsc.

Traditional foundation ch method:
Ch 55 (59, 63, 67).
Row 1: Sc in second ch from hook and in each ch to end. Total 54 (58, 62, 66) sc.

Both methods:
Row 2: Ch 1, turn. Sc in each of first 2 sc. *Ch 2, sk 2 sc, sc in each of next 2 sc. Repeat from * across. Total 28 (30, 32, 34) sc.
Row 3 (RS): Ch 3 (counts as first dc here and throughout), turn. Sk first sc, dc in next sc. *Ch 2, dc in each of next 2 sc. Repeat from * across. Total 28 (30, 32, 34) dc. Place marker anywhere on row to indicate RS.
Row 4: Ch 1, turn. Sc in each of first 2 dc. *Ch 2, sc in each of next 2 dc. Repeat from * to end.
Rows 5– 48 (48, 56, 56): Repeat Rows 3 and 4 twenty-two (22, 26, 26) times. Fasten off.

SIDE PANELS (make 2)
Fsc method:
Row 1: Work 14 (18, 22, 26) fsc.

Traditional foundation ch method:
Ch 15 (19, 23, 27).
Row 1: Sk first ch, sc in each ch to end. Total 14 (18, 22, 26) sc.

Both methods:
Row 2: Ch 1, turn. Sc in each of first 2 sc. *Ch 2, sk 2 sc, sc in each of next 2 sc. Repeat from * across. Total 8 (10, 12, 14) sc.
Row 3 (RS): Ch 3 (counts as first dc here and throughout), turn. Sk first sc, dc in next sc. *Ch 2, dc in each of next 2 sc. Repeat from * across. Total 8 (10, 12, 14) dc. Place marker anywhere on row to indicate RS.
Row 4: Ch 1, turn. Sc in each of first 2 dc. *Ch 2, sc in each of next 2 dc. Repeat from * to end.
Rows 5–34 (34, 38, 38): Repeat Rows 3 and 4 fifteen (15, 17, 17) times. Fasten off.

JOINING PANELS

Panels are crocheted together with sc to make the seams a feature of the garment. All seams are done with the RS facing you.

Before crocheting the seams, pin the panels together from the bottom hem to the armhole, and from outer shoulder to neck. Leave a neck opening of 7½ (7½, 8, 8) inches [19 (19, 20, 20) cm]. Try on the top to ensure you are happy with the armhole depth and the size of the neck opening; adjust as needed. Remove pins as you seam the garment.

First Seam (front panel to left-hand side panel): With WS together, join yarn with sl st through both panels at the bottom. Work from the hem to the armhole around the stitches on the dc rows.

Ch 1, sc in both stitches where joined, 2 sc around end dc on each panel, *ch 1, sk sc row, 2 sc around end dcs on next row. Repeat from * to armhole. End with sc in both panels, through end stitches. Fasten off.

Second Seam (back panel to right-hand side panel): Repeat First Seam.

Third Seam (left-hand side panel to back panel): Repeat First Seam.

Fourth Seam (right-hand side panel to front panel): Repeat First Seam.

SHOULDER SEAMS AND NECK EDGING

Left Shoulder: With front of garment facing you, join yarn through front and back stitches at left shoulder edge. Working through both panels, sl st in first sc, sc in next sc, 2 sc in ch-2 sp. *Sc in each of next 2 sc, 2 sc in ch-2 sp. Repeat from * until last 2 sc. Sc in next sc, sl st in last sc. Fasten off.

Right Shoulder: With back of garment facing you, repeat instructions for Left Shoulder. Do not fasten off.

Neck Edging: [Sc in each sc, 2 sc in each ch-2 sp] to opposite shoulder seam. Sc2tog around sl st at that seam. [Sc in

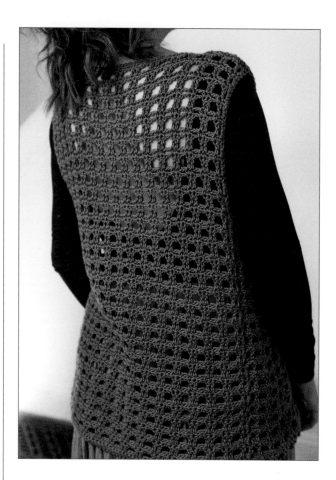

each sc, 2 sc in each ch-2 sp] around to starting point. Sl st to first st of round. Fasten off.

ARMHOLE EDGING

With RS facing you, and working on RS of garment, join yarn at center bottom edge of armhole (near the middle of the side panel) in the first of 2 sc.

NOTE: *For the top and bottom of armhole, sc in each sc, work 2 sc in each ch-2 sp.*

For the sides of armhole, work 2 sc around each dc post; work ch-1 over each set of 2 scs.
Work sc2tog around the seams that join the bottom to the sides.
Sl st to first st of round. Fasten off.

HEM EDGING

With RS facing you, join yarn on the bottom edge of a side panel, through a foundation ch or fsc. Ch 1. Sc in each st around, working sc2tog around seams. Sl st to first st of round. Fasten off.

FINISHING

Using tapestry needle, weave in ends.
Steam block or wet block garment to shape and size.

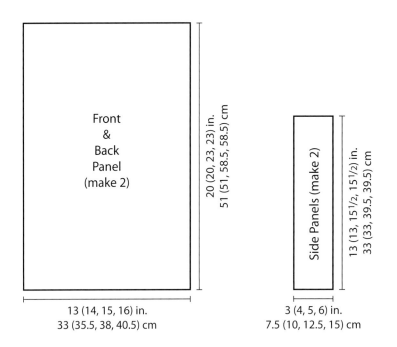

Front
&
Back
Panel
(make 2)

20 (20, 23, 23) in.
51 (51, 58.5, 58.5) cm

13 (14, 15, 16) in.
33 (35.5, 38, 40.5) cm

Side Panels (make 2)

13 (13, 15½, 15½) in.
33 (33, 39.5, 39.5) cm

3 (4, 5, 6) in.
7.5 (10, 12.5, 15) cm

Seaming Diagram

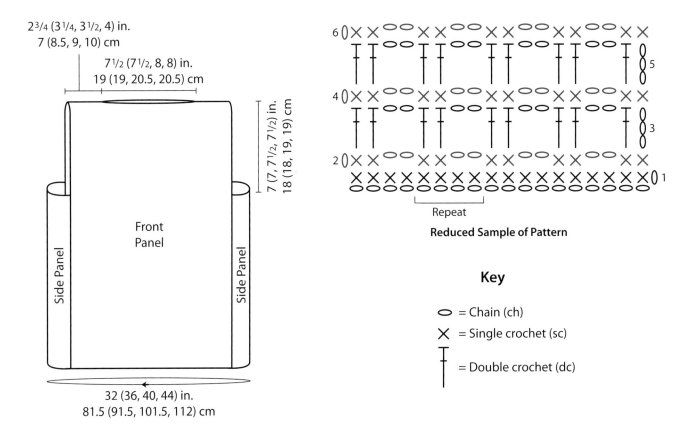

2¾ (3¼, 3½, 4) in.
7 (8.5, 9, 10) cm

7½ (7½, 8, 8) in.
19 (19, 20.5, 20.5) cm

7 (7, 7½, 7½) in.
18 (18, 19, 19) cm

Side Panel

Side Panel

Front
Panel

32 (36, 40, 44) in.
81.5 (91.5, 101.5, 112) cm

Repeat

Reduced Sample of Pattern

Key

○ = Chain (ch)

✕ = Single crochet (sc)

┬ = Double crochet (dc)

Fingerless Gloves

Designed by Amy Solovay

R ibbons and a lace ruffle accent these feminine fingerless gloves, which have just the right amount of stretch for a perfect fit. The predominant stitch pattern is an easy mesh. Hand-painted yarn adds playful speckles of color.

SKILL LEVEL

EASY

MEASUREMENTS

Small/Medium for hands measuring up to 7½ in. (19 cm) in circumference, measured at the widest point around the hand between thumb and knuckles. Length is 7 in. (17.8 cm).

Medium/Large for hands measuring between 7½ in. (19 cm) and 8½ in. (21.6 cm) in circumference, measured at the widest point around the hand between thumb and knuckles. Length is 7½ in. (19 cm).

Instructions are for size S/M, with size M/L in parentheses.

MATERIALS

1

Super Fine

Knit Picks Hawthorne Fingering (80% superwash fine highland wool, 20% polyamide); 3½ oz./ 100 g; 357 yd./326.4 m)
   » Blueberry Speckle (27219): 1 skein, or Italian Ice Speckle (27221): 1 skein
» U.S. size F-5 (4.0 mm) crochet hook
» U.S. size D-3 (3.25 mm) crochet hook
» Polyester ribbon, ¼-in. (0.64 cm) to ¾-in (1.9 cm) wide, 48 in. (122 cm) long, royal blue or teal green
» Stitch marker
» Tapestry needle
» Blocking pins
» Blocking board or towel
» Clear nail polish (optional)

GAUGE

24 sts and 17 rows = 4 in. (10.2 cm), unblocked.

For gauge swatch, with F hook, ch 35. Last 3 chs count as first hdc and first ch on Row 1.

Row 1: Hdc into fifth ch from hook. *Ch 1, sk next ch, hdc in next ch. Rep from * across.

Row 2: Ch 1 (does not count as st), turn. Sc in first hdc. *Ch 1, sk next ch, sc in next hdc. Rep from * across.

Row 3: Ch 3 (counts as hdc and ch-1 here and throughout), turn. Sk first sc and ch, hdc in next sc. *Ch 1, sk next ch, hdc in next sc. Rep from * across.

Rep Rows 2 and 3 until swatch measures at least 4½ in. (11.4 cm).

NOTE: *On gauge swatch, odd-numbered rows will have hdc sts separated by ch-1; even-numbered rows will have sc sts separated by ch-1. Each row should have 16 ch-sps.*

PATTERN NOTES

   » Rows are crocheted from wrist to fingers and back again. Odd-numbered rows start with the wrist ruffle, then a ch-2 sp where the ribbon will be woven through, then the body of the glove; even-numbered rows start with the body of the glove, then the ch-2 sp for the ribbon, then the ruffle.

Pattern (make 2)

With F hook, ch 40 (44). Last 6 stitches make scallop along ruffled edge.

Row 1 (RS, begins with ruffle): Tr in seventh ch from hook.

Ch 1, sk next ch, tr in next ch, ch 1, sk next ch, dc in next ch, hdc in each of the next 2 chs. Ch 2 (makes opening for ribbon), sk next 2 chs. Begin working the body of the glove: Hdc in next ch. *Ch 1, sk next ch, hdc in next ch. Rep from * to end. Place marker to indicate RS.

Row 2: Ch 1 (does not count as a st), turn. Sc in first hdc. *Ch 1, sk next ch, sc in next hdc. Rep from * until you've worked a total of 12 (14) chs and 13 (15) sc. Ch 2, sk 2 chs (makes ribbon opening). Work ruffle: Hdc in each of the next 2 hdc, dc in next dc, ch 1, sk next ch, tr in next tr, ch 1, sk next ch, tr in next tr.

Row 3: Ch 6 (makes scallop along ruffled edge), turn. Tr in first tr, ch 1, sk next ch, tr in next tr, ch 1, sk next ch, dc in next dc, hdc in each of the next 2 hdc, ch 2, sk next 2 chs. Hdc in next sc. *Ch 1, sk next ch, hdc in next sc. Rep from * to end.

Rows 4–29 (4–33), or until circumference of body of glove measures ½ in. (1.25 cm) less than hand circumference: Rep Rows 2–3.

Row 30 (34): Rep Row 2. Do not fasten off.

Wrist Edging: Turn work 90 degrees with the WS facing you. Working around the wrist ruffle, *[sc, ch 1, sc] in sp under next tr, [sc, ch 2, sc, ch 4, sc, ch 2, sc] in next ch-6 sp. Rep from * to end. Sl st in the ch that anchors the next tr. Fasten off, leaving a 5-in. (12.7-cm) tail for seaming.

SEAMS

Orient glove with RS facing out. Starting at the ruffle, whipstitch the side seams on the gloves until you are 4 sts above the ribbon channel. Fasten off. Skip 2¼ in. (5.8 cm) for the thumb opening. Whipstitch remaining edges of glove together.

COMPLETING THUMB OPENING

Insert F hook into any st along edge of thumb opening, pull up a loop, ch 2 (counts as first sc and first ch). [Sc, ch 1] evenly around thumb opening. Sl st to first sc. Fasten off.

EDGE AROUND FINGERS

***NOTE:** Work perpendicular to the body of the glove, into the ch-sps under the sc and the hdc stitches. Pull up the first loop of each sc to the height of where the border should be.*

Using D hook (or size needed to keep stitches flat), insert hook into any ch-1 sp along upper edge of glove, pull up a loop, ch 2 (counts as sc and ch-1). *Sc in next ch-1 sp, ch 1. Rep from * around. Join with sl st to first sc. Fasten off.

FINISHING

Using tapestry needle, weave in ends.

Only the ruffled wrist of the glove needs blocking. Arrange the ruffle in a circle like a doily, with the body of the glove sticking up into the air (you can stuff with a plastic bag to hold it in position if desired). Wet block the ruffle and pin into place, being sure to stretch each scallop. Let dry completely before unpinning.

Cut a length of ribbon approximately 21 in. (53 cm). Starting at center back of glove, weave ribbon over and under the ch-2 spaces around the wrist. Tie in a bow.

NOTE: *To keep cut ends of ribbon from fraying, dip in clear nail polish and let dry.*

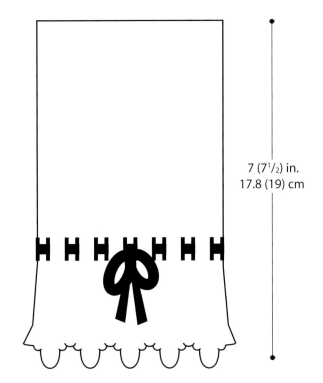

7 (7½) in.
17.8 (19) cm

**Glove Size Medium/Large
Section of Pattern**

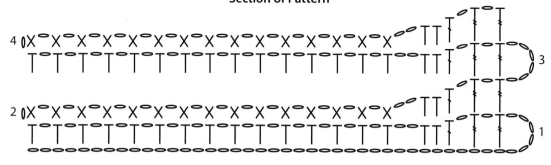

**Glove Size Small/Medium
Section of Pattern**

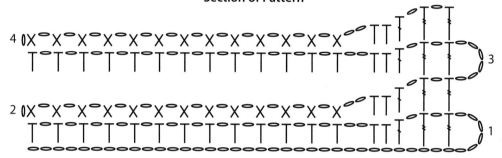

**Lower Edging at Wrist
Section of Pattern**

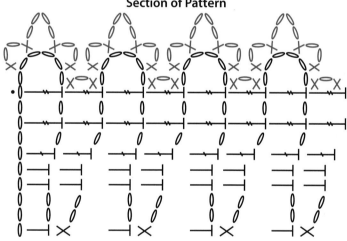

Key

◡ = Chain (ch)

• = Slip stitch (sl st)

X = Single crochet (sc)

T = Half double crochet (hdc)

⊤ = Double crochet (dc)

⊤ = Treble crochet (tr)

**Upper Edging at Fingers
Section of Pattern**

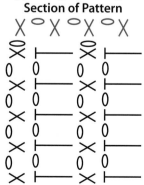

Flirt Cardigan

Designed by Karen McKenna

This Tunisian crochet cardigan has a hint of sparkle and a soft halo effect. Wear it to add a touch of elegance to anything from jeans to a little black dress.

SKILL LEVEL

EXPERIENCED

MEASUREMENTS

	CHEST	LENGTH (shoulder to hem)
Small	32 in. (81.5 cm)	18½ in. (47 cm)
Medium	36 in. (91.5 cm)	20½ in. (52 cm)
Large	40 in. (101.5 cm)	21½ in. (54.5 cm)
Extra Large	44 in. (111.75 cm)	22½ in. (57 cm)

Instructions are for size S, with sizes M, L, and XL in parentheses.

MATERIALS

3

Light

Universal Yarn Classic Shades Sequins Lite (74% acrylic, 22% wool, 4% payette; 3.5 oz./100 g; 264 yd./240 m)
» Lucky Rose (409): 3 (3, 4, 5) balls
» U.S. size I-9 (5.5 mm) Tunisian crochet hook
» Stitch markers (4)
» Tapestry needle
» Blocking pins
» Blocking mat or towel

GAUGE

16 sts and 8 rows in pattern = 4 in. (10.2 cm), blocked.

For gauge swatch, ch 29.
Row 1: Insert hook in back bump of second ch from hook, yo, pull up lp. *Insert hook in back bump of next ch, yo, pull up lp. Rep from * across. Total 29 lps on hook. Return.

Row 2 forward: Ch 1. Tdc in each of next 2 sts. *Tss in each of next 3 sts, Tdc in each of next 3 sts. Rep from * to last 2 sts. Tss in each of last 2 sts.
Row 2 return: Ch 1, yo, pull through 3 lps. *Ch 2, yo, pull through 2 lps, ch 2, yo, pull through 6 lps. Rep from * until 3 lps remain on hook. Ch 2, [yo, pull through 2 lps] twice.
Row 3 forward: Sk first vertical bar. Tss in next vertical bar. *Pull up lp in ch-2 sp, 3 Tdc in top of CL, pull up lp in ch-2 sp, Tss in next st. Rep from * until 1 ch-2 sp and 1 PCL remain. Pull up lp in ch-2 sp, 2 Tdc in top of PCL.
Row 3 return: Yo, pull through 1 lp. *Ch 2, yo, pull through 6 lps, ch 2, yo, pull through 2 lps. Rep from * until 5 lps remain on hook. Ch 2, yo, pull through 4 lps, yo, pull through 2 lps.
Row 4 forward: Ch 1, 2 Tdc in top of PCL, pull up lp in ch-2 sp. *Tss, pull up lp in ch-2 sp, 3 Tdc in top of CL, pull up lp in ch-2 sp. Rep from * until 1 st remains. Tss in last st.
Row 4 return: Rep Row 2 Return.
Rep Rows 3 and 4 until swatch measures at least 4½ in. (11.4 cm).

SPECIAL STITCHES

Tunisian double crochet (Tdc): Yo, insert hook as for Tss, yo, pull up lp, yo, pull through 2 lps. Each Tdc adds 1 lp to the hook.
1. Yo, insert hook as for Tss.

2. Yo, pull up lp, yo, pull through 2 lps.

3. Each Tdc adds 1 lp to the hook.

Tunisian double crochet increase (Tdc inc): Yo, insert hook in sp between 2 vertical bars, yo, pull up lp, yo, pull through 2 lps on hook. (The stitch is the same as a regular Tdc except it is worked into a space, not into a stitch.)

2 Tunisian double crochet increase (2 Tdc inc): Work 2 Tdc stitches into the same space between 2 vertical bars.

PATTERN NOTES

» To pull up a lp in ch-2 sp, insert hook in sp front to back, yo, pull up lp.

» To work final st on forward pass, insert hook behind the final vertical bar and the horizontal thread that runs behind it, yo, pull up lp. This creates stability along the edge of the piece.

» Standard return pass is as follows: Yo, pull through 1 lp. *Yo, pull through 2 lps. Rep from * until 1 lp remains on hook.

» Work standard return unless instructed to do otherwise. Nonstandard returns are explained in pattern instructions.

» A cluster (CL) is created on the return pass with yo, pull through 6 lps. A partial cluster (PCL) is created on the return pass with yo, pull through 3 or 4 lps as instructed.

Pattern

BACK

Ch 65 (71, 83, 89)

Row 1: Insert hook in back bump of second ch from hook, yo, pull up lp. *Insert hook in back bump of next ch, yo, pull up lp. Rep from * across. Total 65 (71, 83, 89) loops on hook. Return.

Row 2 forward: Ch 1. Tdc in each of next 2 sts. *Tss in each of next 3 sts, Tdc in each of next 3 sts. Rep from * to last 2 sts. Tss in each of last 2 sts.

Row 2 return: Ch 1, yo, pull through 3 lps. *Ch 2, yo, pull through 2 lps, ch 2, yo, pull through 6 lps. Rep from * until 3 lps remain on hook. Ch 2, [yo, pull through 2 lps] twice.

Row 3 forward: Sk first vertical bar. Tss in next vertical bar. *Pull up lp in ch-2 sp, 3 Tdc in top of CL, pull up lp in ch-2 sp, Tss in next st. Rep from * until 1 ch-2 sp and 1 PCL remain. Pull up lp in ch-2 sp, 2 Tdc in top of PCL.

Row 3 return: Yo, pull through 1 lp. *Ch 2, yo, pull through 6 lps, ch 2, yo, pull through 2 lps. Rep from * until 5 lps remain on hook. Ch 2, yo, pull through 4 lps, yo, pull through 2 lps.

Row 4 forward: Ch 1. 2 Tdc in top of PCL, pull up lp ch-2 sp. *Tss in next st, pull up lp in ch-2 sp, 3 Tdc in top of CL, pull up lp in ch-2 sp. Rep from * until 1 st remains. Tss in last st.

Row 4 return: Rep Row 2 return.

Rows 5–34 (5–36, 5–40, 5–42): Rep Rows 3 and 4.

RIGHT SHOULDER/NECKLINE SHAPING

Row 35 (37, 41, 43) forward: Work Row 3 forward for 19 (19, 25, 28) sts. Total 20 (20, 26, 29) lps on hook.

Small, Medium, and Large Only

Row 35 (37, 41) return: Ch 1, yo, pull through 3 lps. Ch 2, yo, pull through 2 lps. *Ch 2, yo, pull through 6 lps, ch 2, yo, pull through 2 lps. Rep from * until 5 lps remain on hook. Ch 2, yo, pull through 4 lps, yo, pull through 2 lps.

Row 36 (38, 42) forward: Ch 1, 2 Tdc in top of PCL, pull up lp in ch-2 sp, Tss. *Pull up lp in ch-2 sp, 3 Tdc in top of CL, pull up lp in ch-2 sp, Tss. Rep from * until 1 ch-2 sp and 1 PCL remain. Pull up lp in ch-2 sp, 2 Tdc in top of PCL. Total 20 (20, 26) lps on hook.

Row 36 (38, 42) return: Yo, pull through 1 lp. Ch 2, yo, pull through 6 lps. *Ch 2, yo, pull through 2 lps, ch 2, yo, pull through 6 lps. Rep from * until 3 lps remain on hook. Ch 2, [yo, pull through 2 loops] twice.

Row 37 (39, 43) forward: Sk first vertical bar. Tss in next vertical bar, pull up lp in ch-2 sp, 3 Tdc in top of CL. *Pull up lp in ch-2 sp, Tss in next st, pull up lp in ch-2 sp, 3 Tdc in top of CL. Rep from * until 1 ch-2 sp and 1 st remain. Pull up lp in ch-2 sp, Tss in final st. Total 20 (20, 26) lps on hook.

Row 37 (39, 43) return: Ch 1, yo, pull through 3 lps. Ch 2, yo, pull through 2 lps. *Ch 2, yo, pull through 6 loops, ch 2, yo, pull through 2 lps. Rep from * until 5 lps remain on hook. Ch 2, yo, pull through 4 lps, yo, pull through 2 lps.

Row 38 (40, 44): Rep Row 36 (38, 42) forward and return. Fasten off.

Extra Large Only

Row 43 return: Rep Row 3 return.

Row 44: Rep Row 4 forward and Row 2 return.

Row 45: Rep Row 3 forward and return.

Row 46: Rep Row 4 forward and Row 2 return. Fasten off.

LEFT SHOULDER/NECKLINE SHAPING

Small, Medium, and Large Only

Row 35 (37, 41) forward: Sk 24 (30, 30) sts.

> **NOTE:** Ch-2 sps count as 2 sts; Tss and CL count as 1 each.

Join yarn in ch-2 sp to the right of a CL by pulling up a lp. Ch 1, 2 Tdc in top of CL, pull up lp in ch-2 sp, Tss in next st. *Pull up lp in ch-2 sp, 3 Tdc in top of CL, pull up lp in ch-2 sp, Tss in next st. Rep from * until 1 ch-2 sp and PCL remain. Pull up lp in ch-2 sp, 2 Tdc in top of PCL. Total 20 (20, 26) lps on hook.

Row 35 (37, 41) return: Yo, pull through 1 lp. Ch 2, yo, pull through 6 lps *Ch 2, yo, pull through 2 lps, ch 2, yo, pull through 6 lps. Rep from * until 3 lps remain on hook. Ch 2, [yo, pull through 2 lps] twice.

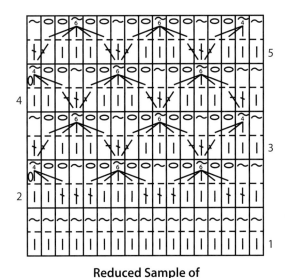

**Reduced Sample of
Main Stitch Pattern**

Key

☐ | = Tunisian Simple Stitch (Tss)

☐ † = Tunisian double crochet (Tdc)

Return Symbols

☐ ~ = yo, draw through 1 lp for first st, yo,
draw through 2 lps for each rem st

☐ ○ = ch 1

☐☐ or ☐☐ = yo, draw through
4 lps on hook

☐☐☐ = yo, draw through
6 lps on hook

Row 36 (38, 42) forward: Sk first vertical bar. *Tss in next st, pull up lp in ch-2 sp, 3 Tdc in CL, pull up lp in ch-2 sp. Rep from * until 1 st remains. Tss in last st.

Row 36 (38, 42) return: Ch 1, yo, pull through 3 lps, ch 2, yo pull through 2 lps, *Ch 2, yo, pull through 6 lps, ch 2, yo, pull through 2 lps. Rep from * until 5 lps remain on hook. Ch 2, yo, pull through 4 lps, yo, pull through 2 lps.

Row 37 (39, 43) forward: Ch 1, 2 Tdc in top of PCL, pull up lp in ch-2 sp, Tss in next st. *Pull up lp in ch-2 sp, 3 Tdc in top of CL, pull up lp in ch-2 sp, Tss in next st. Rep from * until 1 ch-2 sp and 1 PCL remain. Pull up lp in ch-2 sp, 2 Tdc in top of PCL.

Row 37 (39, 43) return: Yo, pull through 1 lp, ch 2, yo, pull through 6 lps. *Ch 2, yo, pull through 2 lps, ch 2, yo, pull through 6 lps. Rep from * until 3 lps remain on hook. Ch 2, [yo, pull through 2 lps] twice.

Row 38 (40, 44): Rep Row 36 (38, 42) forward and return. Fasten off.

Extra Large Only
Row 43 forward: Sk 31 sts.

NOTE: *Ch-2 sps count as 2 sts; Tss and CL count as 1 each. The last skipped sp is the first ch of a ch-2 sp; join the yarn in the same ch-2 sp, to the right of a Tss.*

Join yarn in ch-2 sp by pulling up a lp. Ch 1. Tss in next st. *Pull up lp in ch-2 sp, 3 Tdc in top of CL, pull up lp in ch-2 sp, Tss in next st. Rep from * until 1 ch-2 sp and PCL remain. Pull up lp in ch-2 sp, 2 Tdc in top of PCL. Total 29 lps on hook.

Row 43 return: Rep Row 3 return.
Row 44: Rep Row 4 forward and Row 2 return.
Row 45: Rep Row 3 forward and return.
Row 46: Rep Row 4 forward and Row 2 return. Fasten off.

Ch 29 (35, 41, 41).

Row 1: Insert hook in back bump of second ch from hook, yo, pull up lp. *Insert hook in back bump of next ch, yo, pull up lp. Rep fro m * across. Total 29 (35, 41, 41) lps on hook. Return.

Row 2 forward: Ch 1, Tdc in each of next 2 sts. *Tss in each of next 3 sts, Tdc in each of next 3 sts. Rep from * to last 2 sts. Tss in each of last 2 sts.

Row 2 return: Ch 1, yo, pull through 3 lps. *Ch 2, yo, pull through 2 lps, ch 2, yo, pull through 6 lps. Rep from * until 3 lps remain on hook. Ch 2, [yo, pu ll through 2 lps] twice.

Row 3 forward: Sk first vertical bar. Tss in next vertical bar. *Pull up lp in ch-2 sp, 3 Tdc in top of CL, pull up lp in ch-2 sp, Tss in next st. Rep from * until 1 ch-2 sp and 1 PCL remain. Pull up lp in ch-2 sp, 2 Tdc in top of PCL.

Row 3 return: Yo, pull through 1 lp. *Ch 2, yo, pull through 6 lps, ch 2, yo, pull through 2 lps. Rep from * until 5 lps remain on hook. Ch 2, yo, pull through 4 lps, yo, pull through 2 lps.

Row 4 forward: Ch 1, 2 Tdc in top of PCL, pull up lp in ch-2 sp. *Tss in next st, pull up lp in ch-2 sp, 3 Tdc in top of CL, pull up lp in ch-2 sp. Rep from * until 1 st remains. Tss in last st.

Row 4 return: Rep Row 2 return.
Rows 5–28 (5–32, 5–34, 5–36): Rep Rows 3 and 4.
Row 29 (33, 35, 37): Rep Row 3. Fasten off.

SHOULDER/NECKLINE SHAPING
Sizes Small, Medium, and Large
Row 30 (34, 36) forward: Sk 9 (15, 15) sts.

NOTE: *Ch-2 sps count as 2 sts; Tss and CL count as 1 each. The last skipped sp is the first ch of a ch-2 sp to the right of a Tss; join the yarn in the same ch-2 sp.*

Join yarn in ch-2 sp by pulling up a lp. Ch 1. *Tss in next st, pull up lp in ch-2 sp, 3 Tdc in top of CL, pull up lp in ch-2 sp. Rep from * until 1 st remains. Tss in last st. 20 (20, 26) lps on hook.

Row 30 (34, 36) return: Ch 1, yo, pull through 3 lps. Ch 2, yo, pull through 2 lps. *Ch 2, yo, pull through 6 lps, ch 2, yo, pull through 2 lps. Rep from * until 5 lps remain on hook. Ch 2, yo, pull through 4 lps, yo, pull through 2 lps.

Row 31 (35, 37) forward: Ch 1, 2 Tdc in top of PCL, pull up lp in ch-2 sp, Tss in next st. *Pull up lp in ch-2 sp, 3 Tdc in top of CL, pull up lp in ch-2 sp, Tss. Rep from * until 1 ch-2 sp and 1 PCL remain. Pull up lp in ch-2 sp, 2 Tdc in top of next st.

Row 31 (35, 37) return: Yo, pull through 1 lp. Ch 2, yo, pull through 6 lps. *Ch 2, yo, pull through 2 lps, ch 2, yo, pull through 6 lps. Rep from * until 3 lps remain on hook. Ch 2, [yo, pull through 2 lps] twice.

Row 32 (36, 38) forward: Sk first vertical bar. *Tss in next vertical bar, pull up lp in ch-2 sp, 3 Tdc in top of CL, pull up lp in ch-2 sp. Rep from * until 1 st remains. Tss in last st.

Row 32 (36, 38) return: Ch 1, yo, pull through 3 lps, ch 2, yo, pull through 2 lps. *Ch 2, yo, pull through 6 lps, ch 2, yo, pull through 2 lps. Rep from * until 5 lps remain on hook. Ch 2, yo, pull through 4 lps, yo, pull through 2 lps.

Rows 33–36 (37–40, 39–42): Rep Rows 31–32 (35–36, 37–38) twice. Size Medium, fasten off.

Sizes Small and Large
Rows 37–38 (43–44): Rep Rows 31–32 (37–38). Fasten off.

Size Extra Large
Row 38 forward: Sk 12 sts.

> **NOTE:** *Ch-2 sps count as 2 sts; Tss and CL count as 1 each. The last skipped sp is the first ch of a ch-2 sp; join the yarn in the same ch-2 sp to the right of a CL.*

Join yarn in ch-2 sp by pulling up a lp. Ch 1. 2 Tdc in top of CL, pull up lp in ch-2 sp. *Tss in next st, pull up lp in ch-2 sp, 3 Tdc in top of CL, pull up lp in ch-2 sp. Rep from * until 1 st remains. Tss in last st. 29 lps on hook.

Row 38 return: Ch 1, yo, pull through 3 lps. *Ch 2, yo, pull through 2 lps, ch 2, yo, pull through 6 lps. Rep from * until 3 lps remain on hook. Ch 2, [yo, pull through 2 lps] twice.

Row 39 forward: Sk first vertical bar. Tss in next st. *Pull up lp in ch-2 sp, 3 Tdc in top of CL, pull up lp in ch-2 sp, Tss in next st. Rep from * until 1 ch-2 sp and 1 PCL remain. Pull up lp in ch-2 sp, 2 Tdc in top of PCL.

Row 39 return: Yo, pull through 1 lp. *Ch 2, yo, pull through 6 lps, ch 2, yo, pull through 2 lps. Rep from * until 5 lps remain on hook. Ch 2, yo, pull through 4 lps, yo, pull through 2 lps.

Row 40 forward: Ch 1. 2 Tdc in PCL, pull up lp in ch-2 sp, *Tss, pull up lp in ch-2 sp, 3 Tdc in CL, pull up lp in ch-2 sp. Rep from * until 1 st remains. Tss in last st.

Row 40 return: Ch 1, yo, pull through 3 lps. *Ch 2, yo, pull through 2 lps, ch 2, yo, pull through 6 lps. Rep from * until 3 lps remain on hook. Ch 2, [yo, pull through 2 lps] twice.

Row 41 forward: Sk first vertical bar. Tss in next vertical bar. *Pull up lp in ch-2 sp, 3 Tdc in top of CL, pull up lp in ch-2 sp, Tss in next st. Rep from * until 1 ch-2 sp and 1 PCL remain. Pull up lp in ch-2 sp, 2 Tdc in top of PCL.

Row 41 return: Yo, pull through 1 lp. *Ch 2, yo, pull through 6 lps, ch 2, yo, pull through 2 lps. Rep from * until 5 lps remain on hook. Ch 2, yo, pull through 4 lps, yo, pull through 2 lps.

Rows 42–45: Repeat Rows 40 and 41 twice.
Row 46: Repeat Row 40. Fasten off.

LEFT FRONT
Ch 29 (35, 41, 41).

Row 1: Insert hook in back bump of second ch from hook, yo, pull up lp. *Insert hook in back bump of next ch, yo, pull up lp. Rep from * across. Total 29 (35, 41, 41) lps on hook. Return.

Row 2 forward: Ch 1. Tdc in each of next 2 sts. *Tss in each of next 3 sts, Tdc in each of next 3 sts. Rep from * to last 2 sts. Tss in each of last 2 sts.

Row 2 return: Ch 1, yo, pull through 3 lps. *Ch 2, yo, pull through 2 lps, ch 2, yo, pull through 6 lps. Rep from * until 3 lps remain on hook. Ch 2, [yo, pull through 2 lps] twice.

Row 3 forward: Sk first vertical bar. Tss in next vertical bar. *Pull up lp in ch-2 sp, 3 Tdc in top of CL, pull up lp in ch-2 sp, Tss in next st. Rep from * until 1 ch-2 sp and 1 PCL remain. Pull up lp in ch-2 sp, 2 Tdc in top of PCL.

Row 3 return: Yo, pull through 1 lp. *Ch 2, yo, pull through 6 lps, ch 2, yo, pull through 2 lps. Rep from * until 5 lps remain on hook. Ch 2, yo, pull through 4 lps, yo, pull through 2 lps.

Row 4 forward: Ch 1. 2 Tdc in top of PCL, pull up lp in ch-2 sp. *Tss in next st, pull up lp in ch-2 sp, 3 Tdc in top of CL, pull up lp in ch-2 sp. Rep from * until 1 st remains. Tss in last st.

Row 4 return: Rep Row 2 return.

Rows 5–28 (5–32, 5–34, 5–36): Rep Rows 3 and 4.

Row 29 (33, 35, 37): Rep Row 3. Do not fasten off.

SHOULDER/NECKLINE SHAPING

Sizes Small, Medium and Large

Row 30 (34, 36) forward: Rep Row 4 forward for 19 (19, 25) sts. Total 20 (20, 26) lps on hook.

Row 30 (34, 36) return: Yo, pull through 1 lp. Ch 2, yo, pull through 6 lps. *Ch 2, yo, pull through 2 lps, ch 2, yo, pull through 6 lps. Rep from * until 3 lps remain on hook. Ch 2, [yo, pull through 2 lps] twice.

Row 31 (35, 37) forward: Sk first vertical bar. *Tss, pull up lp in ch-2 sp, 3 Tdc in top of CL, pull up lp in ch-2 sp. Rep from * until 1 st remains. Tss in last st.

Row 31 (35, 37) return: Ch 1, yo, pull through 3 lps, ch 2, yo, pull through 2 lps. *Ch 2, yo, pull through 6 lps, ch 2, yo, pull through 2 lps. Rep from * until 5 lps remain on hook. Ch 2, yo, pull through 4 lps, yo, pull through 2 lps.

Row 32 (36, 38) forward: Ch 1. 2 Tdc in top of PCL, pull up lp in ch-2 sp, Tss in next st. *Pull up lp in ch-2 sp, 3 Tdc in top of CL, pull up lp in ch-2 sp, Tss in next st. Rep from * until 1 ch-2 sp and 1 PCL remains. Pull up lp in ch-2 sp, 2 Tdc in top of PCL.

Row 32 (36, 38) return: Yo, pull through 1 lp. Ch 2, yo, pull through 6 lps. *Ch 2, yo, pull through 2 lps, ch 2, yo, pull through 6 lps. Rep from * until 3 lps remain on hook. Ch 2, [yo, pull through 2 lps] twice.

Rows 33–36 (37–40, 39–42): Rep Rows 31–32 (35–36, 37–38) twice. Medium only, fasten off.

Sizes Small and Large only

Rows 37–38 (43–44): Rep Row 31–32 (37–38). Fasten off.

Size Extra Large

Row 38 forward: Rep Row 4 forward for 28 sts. Total 29 lps on hook.

Row 38 return: Ch 1, yo, pull through 3 lps. *Ch 2, yo, pull through 2 lps, ch 2, yo, pull through 6 lps. Rep from * until 3 lps remain on hook. Ch 2, [yo, pull through 2 lps] twice.

Row 39 forward: Sk first vertical bar. Tss in next vertical bar.

*Pull up lp in ch-2 sp, 3 Tdc in top of CL, pull up lp in ch-2 sp, Tss in next st. Rep from * until 1 ch-2 sp and 1 PCL remains. Pull up lp in ch-2 sp, 2 Tdc in top of PCL.

Row 39 return: Yo, pull through 1 lp. *Ch 2, yo, pull through 6 lps, ch 2, yo, pull through 2 lps. Rep from * until 5 lps remain on hook. Ch 2, yo, pull through 4 lps, yo, pull through 2 lps.

Rows 40–45: Rep Rows 38 and 39 three times.

Row 46: Rep Row 38. Fasten off.

SLEEVE (make 2)

NOTE: *Sleeve is worked from cuff to shoulder.*

Sizes Small and Medium Only

Ch 53 (59).

Row 1: Insert hook in back bump of second ch from hook, yo, pull up lp. *Insert hook in back bump of next ch, yo, pull up lp. Rep from * across. Total 53 (59) lps on hook. Return.

Row 2 forward: Ch 1, Tdc inc (see Special Stitches), Tdc in each of next 2 sts. *Tss in each of next 3 sts, Tdc in each of next 3 sts. Rep from * to last 2 sts. Tdc, Tdc inc, Tdc in last st. Total 55 (61) lps on hook.

Row 2 return: Ch 1, yo, pull through 1 lp, yo, pull through 4 lps. *Ch 2, yo, pull through 2 lps, ch 2, yo, pull through 6 lps. Rep from * until 4 lps remain on hook. Ch 2, [yo, pull through 2 lps] 3 times.

Row 3 forward: Ch 1, Tdc inc, Tdc in next st, Tdc inc, Tss in next st, pull up lp in ch-2 sp. *3 Tdc in top of CL, pull up lp in ch-2 sp, Tss in next st, pull up lp in ch-2 sp. Rep from * to last PCL. 2 Tdc in top of PCL, 2 Tdc inc, Tdc in last st. Total 59 (65) lps on hook.

Row 3 return: Yo, pull through 1 lp, [yo, pull through 2 lps] 3 times, ch 2, yo, pull through 6 lps. *Ch 2, yo, pull through 2 lps, ch 2, yo, pull through 6 lps. Rep from * until 9 lps remain on hook. Ch 2, yo, pull through 2 lps, ch 2, yo, pull through 4 lps, [yo, pull through 2 lps] 4 times.

Row 4 forward: Ch 1, Tdc inc, Tdc in each of next 2 sts, Tss, 2 Tdc in top of PCL. *Pull up lp in ch-2 sp, Tss in next st, pull up lp in ch-2 sp, 3 Tdc in top of CL. Rep from * to last ch-2 sp. Pull up lp in ch-2 sp, Tss in next st, Tdc in each of next 2 sts, Tdc inc, Tdc in last st. Total 61 (67) lps on hook.

Row 4 return: Ch 1, [yo, pull through 2 lps] 3 times, yo, pull through 4 lps. *Ch 2, yo, pull through 2 lps, ch 2, yo, though 6 lps. Rep from * until 7 lps remain on hook. Ch 2, [yo, pull through 2 lps] 6 times.

Row 5 forward: Ch 1, Tdc inc, Tdc in next st, Tdc inc, Tdc in each of next 2 sts, Tss in each of next 2 sts. *Pull up lp in ch-2 sp, 3 Tdc in top of CL, pull up lp in ch-2 sp, Tss in next st. Rep from * to last ch-2 sp. Pull up lp in ch-2 sp, 2 Tdc in top of PCL, Tdc in each of next 2 sts, Tdc inc, Tdc in next st, Tdc inc, Tdc in last st. Total 65 (71) lps on hook.

Row 5 return: Ch 1, [yo, pull through 2 lps] 6 times. *Ch 2, yo, pull through 6 lps, ch 2, yo, pull through 2 lps. Rep from * until 11 lps remain on hook. Ch 2, yo, pull through 4 lps, [yo, pull through 2 lps] 7 times.

Row 6 forward: Ch 1, Tdc inc, Tdc in each of next 4 sts, Tss in each of next 2 sts, 2 Tdc in top of PCL. *Pull up lp in ch-2 sp, Tss in next st, pull up lp in ch-2 sp, 3 Tdc in top of CL. Rep from * to last ch-2 sp. Pull up lp in ch-2 sp, Tss in next st, Tdc in each of next 5 sts, Tdc inc, Tdc in last st. Total 67 (73) lps on hook.

Row 6 return: Ch 1, [yo, pull through 2 lps] 6 times, yo, pull through 4 lps. *Ch 2, yo, pull through 2 lps, ch 2, yo, pull through 6 lps. Rep from * until 10 lps remain on hook. Ch 2, [yo, pull through 2 lps] 9 times.

Row 7 forward: Ch 1, Tdc inc, Tdc in next st, Tdc inc, Tdc in each of next 5 sts, Tss in each of next 2 sts. *Pull up lp in ch-2 sp, 3 Tdc in top of CL, pull up lp in ch-2 sp, Tss in next st. Rep from * to last ch-2 sp. Pull up lp in ch-2 sp, 2 Tdc in top of PCL, Tdc in each of next 5 sts, Tdc inc, Tdc in next st, Tdc inc, Tdc in last st. Total 71 (77) lps on hook.

Row 7 return: Ch 1, [yo, pull through 2 lps] 9 times, ch 2, yo, pull through 6 lps. *Ch 2, yo, pull through 2 lps, ch 2, yo, pull through 6 lps. Rep from * until 15 lps remain on hook. Ch 2, yo, pull through 2 lps, ch 2, yo, pull through 4 lps, [yo, pull through 2 lps] 10 times.

Row 8 forward: Ch 1, Tdc inc, Tdc in next st, Tdc inc, Tdc in each of next 6 sts, Tss in each of next 2 sts, 2 Tdc in top of PCL. *Pull up lp in ch-2 sp, Tss in next st, pull up lp in ch-2 sp, 3 Tdc in top of CL. Rep from * to last ch-2 sp. Pull up lp in ch-2 sp, Tss in next st, Tdc in each of next 8 sts, Tdc inc, Tdc in last st. Total 74 (80) lps on hook.

Row 8 return: Ch 1, [yo, pull through 2 lps] 10 times. Yo, pull through 3 lps. *Ch 2, yo, pull through 2 lps, ch 2, yo, pull through 6 lps. Rep from * until 14 lps remain on hook. Ch 2, [yo, pull through 2 lps] 13 times. Fasten off.

Sizes Large and Extra Large Only

Ch 65 (71).

Row 1: Insert hook in back bump of second ch from hook, yo, pull up lp. *Insert hook in back bump of next ch, yo, pull up lp. Rep from * across. Total 65 (71) lps on hook. Return.

Row 2 forward: Ch 1, Tdc inc, Tdc in each of next 2 sts. *Tss in each of next 3 sts, Tdc in each of next 3 sts. Rep from * to last 2 sts. Tss in next, Tdc inc, Tdc in last st. Total 67 (73) lps on hook.

Row 2 return: Ch 2, yo, pull through 4 lps. *Ch 2, pull through 2 lps, ch 2, pull through 6 lps. Rep from * until 4 lps remain on hook. Ch 2, [yo, pull through 2 lps] 3 times.

Row 3 forward: Ch 1, Tdc inc, Tss in each of next 2 sts, pull up lp in ch-2 sp. *3 Tdc in top of CL, pull up lp in ch-2 sp, Tss in next st, pull up lp in ch-2 sp. Rep from * to last PCL. 2 Tdc in PCL, Tdc inc, Tdc in last st. Total 69 (75) lps on hook.

Row 3 return: Yo, pull through 1 lp, [yo, pull through 2 lps] twice, ch 2, yo, pull through 6 lps. *Ch 2, yo, pull through 2 lps, ch 2, yo, pull through 6 lps. Rep from * until 8 lps remain on hook. Ch 2, yo, pull though 2 lps, ch 2, yo, pull though 4 lps, [yo, pull through 2 lps] 3 times.

Row 4 forward: Ch 1, Tdc inc, Tdc in next st, Tss in next st, 2 Tdc in PCL. *Pull up lp in ch-2 sp, Tss in next st, pull up lp in ch-2 sp, 3 Tdc in top of CL. Rep from * to last ch-2 sp. Pull up lp in ch-2 sp, Tss in next st, Tdc in next st, Tdc inc, Tdc in last st. Total 71 (77) lps on hook.

Row 4 return: Ch 1, [yo, pull through 2 lps] 2 times, yo, pull through 4 lps. *Ch 2, yo, pull through 2 lps, ch 2, yo, pull through 6 lps. Rep from * until 6 lps remain on hook. Ch 2, [yo, pull through 2 lps] 5 times.

Row 5 forward: Ch 1, Tdc inc, Tdc in each of next 2 sts, Tss in each of next 2 sts, pull up lp in ch-2 sp. *3 Tdc in CL, pull up lp in ch-2 sp, Tss in next st, pull up lp in ch-2 sp. Rep from * to last PCL. 2 Tdc in PCL, Tdc in each of next 2 sts, Tdc inc, Tdc in last st. Total 73 (79) lps on hook.

Row 5 return: Ch 1, [yo, pull through 2 lps] 4 times. *Ch 2, yo, pull through 6 lps, ch 2, yo, pull through 2 lps. Rep from * until 9 lps remain on hook. Ch 2, yo, pull though 4 lps, [yo, pull through 2 lp] 5 times.

Row 6 forward: Ch 1, Tdc inc, Tdc in each of next 3 sts, Tss in next st, 2 Tdc in PCL. *Pull up lp in ch-2 sp, Tss in next st, pull up lp in ch-2 sp, 3 Tdc in top of CL. Rep from * to last ch-2 sp. Pull up lp in ch-2 sp, Tss in next st, Tdc in each of next 3 sts, Tdc inc, Tdc in last st. Total 75 (81) lps on hook.

Row 6 return: Ch 1, [yo, pull though 2 lps] 4 times, yo, pull through 4 lps. *Ch 2, yo, pull through 2 lps, ch 2, yo, pull though 6 lps. Rep from * until 8 lps remain on hook. Ch 2, [yo, pull through 2 lps] 7 times.

Row 7 forward: Ch 1, Tdc inc, Tdc in each of next 4 sts, Tss in each of next 2 sts. *Pull up lp in ch-2 sp, 3 Tdc in top of CL, pull up lp in ch-2 sp, Tss in next st. Rep from * to last ch-2 sp. Pull up lp in ch-2 sp, 2 Tdc in PCL, Tdc in each of next 4 sts, Tdc inc, Tdc in last st. Total 77 (83) lps on hook.

Row 7 return: Ch 1, [yo, pull through 2 lps] 6 times, ch 2, yo, pull through 6 lps. *Ch 2, yo, pull through 2 lps, ch 2, yo, pull through 6 lps. Rep from * until 12 lps remain on hook. Ch 2, yo, pull though 2 lps, ch 2, yo, pull though 4 lps, [yo, pull though 2 lps] 7 times.

Row 8 forward: Ch 1, Tdc inc, Tdc in each of next 4 sts, Tss in each of next 2 sts, 2 Tdc in PCL. *Pull up lp in ch-2 sp, Tss in next st, pull up lp in ch-2 sp, 3 Tdc in top of CL. Rep from * to last ch-2 sp. Pull up lp in ch-2 sp, Tss in next st, Tdc in each of next 5 sts, Tdc inc, Tdc in last st. Total 79 (85) lps on hook.

Row 8 return: Ch 1, [yo, pull through 2 lps] 6 times, yo, pull though 4 lps. *Ch 2, yo, pull through 2 lps, ch 2, yo, pull though 6 lps. Rep from * until 10 lps remain on hook. Ch 2, [yo, pull though 2 lps] 9 times.

Row 9 forward: Ch 1, Tdc inc, Tdc in next st, Tdc inc, Tdc in each of next 5 sts, Tss in each of next 2 sts. *Pull up lp in ch-2 sp, 3 Tdc in top of CL, pull up lp in ch-2 sp, Tss in next st. Rep from * to last ch-2 sp. Pull up lp in ch-2 sp, 2 Tdc in PCL, Tdc in each of next 5 sts, Tdc inc, Tdc in next st, Tdc inc, Tdc. Total 83 (89) lps on hook.

Row 9 return: Ch 1, [yo, pull though 2 lps] 9 times. *Ch 2, yo, pull through 6 lps, ch 2, yo, pull through 2 lps. Rep from * until 14 lps remain on hook. Ch 2, yo, pull through 4 lps, [yo, pull through 2 lps] 10 times.

Row 10 forward: Ch 1, Tdc inc, Tdc in next st, Tdc inc, Tdc in each of next 6 sts, Tss in each of next 2 sts, 2 Tdc in top of PCL. *Pull up lp in ch-2 sp, Tss in next st, pull up lp in ch-2 sp, 3 Tdc in top of CL. Rep from * to last ch-2 sp. Pull up lp in ch-2 sp, Tss in next st, Tdc in each of next 8 sts, Tdc inc, Tdc. Total 86 (92) lps on hook.

Row 10 return: Ch 1, [yo, pull though 2 lps] 9 times, yo, pull through 4 lps. *Ch 2, yo, pull though 2 lps, ch 2, yo, pull though 6 lps. Rep from * until 14 lps remain on hook. Ch 2. [Yo, pull through 2 lps] 13 times. Fasten off.

FINISHING

Using tapestry needle, weave in all ends.
Wet block each piece to schematic measurements.
With RS together, whipstitch shoulder seams.
PM at indicated distance for armhole on each side (see schematic). Whipstitch seam from underarm to bottom edge.
Position sleeve in armhole with unsewn sleeve seam on underside of arm. Make sure that when you turn the garment right-side out, the RS of the sleeve and the body are both showing. Sew sleeves to armhole opening, starting at underarm. When you get all the way around to where you started, continue seaming down the sleeve.

EDGING

The edging is done in Tunisian crochet. Starting at RS bottom right front, attach yarn with a sl st to first st. Pull up lps evenly up front, around neckline, and down left front. Return.

NOTE: *If your garment is puckering, your sts are too far apart; if it is ruffling, they are too close together. The edging and the garment should lie flat.*

With tapestry needle, weave in ends.

TIE

Attach yarn with a sl st to front top corner. Ch 55.
Sc in back bump of second ch from hook. Sc in back bump of each ch to end, sl st to corner of front. Fasten off. Rep for other side.
With tapestry needle, weave in ends.

Schematic of Back

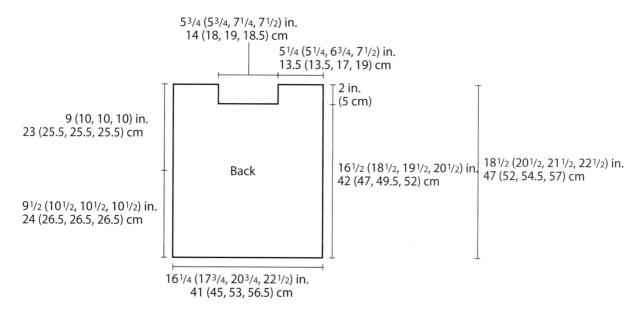

5³/4 (5³/4, 7¹/4, 7¹/2) in.
14 (18, 19, 18.5) cm

5¹/4 (5¹/4, 6³/4, 7¹/2) in.
13.5 (13.5, 17, 19) cm

2 in.
(5 cm)

9 (10, 10, 10) in.
23 (25.5, 25.5, 25.5) cm

Back

16¹/2 (18¹/2, 19¹/2, 20¹/2) in.
42 (47, 49.5, 52) cm

18¹/2 (20¹/2, 21¹/2, 22¹/2) in.
47 (52, 54.5, 57) cm

9¹/2 (10¹/2, 10¹/2, 10¹/2) in.
24 (26.5, 26.5, 26.5) cm

16¹/4 (17³/4, 20³/4, 22¹/2) in.
41 (45, 53, 56.5) cm

Schematic of Sleeve

18 1/2 (20, 21 1/2, 23) in.
47 (51, 54.5, 58.5) cm

Sleeve

4 in.
(10 cm)

13 (15, 16, 18) in.
33 (38, 40.5, 45.5) cm

Schematic of Front

5 1/4 (5 1/4, 6 3/4, 7 1/2) in.
13.5 (13.5, 17, 19) cm

2 (3 1/2, 3 1/2, 2 3/4) in.
5 (9, 9, 7) cm

4 in.
(10 cm)

9 (10, 10, 10) in.
23 (25.5, 25.5, 25.5) cm

Front

14 1/2 (16 1/2, 17 1/2, 18 1/2) in.
37 (42, 44.5, 47) cm

18 1/2 (20 1/2, 21 1/2, 22 1/2) in.
47 (52, 54.5, 57) cm

9 1/2 (10 1/2, 10 1/2, 10 1/2) in.
24 (26.5, 26.5, 26.5) cm

7 1/4 (8 3/4, 10 1/4, 10 1/4) in.
18.5 (22.2, 26, 26) cm

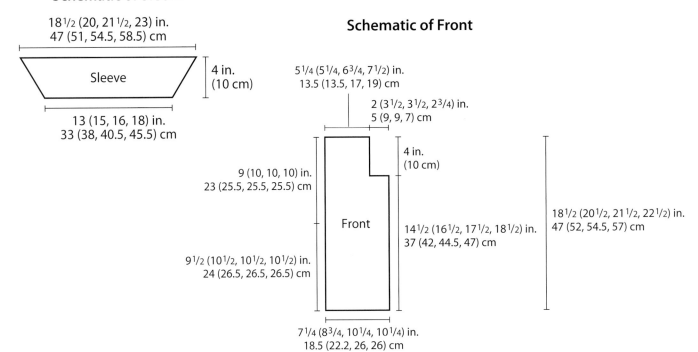

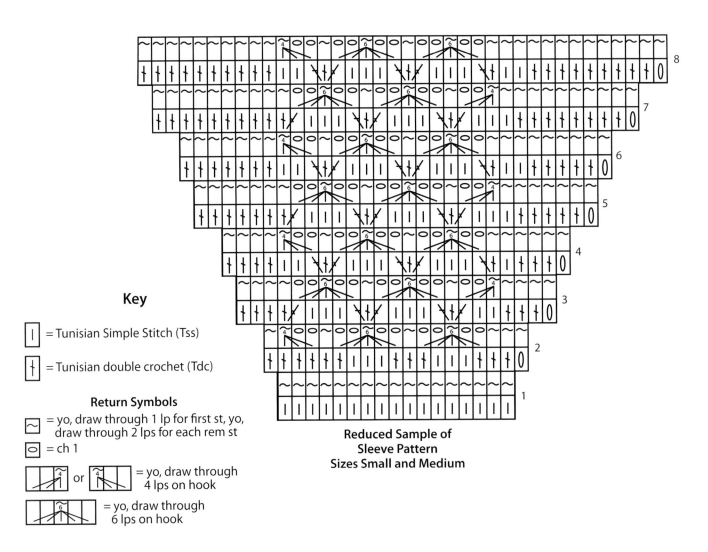

Key

| | = Tunisian Simple Stitch (Tss)

┼ = Tunisian double crochet (Tdc)

Return Symbols

⌒ = yo, draw through 1 lp for first st, yo, draw through 2 lps for each rem st

○ = ch 1

= yo, draw through 4 lps on hook

= yo, draw through 6 lps on hook

**Reduced Sample of
Sleeve Pattern
Sizes Small and Medium**

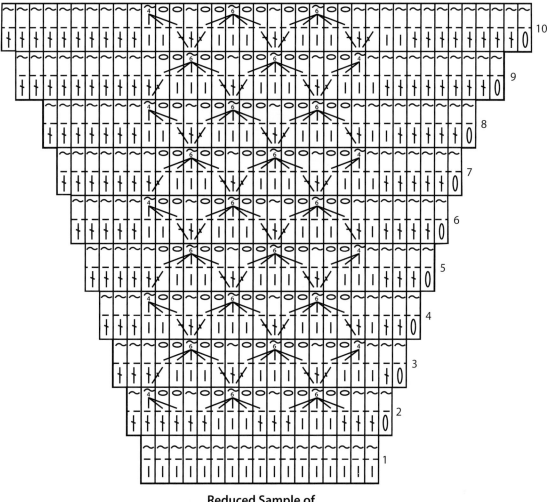

**Reduced Sample of
Sleeve Pattern
Sizes Large and Extra Large**

Key

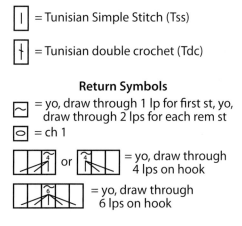

| = Tunisian Simple Stitch (Tss)

† = Tunisian double crochet (Tdc)

Return Symbols

~ = yo, draw through 1 lp for first st, yo, draw through 2 lps for each rem st

⊙ = ch 1

= yo, draw through 4 lps on hook

= yo, draw through 6 lps on hook

Gentle Whisper Shawl

Designed by Judith Butterworth

Soft as a whisper, a blend of merino wool and silk
yarn gives this shawl an opulent look. Gentle
Whisper is light and airy but still warm enough for
a chilly summer evening. This luxurious garment is
worked from the neck down.

SKILL LEVEL

EXPERIENCED

MEASUREMENTS
Before Blocking: 21 in. (53 cm) by 52 in. (130 cm).
After Blocking: 26 in. (66 cm) by 60 in. (152 cm).

MATERIALS

Super Fine

Manos Del Uruguay Silk Blend Fino (70%
extrafine merino wool, 30% silk; 3.5 oz./100 g;
450 yds./490 m)

» Watered Silk (SF404): 1 skein
» U.S. size H-8 (5 mm) crochet hook
» Stitch marker
» Tapestry needle
» Blocking pins
» Blocking board or towel

GAUGE
6 rows in pattern = 7 in. (17.5 cm) x 4 in. (10.2 cm), unblocked.
For gauge swatch, work first 6 rows of pattern. If your gauge
matches, you may use the swatch as the beginning of the
garment and continue with Row 7.

SPECIAL STITCHES
Double crochet 2 together (dc2tog): Yo, enter stitch as
    instructed, yo, pull up lp, yo, pull through 2 lps (2 lps
    remain on hook), yo, enter stitch as instructed, yo, pull up
    lp, yo, pull through 2 lps, yo, pull through all 3 lps.
End V-stitch (EV-st): (Dc, ch 3, dc) in same st.
Half double crochet V-stitch (HV-st): (Hdc, ch 3, hdc) in
    same st.
Large V-Stitch (LV-st): (Tr, ch 4, tr) in same st.
V-stitch (V-st): (Dc, ch 2, dc) in same st.
Picot (P): Ch 3, sc in third ch from hook.

Wing stitch (W-st): (Tr, ch 3, sc, ch 3, tr) in same st.
Y-stitch (Y-st): [Tr, ch 5, dc into side of tr].
1. Tr, ch 5, dc into side of tr. The toothpick shows where you
    will dc into side of tr.

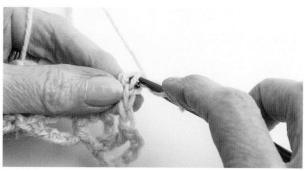

2. The completed Y-stitch.

PATTERN NOTES

» Practice working with the fingering yarn until your stitches have an even tension. Be careful not to pull your stitches too tight.

» When instructions say to work in EV-st, HV-st, LV-st, V-st, or Y-st, work under the chains between the two halves of the stitch.

» When instructions say to work in a ch lp, work under the chains.

» When instructions say to work in the middle chain of a ch lp, work into that ch, not under the ch lp.

» For Y-st, work the dc into the bottom 2 lps in the front of the tr.

» Blocking is essential to give your garment ideal size and drape.

Pattern

Ch 11. Sl st into first ch to make ring.

Row 1 (RS): Ch 6, dc into ring. [Ch 1, dc into ring] 3 times. Ch 1, HV-st into ring, PM. [Ch 1, dc into ring] 4 times, ch 3, dc into ring.

Row 2: Ch 6, turn. Dc in ch-3 lp, ch 1, dc in ch-1 lp, ch 3, sc in ch-1 lp, ch 5, sc in ch-1 lp, ch 3, dc in ch-1 lp, ch 1, HV-st in HV-st, MM, ch 1, dc in ch-1 lp, ch 3, sc in ch-1 lp, ch 5, sc in ch-1 lp, ch 3, dc in ch-1 lp, ch 1, EV-st in ch-6 lp.

***NOTE:** Continue to move marker for center stitch up as you work.*

Row 3: Ch 6, turn. Dc in EV-st, ch 1, dc in ch-1 lp, ch 3, sc in ch-3 lp, ch 5, sc in ch-5 lp, ch 5, sc in ch-3 lp, ch 3, dc in ch-1 lp, ch 1, HV-st in HV-st, ch 1, dc in ch-1 lp, ch 3, sc in ch-3 lp, ch 5, sc in ch-5 lp, ch 5, sc in ch-3 lp, ch 3, dc in ch-1 lp, ch 1, EV-st in ch-6 lp. Total 2 ch-5 lps each side.

Row 4: Ch 6, turn. Dc in EV-st, ch 1, dc in ch-1 lp, ch 3, sc in ch-3 lp. [Ch 5, sc in ch-5 lp] twice. Ch 5, sc in ch-3 lp, ch 3, dc in ch-1 lp, ch 1, HV-st in HV-st, ch 1, dc in ch-1 lp, ch 3, sc in ch-3 lp. [Ch 5, sc in ch-5 lp] twice. Ch 5, sc in ch-3 lp, ch 3, dc in ch-1 lp, ch 1, EV-st in ch-6 lp. Total 3 ch-5 lps each side.

Row 5: Ch 6, turn. Dc in EV-st, ch 1, dc in ch-1 lp, ch 3, sc in ch-3 lp. [Ch 5, sc in ch-5 lp] 3 times. Ch 5, sc in ch-3 lp, ch 3, dc in ch-1 lp, ch 1, HV-st in HV-st, ch 1, dc in ch-1 lp, ch 3, sc in ch-3 lp. [Ch 5, sc in ch-5 lp] 3 times. Ch 5, sc in ch-3 lp, ch 3, dc in ch-1 lp, ch 1, EV-st in ch-6 lp. Total 4 ch-5 lps each side.

Row 6: Ch 6, turn. Dc in EV-st, ch 1, dc in ch-1 lp, ch 3, sc in ch-3 lp. [Ch 5, sc in ch-5 lp] 4 times. Ch 5, sc in ch-3 lp, ch 3, dc in ch-1 lp, ch 1, HV-st in HV-st, ch 1, dc in ch-1 lp, ch 3, sc in ch-3 lp. [Ch 5, sc in ch-5 lp] 4 times. Ch 5, sc in ch-3 lp, ch 3, dc in ch-1 lp, ch 1, EV-st in ch-6 lp. Total 5 ch-5 lps each side.

Row 7: Ch 6, turn. Dc in EV-st, ch 1, dc in ch-1 lp, ch 3, 5 sc in ch-3 lp. [Ch 5, sk next ch-5 lp, 5 sc in ch-5 lp] twice. Ch 5, sk next ch-5 lp, 5 sc in ch-3 lp, ch 3, dc in ch-1 lp, ch 1, HV-st in HV-st, ch 1, dc in ch-1 lp, ch 3, 5 sc in ch-3 lp. [Ch 5, sk next ch-5 lp, 5 sc in ch-5 lp] twice. Ch 5, sk next ch-5 lp, 5 sc in ch-3 lp, ch 3, dc in ch-1 lp, ch 1, EV-st in ch-6 lp. Total 3 ch-5 lps each side.

Row 8: Ch 6, turn. Dc in EV-st, ch 1, dc in ch-1 lp, ch 3, sc in ch-3 lp. [Ch 3, sk next sc, sc in each of next 3 sc, ch 3, sc in ch-5 lp] 3 times. Ch 3, sk next sc, sc in next 3 sc, ch 3, sc in ch-3 lp, ch 3, dc in ch-1 lp, ch 1, HV-st in HV-st, ch 1, dc in ch-1 lp, ch 3, sc in ch-3 lp. [Ch 3, sk next sc, sc in each of next 3 sc, ch 3, sc in ch-5 lp] 3 times. Ch 3, sk next sc, sc in next 3 sc, ch 3, sc in ch-3 lp, ch 3, dc in ch-1 lp, ch 1, EV-st in ch-6 lp.

Row 9: Ch 6, turn. Dc in EV-st, ch 1, dc in ch-1 lp. [Ch 3, sc in ch-3 lp, sc in sc, sc in ch-3 lp, ch 3, sk next sc, sc in sc] 4 times. Ch 3, sc in ch-3 lp, sc in sc, sc in ch-3 lp, ch 3, dc in ch-1 lp, ch 1, HV-st in HV-st, ch 1, dc in ch-1 lp. [Ch 3, sc in ch-3 lp, sc in sc, sc in ch-3 lp, ch 3, sk next sc, sc in sc] 4 times. Ch 3, sc in ch-3 lp, sc in sc, sc in ch-3 lp, ch 3, dc in ch-1 lp, ch 1, EV-st in ch-6 lp.

Row 10: Ch 6, turn. Dc in EV-st, ch 1, dc in ch-1 lp, ch 5. [Sc in ch-3 lp, sc in each of next 3 sc, sc in ch-3 lp, ch 5] 5 times. Dc in ch-1 lp, ch 1, HV-st in HV-st, ch 1, dc in ch-1 lp, ch 5. [Sc in ch-3 lp, sc in each of next 3 sc, sc in ch-3 lp, ch 5] 5 times. Dc in ch-1 lp, ch 1, EV-st in ch-6 lp. Total 6 ch-5 lps each side.

Row 11: Ch 6, turn. Dc in EV-st, ch 1, dc in ch-1 lp, ch 3, sc in ch-5 lp. [Ch 3, sk next sc, sc in each of next 3 sc, ch 3, sc in ch-5 lp] 5 times. Ch 3, dc in ch-1 lp, ch 1, HV-st in HV-st, ch 1, dc in ch-1 lp, ch 3, sc in ch-5 lp. [Ch 3, sk next sc, sc in each of next 3 sc, ch 3, sc in ch-5 lp] 5 times. Ch 3, dc in ch-1 lp, ch 1, EV-st in ch-6 lp.

Row 12: Ch 6, turn. Dc in EV-st, ch 1, dc in ch-1 lp. [Ch 3, sc in ch-3 lp, sc in sc, sc in ch-3 lp, ch 3, sk next sc, sc in sc] 5 times. Ch 3, sc in ch-3 lp, sc in sc, sc in ch-3 lp, ch 3, dc in ch-1 lp, ch 1, HV-st in HV-st, ch 1, dc in ch-1 lp. [Ch 3, sc in ch-3 lp, sc in sc, sc in ch-3 lp, ch 3, sk next sc, sc in sc] 5 times. Ch 3, sc in ch-3 lp, sc in sc, sc in ch-3 lp, ch 3, dc in ch-1 lp, ch 1, EV-st in ch-6 lp.

Row 13: Ch 6, turn. Dc in EV-st, ch 1, dc in ch-1 lp, ch 5. [Sc in ch-3 lp, sc in each of next 3 sc, sc in ch-3 lp, ch 5] 6 times.

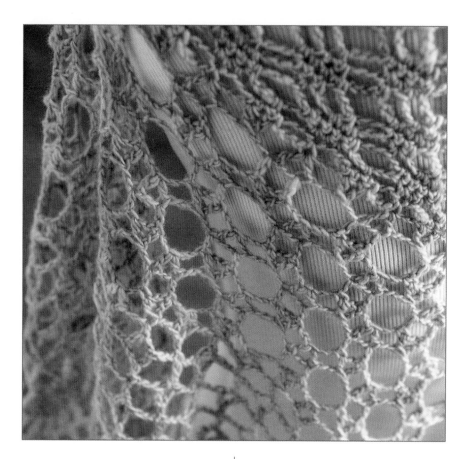

Dc in ch-1 lp, ch 1, HV-st in HV-st, ch 1, dc in ch-1 lp, ch 5. [Sc in ch-3 lp, sc in each of next 3 sc, sc in ch-3 lp, ch 5] 6 times. Dc in ch-1 lp, ch 1, EV-st in ch-6 lp. Total 7 ch-5 lps each side.

Row 14: Ch 6, turn. Dc in EV-st, ch 1, dc in ch-1 lp, ch 3, sc in ch-5 lp. [Ch 3, sk next sc, sc in each of next 3 sc, ch 3, sc in ch-5 lp] 6 times. Ch 3, dc in ch-1 lp, ch 1, HV-st in HV-st, ch 1, dc in ch-1 lp, ch 3, sc in ch-5 lp. [Ch 3, sk next sc, sc in each of next 3 sc, ch 3, sc in ch-5 lp] 6 times. Ch 3, dc in ch-1 lp, ch 1, EV-st in ch-6 lp.

Row 15: Ch 6, turn. Dc in EV-st, ch 1, dc in ch-1 lp. [Ch 3, sc in ch-3 lp, sc in sc, sc in ch-3 lp, ch 3, sk next sc, sc in sc] 6 times. Ch 3, sc in ch-3 lp, sc in sc, sc in ch-3 lp, ch 3, dc in ch-1 lp, ch 1, HV-st in HV-st, ch 1, dc in ch-1 lp. [Ch 3, sc in ch-3 lp, sc in sc, sc in ch-3 lp, ch 3, sk next sc, sc in sc] 6 times. Ch 3, sc in ch-3 lp, sc in sc, sc in ch-3 lp, ch 3, dc in ch-1 lp, ch 1, EV-st in ch-6 lp.

Row 16: Ch 6, turn. Dc in EV-st, ch 1, dc in ch-1 lp, ch 5. [Sc in ch-3 lp, sc in each of next 3 sc, sc in ch-3 lp, ch 5] 7 times. Dc in ch-1 lp, ch 1, HV-st in HV-st, ch 1, dc in ch-1 lp, ch 5. [Sc in ch-3 lp, sc in each of next 3 sc, sc in ch-3 lp, ch 5] 7 times. Dc in ch-1 lp, ch 1, EV-st in ch-6 lp. Total 8 ch-5 lps each side.

Row 17: Ch 6, turn. Dc in EV-st, ch 1, dc in ch-1 lp, ch 3, sc in ch-5 lp. [Ch 3, sk next sc, sc in each of next 3 sc, ch 3, sc in ch-5 lp] 7 times. Ch 3, dc in ch-1 lp, ch 1, HV-st in HV-st, ch 1, dc in ch-1 lp, ch 3, sc in ch-5 lp. [Ch 3, sk next sc, sc in each of next 3 sc, ch 3, sc in ch-5 lp] 7 times. Ch 3, dc in ch-1 lp, ch 1, EV-st in ch-6 lp.

Row 18: Ch 6, turn. Dc in EV-st, ch 1, dc in ch-1 lp. [Ch 3, sc in ch-3 lp, sc in sc, sc in ch-3 lp, ch 3, sk next sc, sc in sc] 7 times. Ch 3, sc in ch-3 lp, sc in sc, sc in ch-3 lp, ch 3, dc in ch-1 lp, ch 1, HV-st in HV-st, ch 1, dc in ch-1 lp. [Ch 3, sc in ch-3 lp, sc in sc, sc in ch-3 lp, ch 3, sk next sc, sc in sc] 7 times. Ch 3, sc in ch-3 lp, sc in sc, sc in ch-3 lp, ch 3, dc in ch-1 lp, ch 1, EV-st in ch-6 lp.

Row 19: Ch 6, turn. Dc in EV-st, ch 1, dc in ch-1 lp, ch 5. [Sc in ch-3 lp, sc in each of next 3 sc, sc in ch-3 lp, ch 5] 8 times. Dc in ch-1 lp, ch 1, HV-st in HV-st, ch 1, dc in ch-1 lp, ch 5. [Sc in ch-3 lp, sc in each of next 3 sc, sc in ch-3 lp, ch 5] 8 times. Dc in ch-1 lp, ch 1, EV-st in ch-6 lp. Total 9 ch-5 lps each side.

Row 20: Ch 6, turn. Dc in EV-st, ch 1, dc in ch-1 lp, ch 3, sc in ch-5 lp. [Ch 3, sk next sc, sc in each of next 3 sc, ch 3, sc in ch-5 lp] 8 times. Ch 3, dc in ch-1 lp, ch 1, HV-st in HV-st, ch 1, dc in ch-1 lp, ch 3, sc in ch-5 lp. [Ch 3, sk next sc, sc in each of next 3 sc, ch 3, sc in ch-5 lp] 8 times. Ch 3, dc in ch-1 lp, ch 1, EV-st in ch-6 lp.

Row 21: Ch 6, turn. Dc in EV-st, ch 1, dc in ch-1 lp. [Ch 3, sc in ch-3 lp, sc in sc, sc in ch-3 lp, ch 3, sk next sc, sc in sc] 8 times. Ch 3, sc in ch-3 lp, sc in sc, sc in ch-3 lp, ch 3, dc in ch-1 lp, ch 1, HV-st in HV-st, ch 1, dc in ch-1 lp. [Ch 3, sc in ch-3 lp, sc in sc, sc in ch-3 lp, ch 3, sk next sc, sc in sc] 8 times. Ch 3, sc in ch-3 lp, sc in sc, sc in ch-3 lp, ch 3, dc in ch-1 lp, ch 1, EV-st in ch-6 lp.

Row 22: Ch 6, turn. Dc in EV-st, ch 1, dc in ch-1 lp, ch 2, V-st in middle ch of ch-3 lp. [Ch 2, dc2tog over first and third sc of 3-sc group, ch 2, V-st in sc] 8 times. Ch 2, dc2tog over first

and third sc of 3-sc group, ch 2, V-st in middle ch of ch-3 lp, ch 2, dc in ch-1 lp, ch 1, HV-st in HV-st, ch 1, dc in ch-1 lp, ch 2, V-st in middle ch of ch-3 lp. [Ch 2, dc2tog over first and third sc of 3-sc group, ch 2, V-st in sc] 8 times. Ch 2, dc2tog over first and third sc of 3-sc group, ch 2, V-st in middle ch of ch-3 lp. Ch 2, dc in ch-1 lp, ch 1, EV-st in ch-6 lp. Total 10 V-sts each side.

Row 23: Ch 6, turn. Dc in EV-st, ch 1, dc in ch-1 lp, ch 5, sk next dc. [Dc in dc, ch 2, dc in dc, ch 5, sk dc2tog] 9 times. Dc in dc, ch 2, dc in dc, ch 3, dc in ch-1 lp, ch 1, HV-st in HV-st, ch 1, dc in ch-1 lp, ch 3, sk next dc. [Dc in dc, ch 2, dc in dc, ch 5, sk dc2tog] 9 times. Dc in dc, ch 2, dc in dc, ch 5, dc in ch-1 lp, ch 1, EV-st in ch-6 lp. Total 10 ch-5 lps.

Row 24: Ch 6, turn. Dc in EV-st, ch 1, dc in ch-1 lp, ch 3. [V-st in middle ch of ch-5 lp, ch 2, dc2tog over next 2 dc, ch 2] 10 times. V-st in middle ch of ch-3 lp, ch 2, dc in ch-1 lp, ch 1, HV-st in HV-st, ch 1, dc in ch-1 lp, ch 2, V-st in middle ch of ch-3 lp. [Ch 2, dc2tog over next 2 dc, ch 2, V-st in middle ch of ch-5 lp] 10 times. Ch 3, dc in ch-1 lp, ch 1, EV-st in ch-6 lp. Total 11 V-sts each side.

Row 25: Ch 6, turn. Dc in EV-st, ch 1, dc in ch-1 lp, ch 5, sk next dc. [Dc in dc, ch 2, dc in dc, ch 5, sk dc2tog] 10 times. Dc in dc, ch 2, dc in dc, ch 3, dc in ch-1 lp, ch 1, HV-st in HV-st, ch 1, dc in ch-1 lp, ch 3, sk next dc. [Dc in dc, ch 2, dc in dc, ch 5, sk dc2tog] 10 times. Dc in dc, ch 2, dc in dc, ch 5, dc in ch-1 lp, ch 1, EV-st in ch-6 lp. Total 11 ch-5 lps.

Row 26: Ch 6, turn. Dc in EV-st, ch 1, dc in ch-1 lp, ch 3. [V-st in middle ch of ch-5 lp, ch 2, dc2tog over next 2 dc, ch 2] 11 times. V-st in middle ch of ch-3 lp, ch 2, dc in ch-1 lp, ch 1, HV-st in HV-st, ch 1, dc in ch-1 lp, ch 2, V-st in middle ch of ch-3 lp. [Ch 2, dc2tog over next 2 dc, ch 2, V-st in middle ch of ch-5 lp] 11 times. Ch 3, dc in ch-1 lp, ch 1, EV-st in ch-6 lp. Total 12 V-sts each side.

Row 27: Ch 6, turn. Dc in EV-st, ch 1, dc in ch-1 lp, ch 5, sk next dc. [Dc in dc, ch 2, dc in dc, ch 5, sk dc2tog] 11 times. Dc in dc, ch 2, dc in dc, ch 3, dc in ch-1 lp, ch 1, HV-st in HV-st, ch 1, dc in ch-1 lp, ch 3, sk next dc. [Dc in dc, ch 2, dc in dc, ch 5, sk dc2tog] 11 times. Dc in dc, ch 2, dc in dc, ch 5, dc in ch-1 lp, ch 1, EV-st in ch-6 lp. Total 12 ch-5 lps.

Row 28: Ch 6, turn. Dc in EV-st, ch 1, dc in ch-1 lp, ch 3. [V-st in middle ch of ch-5 lp, ch 2, dc2tog over next 2 dc, ch 2] 12 times. V-st in middle ch of ch-3 lp, ch 2, dc in ch-1 lp, ch 1, HV-st in HV-st, ch 1, dc in ch-1 lp, ch 2, V-st in middle ch of ch-3 lp. [Ch 2, dc2tog over next 2 dc, ch 2, V-st in middle ch of ch-5 lp] 12 times. Ch 3, dc in ch-1 lp, ch 1, EV-st in ch-6 lp. Total 13 V-sts each side.

Row 29: Ch 6, turn. Dc in EV-st, ch 1, dc in ch-1 lp, ch 5, sk next dc. [Dc in dc, ch 2, dc in dc, ch 5, sk dc2tog] 12 times. Dc in dc, ch 2, dc in dc, ch 3, dc in ch-1 lp, ch 1, HV-st in HV-st, ch 1, dc in ch-1 lp, ch 3, sk next dc. [Dc in dc, ch 2, dc in dc, ch 5, sk dc2tog] 12 times. Dc in dc, ch 2, dc in dc, ch 5, dc in ch-1 lp, ch 1, EV-st in ch-6 lp. Total 13 ch-5 lps.

Row 30: Ch 6, turn. Dc in EV-st, ch 1, dc in ch-1 lp, ch 3. [V-st in middle ch of ch-5 lp, ch 2, dc2tog over next 2 dc, ch 2] 13 times. V-st in middle ch of ch-3 lp, ch 2, dc in ch-1 lp, ch

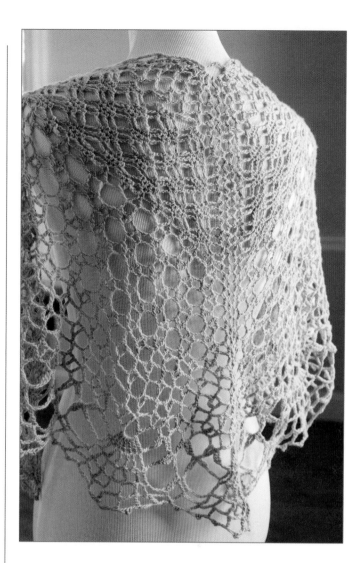

1, HV-st in HV-st, ch 1, dc in ch-1 lp, ch 2, V-st in middle ch of ch-3 lp. [Ch 2, dc2tog over next 2 dc, ch 2, V-st in middle ch of ch-5 lp] 13 times. Ch 3, dc in ch-1 lp, ch 1, EV-st in ch-6 lp. Total 14 V-sts each side.

Row 31: Ch 6, turn. Dc in EV-st, ch 1, dc in ch-1 lp, ch 2, Y-st in ch-3 lp, ch 2, dc in V-st. [Ch 2, Y-st in dc2tog, ch 2, dc in V-st] 13 times. Ch 2, sk ch-2 lp, dc in ch-1 lp, ch 1, HV-st in HV-st, ch 1, dc in ch-1 lp, ch 2, sk ch-2 lp, dc in V-st. [Ch 2, Y-st in dc2tog, ch 2, dc in V-st] 13 times. Ch 2, Y-st in ch-3 lp, ch 2, dc in ch-1 lp, ch 1, EV-st in ch-6 lp. Total 14 Y-sts each side.

Row 32: Ch 6, turn. Dc in EV-st, ch 1, dc in ch-1 lp, ch 2, Y-st in dc. [Ch 2, dc in Y-st, ch 2, Y-st in dc] 14 times. Ch 2, sk ch-2 lp, dc in ch-1 lp, ch 1, HV-st in HV-st, ch 1, dc in ch-1 lp, ch 2, sk ch-2 lp, Y-st in dc. [Ch 2, dc in Y-st, ch 2, Y-st in dc] 14 times. Ch 2, dc in ch-1 lp, ch 1, EV-st in ch-6 lp. Total 15 Y-sts each side.

NOTE: *When working into a dc after working into a Y-st, make sure you are advancing far enough on the previous row to reach the next dc; do not inadvertently work into the base of the Y-st.*

Row 33: Ch 6, turn. Dc in EV-st, ch 1, dc in ch-1 lp, ch 2, Y-st in dc. [Ch 2, dc in Y-st, ch 2, Y-st in dc] 14 times. Ch 2, dc in Y-st, ch 2, Y-st in ch-2 lp, ch 2, dc in ch-1 lp, ch 1, HV-st in HV-st, ch 1, dc in ch-1 lp, ch 2, Y-st in ch-2 lp. [Ch 2, dc in Y-st, ch 2, Y-st in dc] 15 times. Ch 2, dc in ch-1 lp, ch 1, EV-st in ch-6 lp. Total 16 Y-sts each side.

Row 34: Ch 6, turn. Dc in EV-st, ch 1, dc in ch-1 lp, ch 2, Y-st in dc. [Ch 2, dc in Y-st, ch 2, Y-st in dc] 15 times. Ch 2, dc in Y-st, ch 2, Y-st in ch-2 lp, ch 2, dc in ch-1 lp, ch 1, HV-st in HV-st, ch 1, dc in ch-1 lp, ch 2, Y-st in ch-2 lp. [Ch 2, dc in Y-st, ch 2, Y-st in dc] 16 times. Ch 2, dc in ch-1 lp, ch 1, EV-st in ch-6 lp. Total 17 Y-sts each side.

Row 35: Ch 7, turn. Tr in EV-st, ch 1, tr in ch-1 lp, ch 4. [Sc in Y-st, ch 2, LV-st in dc, ch 2] 16 times. Sc in Y-st, ch 2, sk ch-2 lp and ch-1 lp, LV-st in HV-st. Ch 2, sk ch-1 lp and ch-2 lp. [Sc n Y-st, ch 2, LV-st in dc, ch 2] 16 times. Sc in Y-st, ch 4, sk ch-2 lp, tr in ch-1 lp, ch 1, [tr, ch 3, tr] in ch-6 lp. Total 16 LV-sts each side and 1 LV-st in center.

Row 36: Ch 7, turn. Tr in ch-3 lp, ch 1, tr in ch-1 lp, ch 3. Sk to LV st. *7 tr in LV-st, [ch 3, W-st in LV-st] 3 times, ch 3. Rep from * to center. 9 tr in LV-st. *[Ch 3, W-st in LV-st] 3 times, ch 3, 7 tr in LV-st. Rep from * 3 times. Ch 3, sk to ch-1 lp. Tr in ch 1-lp, ch 1, [tr, ch 3, tr] in ch-7 lp. Total 4 tr groups each side.

Row 37: Ch 7, turn. Tr in ch-3 lp, ch 1, tr in ch-1 lp, ch 5. *Sk to tr group, [tr in tr, ch 1] 6 times, tr in tr, sk ch-3 lp, [ch 5, sk W-st, W-st in ch-3 lp] twice, ch 5. Rep from * to central tr group. [Tr in tr, ch 1] 8 times, tr in tr. **Sk ch-3 lp, [ch 5, sk W-st, W-st in ch-3 lp] twice, ch 5, sk to tr group, [tr in tr, ch 1] 6 times, tr in tr. Rep from ** 3 times. Ch 5, skip to ch-1 lp, tr in ch-1 lp, ch 1, [tr, ch 3, tr] in ch-7 lp.

Row 38: Ch 7, turn. Tr in ch-3 lp, ch 1, tr in ch-1 lp, ch 5. *Sk to tr group, [tr in tr, ch 2] 6 times, tr in tr, ch 5, sk ch-5 lp and W-st, W-st in ch-5 lp, ch 5. Rep from * to central tr group.

[Tr in tr, ch 2] 8 times, tr in tr. **Ch 5, sk ch-5 lp and W-st, W-st in ch-5 lp, ch 5, sk to tr group, [tr in tr, ch 2] 6 times, tr in tr. Rep from ** 3 times. Ch 5, sk to ch-1 lp, tr in ch-1 lp, ch 1, [tr, ch 3, tr] in ch-7 lp.

Row 39: Ch 7, turn. Tr in ch-3 lp, ch 1, tr in ch-1 lp, ch 5. *Sk to tr group, [tr in tr, ch 3] 6 times, tr in tr, [ch 5, sc in tr of W-st] twice, ch 5. Rep from * to central tr group. [Tr in tr, ch 3] 8 times, tr in tr. **Ch 5, [sc in tr of W-st, ch 5] twice, sk to tr group, [tr in tr, ch 3] 6 times, tr in tr. Rep from ** 3 times. Ch 5, sk to ch-1 lp, tr in ch-1 lp, ch 1, [tr, ch 3, tr] in ch-7 lp, turn.

Row 40: Ch 7, turn. Tr in ch-3 lp, ch 1, tr in ch-1 lp. *Sk to tr group, [ch 1, P, ch 1, tr in tr] 7 times, ch 1, P, ch 1, sk ch-5 lp, sc in ch-5 lp. Rep from * to central tr group. [Ch 1, P, ch 1, tr in tr] 9 times, **Ch 1, P, ch 1, sk ch-5 lp, sc in ch-5 lp, sk to tr group, [ch 1, P, ch 1, tr in tr] 7 times. Rep from ** 3 times. Ch 1, P, ch 1, sk to ch-1 lp, tr in ch-1 lp, ch 1, [tr, ch 3, tr] in ch-7 lp. Fasten off.

NOTE: *There is a ch on each side of each picot. When the instructions say "ch 1, P, ch 1," do the following: Ch 1, make an additional 3 chs for the picot, sl st into the third ch from hook to complete the picot, ch 1.*

FINISHING

With tapestry needle, weave in ends.

Wet block the garment, pinning it gently to the correct size without overstretching. Pin the picots in place to show them off to their best advantage. Let the wrap dry completely before unpinning it from the board or towel.

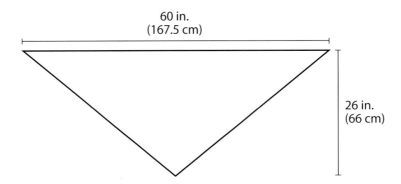

60 in. (167.5 cm)

26 in. (66 cm)

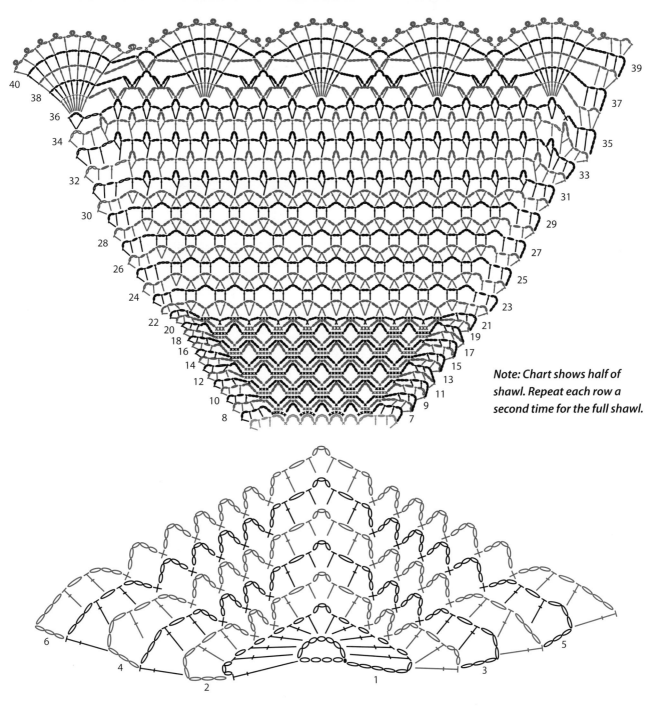

40
38
36
34
32
30
28
26
24
22
20
18
16
14
12
10
8

39
37
35
33
31
29
27
25
23
21
19
17
15
13
11
9
7

Note: Chart shows half of shawl. Repeat each row a second time for the full shawl.

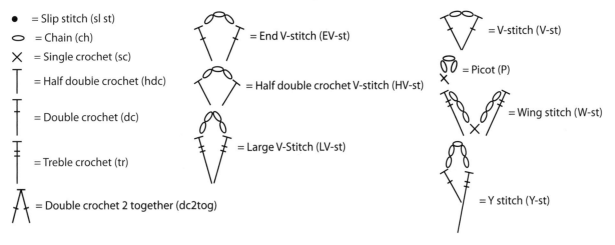

6
4
2

1

3
5

Key

●	= Slip stitch (sl st)
⬭	= Chain (ch)
✕	= Single crochet (sc)
⊤	= Half double crochet (hdc)
⊥	= Double crochet (dc)
	= Treble crochet (tr)
⋀	= Double crochet 2 together (dc2tog)

= End V-stitch (EV-st)

= Half double crochet V-stitch (HV-st)

= Large V-Stitch (LV-st)

= V-stitch (V-st)

= Picot (P)

= Wing stitch (W-st)

= Y stitch (Y-st)

Hourglass Scarf

Designed by Sharon Silverman

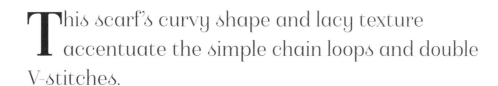

T his scarf's curvy shape and lacy texture accentuate the simple chain loops and double V-stitches.

SKILL LEVEL

EASY

MEASUREMENTS

5½ in. (14 cm) at widest point, 3 in. (7.5 cm) at narrowest point, 60 in. (152.5 cm) long plus 7 in. (18 cm) of fringe at each end.

MATERIALS

Super Fine

Space Cadet Maia (80% bamboo, 20% superwash merino wool; 3.5 oz./100 g; 400 yd./366 m)
  » Dark Skies: 1 skein

  » U.S. size H-8 (5 mm) crochet hook
  » Tapestry needle
  » Blocking pins
  » Blocking board or towel
  » 8-in. (20.3-cm) piece of cardboard

GAUGE

12 sts and 8 rows in dc = 4 in. (10.2 cm), blocked

For gauge swatch, ch 25. Last 3 chs count as first dc on Row 1.
Row 1: Dc in first ch from hook and in each ch across. Total 23 dc.
Row 2: Ch 3 (counts as dc), turn. Sk st at base of chs. Dc in each remaining st across.
Rep Row 2 until swatch measures at least 4½ in. (11.4 cm).

SPECIAL STITCHES

Double V-stitch (DV-st): [2 dc, ch 2, 2 dc] in same st.
Beginning Double V-stitch (beg DV-st): Ch 3, [dc at base of chs, ch 2, 2 dc] in same st.

PATTERN NOTES
  » When instructions say to work in DV-st, work into the ch-2 sp of the DV-st or beg DV-st.

Pattern

Ch 31.
Row 1 (RS): Sc in second ch from hook and in each ch across. Total 30 sc.
Row 2: Ch 1, turn. Sc in each sc across.
Row 3: Ch 3, turn. Beg DV-st. Ch 5, sk 6 sc, sc in next sc. [Ch 5, sk 2 sc, sc in next sc] 5 times. Ch 5, sk 6 sc, DV-st in final sc.
Row 4: Turn. Sl st in each of first 2 dc and into ch-2 sp. Beg DV-st. Ch 5, sk ch-5 lp, sc in next ch-5 lp. [Ch 5, sc into next ch-5 lp] 4 times. Ch 5, sk ch-5 lp, DV-st into DV-st.
Row 5: Turn. Sl st into each of first 2 dc and into ch-2 sp. Beg DV-st. Ch 5, sk ch-5 lp, sc in next ch-5 lp. [Ch 5, sc into next ch-5 lp] 3 times. Ch 5, sk ch-5 lp, DV-st into DV-st.
Row 6: Turn. Sl st into each of first 2 dc and into ch-2 sp. Beg DV-st. Ch 5, sk ch-5 lp, sc in next ch-5 lp. [Ch 5, sc into next ch-5 lp] twice. Ch 5, sk ch-5 lp, DV-st into DV-st.
Row 7: Turn. Sl st into each of first 2 dc and into ch-2 sp. Beg DV-st. Ch 5, sk ch-5 lp, sc in next ch-5 lp. Ch 5, sc into next ch-5 lp. Ch 5, sk ch-5 lp, DV-st into DV-st.
Row 8: Turn. Sl st into each of first 2 dc and into ch-2 sp. Beg DV-st. Ch 5, sk ch-5 lp, DV-st in next ch-5 lp, ch 5, sk next ch-5 lp, DV-st into DV-st.
Row 9: Turn. Sl st into each of first 2 dc and into ch-2 sp. Beg DV-st. Ch 5, sk ch-5 lp, DV-st into DV-st, ch 5, sk next ch-5 lp, DV-st into DV-st.
Rows 10–11: Rep Row 9.
Row 12: Turn. Sl st into each of first 2 dc and into ch-2 sp. Beg DV-st. Ch 5, sc in ch-5 lp, ch 5, sc in DV-st, ch 5, sc in ch-5 lp, ch 5, DV-st into DV-st.
Row 13: Turn. Sl st into each of first 2 dc and into ch-2 sp. Beg DV-st. [Ch 5, sc in next ch-5 lp] 4 times, ch 5, DV-st into DV-st.
Row 14: Turn. Sl st into each of first 2 dc and into ch-2 sp. Beg DV-st. [Ch 5, sc in next ch-5 lp] 5 times, ch 5, DV-st into DV-st.
Row 15: Turn. Sl st into each of first 2 dc and into ch-2 sp. Beg DV-st. [Ch 5, sc in next ch-5 lp] 6 times. Ch 5, DV-st into DV-st.

Row 16: Turn. Sl st into each of first 2 dc and into ch-2 sp. Beg DV-st. [Ch 5, sc in next ch-5 lp] 7 times. Ch 5, DV-st into DV-st.

Row 17: Turn. Sl st into each of first 2 dc and into ch-2 sp. Beg DV-st. Ch 5, sk first ch-5 lp, sc into next ch-5 lp, [ch 5, sc into next ch-5 lp] 5 times, sk next ch-5 sp, DV-st into DV-st.

Row 18: Rep Row 4.

Row 19: Rep Row 5.

Rows 20–89: Rep Rows 6–19 five times.

Rows 90–99: Rep Rows 6–15.

Row 100: Ch 1, turn. Sc in each of first 2 dc, sc in ch-2 sp, sc in each of next 2 dc. 3 sc in each ch-5 sp across, sc in each of next 2 dc, sk ch-2 sp, sc in each of last 2 dc. Total 30 sc.

Row 101: Ch 1, turn. Sc in each sc across. Fasten off.

FINISHING

With tapestry needle, weave in ends. Wet block to size and shape.

FRINGE

Cut a piece of cardboard 8 in. (20.5 cm) long. Wind the yarn loosely and evenly around the cardboard 15 times, then cut across one end.

With WS facing and using a crochet hook, draw the folded end of a single strand through the end stitch along bottom of scarf and pull the loose ends through the folded end. Repeat in every other st across. Make sure there is a fringe in each corner.

Rep for other end of scarf.

Block fringe so it lies flat. Trim to 7 in. (18 cm).

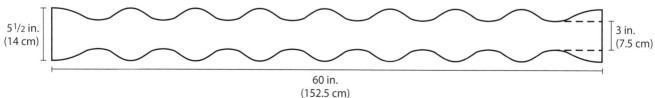

5½ in. (14 cm) 3 in. (7.5 cm)

60 in. (152.5 cm)

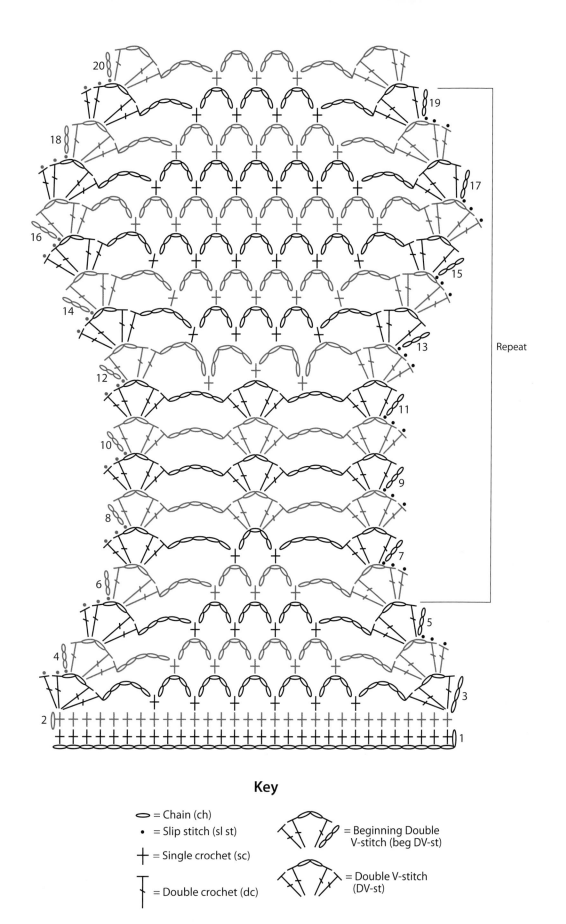

Key

⬭ = Chain (ch)

• = Slip stitch (sl st)

✛ = Single crochet (sc)

ϯ = Double crochet (dc)

⋀ = Beginning Double V-stitch (beg DV-st)

⋀ = Double V-stitch (DV-st)

Iced Silver Fox Sweater

Designed by Kristin Omdahl

This sweater's ingenious assembly was inspired by a floral motif deconstructed into squares and triangles . . . because triangles can be joined together to make squares, and squares can be joined together to make sweaters! The entire garment is composed of only six motifs, pulled together with a simple hem in single crochet.

SKILL LEVEL

EXPERIENCED

FINISHED MEASUREMENTS

	BUST	LENGTH
Small	36 in. (91.5 cm)	21 in. (53.5 cm)
Medium	40 in. (101.5 cm)	23 in. (58.5 cm)
Large	44 in. (112 cm)	25 in. (63.5 cm)
Extra Large	48 in. (121.5 cm)	27 in. (68.5 cm)

MATERIALS

1 Super Fine

Kristin Omdahl Yarns Be So Fine Yarn (100% bamboo; 4 oz./113 g; 650 yd./594 m)
» Iced Silver Fox: 1 (2, 2, 2) hanks

» U.S. size F-5 (3.75 mm) crochet hook
» Stitch markers (6)

GAUGE

Each round of double crochet = 1 in. (2.5 cm) in motif rounds. For gauge swatch, work Diamond Motif through Round 6. If your gauge is accurate, you may use it as the beginning of the motif and continue with Round 7.

SPECIAL STITCHES

2 double-crochet cluster (2dcCL): [Yo, insert hook as indicated, yo, pull up lp, yo, pull through 2 lps] twice, yo, pull through all 3 lps.

3 double-crochet custer (3dcCL): [Yo, insert hook as indicated, yo, pull up lp, yo, pull through 2 lps] 3 times, yo, pull through all 4 lps.

PATTERN NOTES

» Rounds are always worked with the RS facing you. Do not turn until instructed to do so.
» There are two methods for assembling the garment. To join-as-you-go, when working the final row of the bottom triangles and the sleeves, replace the ch 3 with [ch 1, sl st in corresponding ch-3 sp on the adjacent piece, ch 1], then continue with current piece. If you prefer to sew the seams, work each piece to completion, then use a tapestry needle and a length of yarn to sew the pieces together.

Pattern

DIAMOND MOTIF (make 2)

Rnd 1 (RS): Ch 8, sl st to first ch to form ring. Ch 5 (counts as dc, ch-2). *[Dc in ring, ch 2] 7 times. Sl st to third ch of beg ch-5 to join. Total 8 ch-2 sps. Place marker anywhere on round to mark as RS.

Rnd 2: Ch 3 (counts as dc here and throughout), 2 dc in ch-2 sp. *Ch 2, 3 dc in next ch-2 sp. Rep from * around. Ch 2, sl st to top of ch-3 at beg of round to join. Total 8 ch-2 sps.

Rnd 3: Ch 3, dc in each of the next 2 dcs, dc in next ch-2 sp. *Ch 2, dc in same ch-2 sp, dc in each of next 3 dcs, dc in next ch-2 sp. Rep from * around. Ch 2, dc in same ch-2 sp, sl st to top of ch-3 at beg of round to join. Total 8 ch-2 sps.

Rnd 4: Ch 3, dc in each of next 3 dcs, dc in ch-2 sp. *Ch 2, dc in same ch-2 sp, dc in each of next 5 dcs, dc in next ch-2 sp. Rep from * around. Ch 2, dc in same ch-2 sp, dc in next dc, sl st to top of ch-3 at beg of round to join. Total 8 ch-2 sps.

Rnd 5: Ch 3, dc in each of next 3 sts, ch 3, sk next dc, sc in ch-2 sp, ch 3, sk next dc. *Dc in each of next 5 sts, ch 3, sk next dc, sc in ch-2 sp, ch 3, sk next dc. Rep from * around. Dc in next dc, sl st to top of ch-3 at beg of round to join. Total 8 pairs of ch-3 sps.

Rnd 6: Ch 3, dc in each of next 2 sts, ch 4, sc in ch-3 sp, sc in sc, sc in ch-3 sp, ch 4, sk next dc. *Dc in each of next 3 sts, ch 4, sk next dc, sc in ch-3 sp, sc in sc, sc in ch-3 sp, ch 4, sk next dc. Rep from * around. Sl st to top of ch-3 at beg of round to join. Total 16 ch-4 sps.

Rnd 7: Sl st into next dc, [ch 3, 2dcCL (counts as 3dcCL)] in same st, ch 5, sk next dc, sc in ch-4 sp, sc in each of next 3 scs, sc in ch-4 sp, ch 5, sk next dc. *3dcCL in next dc, ch 5, sk next dc, sc in ch-4 sp, sc in each of next 3 scs, sc in ch-4 sp, ch 5, sk next dc. Rep from * around. Sl st to top of CL at beg of round to join. Total 8 3dcCLs.

Rnd 8: Ch 1, sc in same st, ch 4, sk 2 scs, [tr, ch 2] 3 times in next sc, tr in same sc, ch 4, sk 2 scs. *Sc in cluster, ch 4, sk 2 scs, work [tr, ch 2] 3 times in next sc, tr in same sc, ch 4, sk 2 scs. Rep from * around. Sl st to first st at beg of round to join. Total 16 ch-4 sps.

Rnd 9: Ch 6 (counts as dc, ch 3), dc in same st, ch 3, sc in ch-4 sp, sc in tr, sc in ch-2 sp, ch 3. [Dc, ch 3, dc] in next ch-2 sp, ch 3, sc in ch-2 sp, sc in tr, sc in ch-4 sp, ch 3. *[Dc, ch 3, dc] in next sc, ch 3, sc in ch-4 sp, sc in tr, sc in ch-2 sp, ch 3. [Dc, ch 3, dc] in next ch-2 sp, ch 3, sc in ch-2 sp, sc in tr, sc in ch-4 sp, ch 3. Rep from * around. Sl st to third ch of ch-6 at beg of round to join. Total 16 points.

Rnd 10: Sl st into ch-3 sp. Ch 6 (counts as dc, ch 3), dc in same ch-3 sp, ch 3, sc in ch-3 sp, ch 2, sk 1 sc, sc in next sc, ch 2, sk next sc, sc in ch-3 sp, ch 3. *[Dc, ch 3, dc] in next ch-3 sp, ch 3, sc in ch-3 sp, ch 2, sk 1 sc, sc in next sc, ch 2, sk next sc, sc in ch-3 sp, ch 3. Rep from * around. Sl st to third ch of ch-6 at beg of round to join. Total 16 points.

Rnd 11: Sl st into ch-3 sp. Ch 6 (counts as dc, ch 3), dc in same ch-3 sp, sk to center sc of next 3 sc (has a ch-2 on each side), [dtr, ch 3, dtr] in that sc. *Sk to middle ch-3 sp of three, [dc, ch 3, dc] in that sp, sk to center sc of next 3 sc, [dtr, ch 3, dtr] in that st. Rep from * around. Sl st to third ch of ch-6 at beg of round to join. Total 16 (dtr, ch 3, dtr) groups.

Rnd 12: Sl st into ch-3 sp. Ch 6 (counts as dc, ch 3), ([dc, ch 3] twice, dc) in same ch-3 sp (first corner made). [Dc, ch 3, dc] in each of next 7 ch-3 sps. *([Dc, ch 3] 3 times, dc) in next ch-3 sp (next corner made), [dc, ch 3, dc] in each of the next 7 ch-3 sps. Rep from * around. Sl st to third ch of ch-6 at beg of round to join. Total 4 corners.

Rnd 13: Sl st into ch-3 sp. Ch 6 (counts as dc, ch 3), dc in same ch-3 sp, ([dc, ch 3] 3 times, dc) in next ch-3 sp (first corner made), [dc, ch 3, dc] in each of the next 9 ch-3 sps. *([Dc, ch 3] 3 times, dc) in next ch-3 sp (next corner made), [dc, ch 3, dc] in each of the next 9 ch-3 sps. Rep from * once. ([Dc, ch 3] 3 times, dc) in next ch-3 sp (next corner made), [dc, ch 3, dc] in each of the next 8 ch-3 sps. Sl st to third ch of ch-6 at beg of round to join. Total 4 corners.

Rnd 14: Sl st into ch-sp. Ch 6 (counts as dc, ch 3), dc in same ch-3 sp, [dc, ch 3, dc] in next ch-3 sp, ([dc, ch 3] 3 times, dc) in next ch-3 sp (first corner made), [dc, ch 3, dc] in each of the next 11 ch-sps, *([Dc, ch 3] 3 times, dc) in next ch-3 sp (next corner made), [dc, ch 3, dc] in each of the next 11 ch-3 sps. Rep from * once. ([Dc, ch 3] 3 times, dc) in next ch-3 sp (next corner made), [dc, ch 3, dc] in each of next 9 ch-3 sps. Sl st to third ch of ch-6 at beg of round to join. Total 4 corners.

NOTE: *Starting with Row 15, work in rows, not in rounds.*

Row 15: Ch 3, turn. [Dc, ch 3, dc] in each of the next 10 ch-3 sps. *([Dc, ch 3] 3 times, dc) in next ch-3 sp, [dc, ch 3, dc] in each of the next 13 ch-3 sps. Rep from * once. *([Dc, ch 3] 3 times, dc) in next ch-3 sp, [dc, ch 3, dc] in each of the next 10 ch-3 sps, dc in next dc. Do not complete round.

Row 16: Ch 3, turn. [Dc, ch 3, dc] in each of the next 11 ch-3 sps, *([Dc, ch 3] 3 times, dc) in next ch-3 sp, [dc, ch 3, dc] in each of the next 15 ch-3 sps. Rep from * once. ([Dc, ch 3] 3 times, dc) in next ch-3 sp, dc in each of next 11 ch-3 sps, dc under ch-3. Size S, fasten off. Other sizes continue below.

Sizes M, L, XL

Row 17: Ch 3 (counts as dc), turn, [dc, ch 3, dc] in the next 12 ch-3 sps, *([Dc, ch 3] 3 times, dc) in next ch-3 sp, [dc, ch 3, dc] in each of the next 17 ch-3 sps. Rep from * once. ([Dc, ch 3], dc) in next ch-3 sp, [dc, ch 3, dc] in the next 12 ch-3 sps, dc under ch-3. Size M, fasten off. Other sizes continue below.

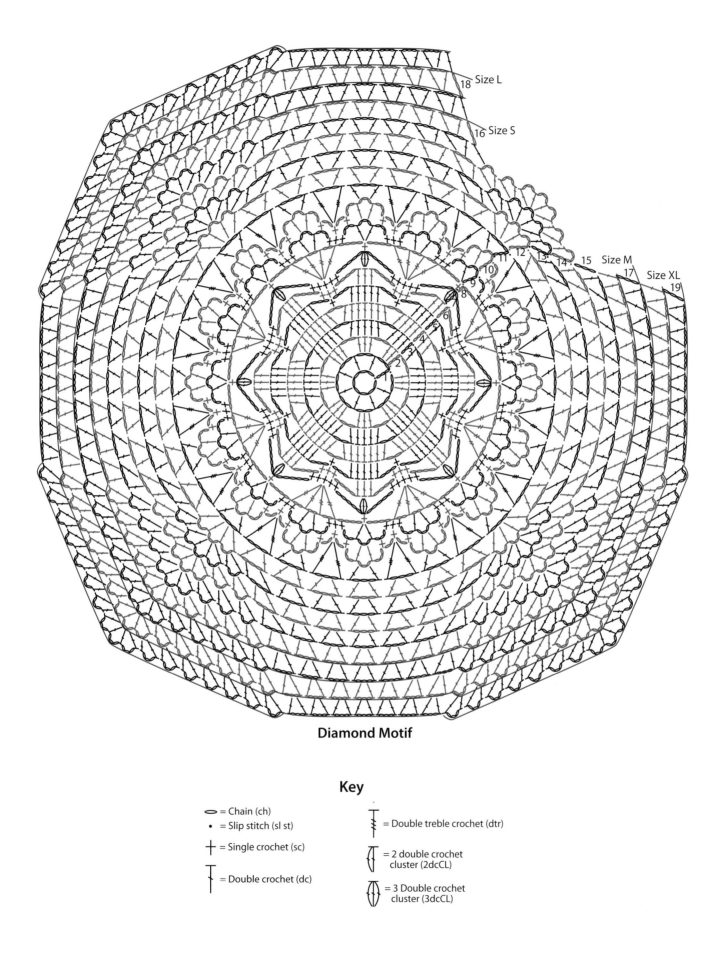

Diamond Motif

Size L — 18

Size S — 16

11 12 13 14 15 Size M — 17

Size XL — 19

9 10

8

6

5 7

3 4

2

Key

⌒ = Chain (ch)

• = Slip stitch (sl st)

+ = Single crochet (sc)

T = Double crochet (dc)

‡ = Double treble crochet (dtr)

⬠ = 2 double crochet cluster (2dcCL)

⬠ = 3 Double crochet cluster (3dcCL)

Sizes L, XL

Row 18: Ch 3 (counts as dc), turn, [dc, ch 3, dc] in the next 13 ch-3 sps, *([Dc, ch 3] 3 times, dc) in next ch-3 sp, [dc, ch 3, dc] in each of the next 19 ch-3 sps. Rep from * once. ([Dc, ch 3] 3 times, dc) in next ch-3 sp, [dc, ch 3, dc] in the last 13 ch-3 sps, dc under ch-3. Size L, fasten off. Size XL, continue below.

Size XL

Row 19: Ch 3 (counts as dc), turn, [dc, ch 3, dc] in the next 14 ch-3 sps, *([Dc, ch 3] 3 times, dc) in next ch-3 sp, [dc, ch 3, dc] in each of the next 21 ch-3 sps. Rep from * once. ([Dc, ch 3] three times, dc) in next ch-3 sp, [dc, ch 3, dc] in next 14 ch-3 sps, dc under ch-3. Fasten off.

LOWER BODY TRIANGLE (make 2)

Ch 4, sl st in fourth ch from hook to form a ring.

Row 1 (RS): Ch 5 (counts as dc, ch 2), ([dc, ch 2] 4 times, dc) in ring. Place marker anywhere on row to mark as RS. Total 5 ch-2 sps.

Row 2: Ch 5 (counts as dc, ch 2), turn. Dc in ch-2 sp, dc in dc, dc in ch-2 sp, ch 2, [dc in same ch-2 sp, dc in dc, dc in ch-2 sp] 3 times, ch 2, dc in last dc. Total 5 ch-2 sps.

Row 3: Ch 5 (counts as dc, ch-2), turn. Dc in ch-2 sp, dc in each of next 3 dc, dc in ch-2 sp, ch 2, [dc in same ch-2 sp, dc in each of next 3 dc, dc in ch-2 sp, ch 2] 3 times, ch 2, dc in last dc. Total 5 ch-2 sps.

Row 4: Ch 5 (counts as dc, ch-2), turn. Dc in ch-2 sp, dc in each of next 5 dc, dc in ch-2 sp, ch 2, [dc in same ch-2 sp, dc in each of next 5 dc, dc in ch-2 sp, ch 2] 3 times, ch 2, dc in last dc. Total 5 ch-2 sps.

Row 5: Ch 5, turn. Sc in ch-2 sp, ch 3, sk dc, dc in each of next 5 dc. [Ch 3, sk dc, sc in ch-2 sp, ch 3, sk dc, dc in each of next 5 dc] 3 times. Ch 3, sc in last ch-2 sp, ch 2, dc in last dc. Total 5 sc.

Row 6: Ch 7 (counts as dc, ch 4), turn. Sc in ch-2 sp, sc in sc, sc in ch-3 sp, ch 4, sk dc, dc in each of next 3 sts. [Ch 4, sk dc, sc in ch-3 sp, sc in sc, sc in ch-3 sp, ch 4, sk dc, dc in each of next 3 dc] 3 times. Ch 4, sk dc, sc in ch-3 sp, sc in sc, sc in ch-2 sp, ch 4, dc in last dc. Total 15 sc.

Row 7: Ch 8 (counts as dc, ch 5), turn. Sc in ch-4 sp, sc in each of next 3 sc, sc in ch-4 sp, ch 5, 3dcCL over next 3 dc. [Ch 5, sc in ch-4 sp, sc in next 3 sc, sc in ch-4 sp, ch 5, 3dcCL over next 3 sts] 3 times. Ch 5, sc in next ch-4 sp, sc in each of next 3 sc, sc in ch-4 sp, ch 5, dc in last dc. Total 25 sc.

Row 8: Ch 1, turn. Sc in same st, ch 4, sk 2 sc, ([tr, ch 2] 3 times, tr) in next sc, ch 4, sk 2 sc. *Sc in cluster, ch 4, sk 2 sc, ([tr, ch 2] 3 times, tr) in next sc, ch 4, sk 2 sc. Rep from * across to last dc, sc in last dc. Total 6 sc.

Row 9: Ch 6 (counts as dc, ch 3), turn. Dc in same st, ch 3, sc in ch-4 sp, sc in tr, sc in ch-2 sp, ch 3. [Dc, ch 3, dc] in next ch-2 sp, ch 3, sc in ch-2 sp, sc in tr, sc in ch-4 sp, ch 3. *[Dc, ch 3, dc] in next sc, ch 3, sc in ch-4 sp, sc in tr, sc in ch-2 sp, ch 3. [Dc, ch 3, dc] in next ch-2 sp, ch 3, sc in ch-2 sp, sc in

tr, sc in ch-4 sp, ch 3. Rep from * across to last sc. [Dc, ch 3, dc] in last sc. Total 11 (dc, ch 3, dc) shells.

Row 10: Ch 6 (counts as dc, ch 3), turn. Dc in ch-3 sp, ch 3, sc in ch-3 sp, ch 2, skip sc, sc in next sc, sk sc, ch 2, sc in ch-3 sp, ch 3, [dc, ch 3, dc] in next ch-3 sp. *Ch 3, sc in next ch-3 sp, ch 2, sk sc, sc in next sc, sk sc, ch 2, sc in ch-3 sp, ch 3, [dc, ch 3, dc] in next ch-3 sp. Rep from * across. Total 11 (dc, ch-3, dc) shells.

Row 11: Ch 6 (counts as dc, ch 3), turn. Dc in ch-3 sp, sk to center sc of next three sc, [dtr, ch 3, dtr] in that sc. *Sk to middle ch-3 sp of three, [dc, ch 3, dc] in that sp, sk to center sc of next three sc, [dtr, ch 3, dtr] in that st. Rep from * to last ch-3 sp. [Dc, ch 3, dc] in last ch-3 sp. Total 21 ch-3 sps.

Row 12: Ch 6 (counts as dc, ch 3), turn. [Dc, ch 3, dc] in same ch-3 sp, [dc, ch 3, dc] in each of next 9 ch-3 sps, ([dc, ch 3] 3 times, dc) in next ch-3 sp, [dc, ch 3, dc] in each of next 9 ch-3 sps, ([dc, ch 3] twice, dc) in last ch-3 sp. Total 25 ch-3 sps.

Row 13: Ch 6 (counts as dc, ch 3), turn. [Dc, ch 3, dc] in same ch-3 sp, [dc, ch 3, dc] in each of next 11 ch-3 sps. ([Dc, ch 3] 3 times, dc) in next ch-3 sp, [dc, ch 3, dc] in each of next 11 ch-3 sps, ([dc, ch 3] twice, dc) in last ch-3 sp. Total 29 ch-3 sps.

Row 14: Ch 6 (counts as dc, ch 3), turn. [Dc, ch 3, dc] in same ch-3 sp, [dc, ch 3, dc] in each of next 13 ch-3 sps, ([dc, ch

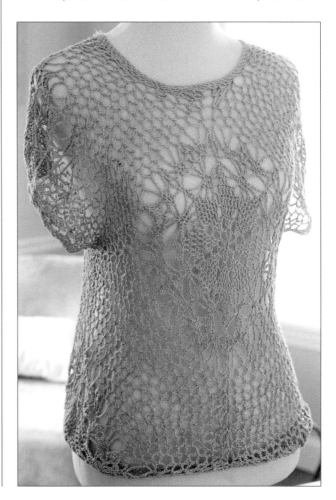

3] 3 times, dc) in next ch-3 sp, [dc, ch 3, dc] in each of next 13 ch-3 sps, ([dc, ch 3] twice, dc) in last ch-3 sp. Total 33 ch-3 sps.

Row 15: Ch 6 (counts as dc, ch 3), turn. [Dc, ch 3, dc] in same ch-3 sp, [dc, ch 3, dc] in each of next 15 ch-3 sps, ([dc, ch 3] 3 times, dc) in next ch-3 sp, [dc, ch 3, dc] in each of next 15 ch-3 sps, ([dc, ch 3] twice, dc) in last ch-3 sp. Total 37 ch-3 sps.

Row 16: Ch 6 (counts as dc, ch 3), turn. [Dc, ch 3, dc] in same ch-3 sp, [dc, ch 3, dc] in each of next 17 ch-3 sps, ([dc, ch 3] 3 times, dc) in next ch-3 sp, [dc, ch 3, dc] in each of next 17 ch-3 sps, ([dc, ch 3] twice, dc) in last ch-3 sp. Total 41 ch-3 sps. Size S fasten off; other sizes continue below.

Sizes M, L, XL

Row 17: Ch 6 (counts as dc, ch 3), turn. [Dc, ch 3, dc] in same ch-3 sp, [dc, ch 3, dc] in each of next 19 ch-3 sps, ([dc, ch 3] 3 times, dc) in next ch-3 sp, [dc, ch3, dc] in each of next 19 ch-3 sps, ([dc, ch 3] twice, dc) in last ch-3 sp. Total 45 ch-3 sps. Size M fasten off; other sizes continue below.

Sizes L, XL

Row 18: Ch 6 (counts as dc, ch 3), turn. [Dc, ch 3, dc] in same ch-3 sp, [dc, ch 3, dc] in each of next 21 ch-3 sps, ([dc, ch 3] 3 times, dc) in next ch-3 sp, [dc, ch 3, dc] in each of next 21 ch-3 sps, ([dc, ch 3] twice, dc) in last ch-3 sp. Total 49 ch-3 sps. Size L fasten off; size XL continue below.

Size XL

Row 19: Ch 6 (counts as dc, ch 3), turn. [Dc, ch 3, dc] in same ch-3 sp, [dc, ch 3, dc] in each of next 23 ch-3 sps, ([dc, ch 3] 3 times, dc) in next ch-3 sp, [dc, ch 3, dc] in each of next 23 ch-3 sps, ([dc, ch 3] twice, dc) in last ch-3 sp. Total 53 ch-3 sps.

Key

⬭ = Chain (ch)

• = Slip stitch (sl st)

+ = Single crochet (sc)

┃ = Double crochet (dc)

╪ = Double treble crochet (dtr)

⋔ = 2 double crochet cluster (2dcCL)

⋔ = 3 Double crochet cluster (3dcCL)

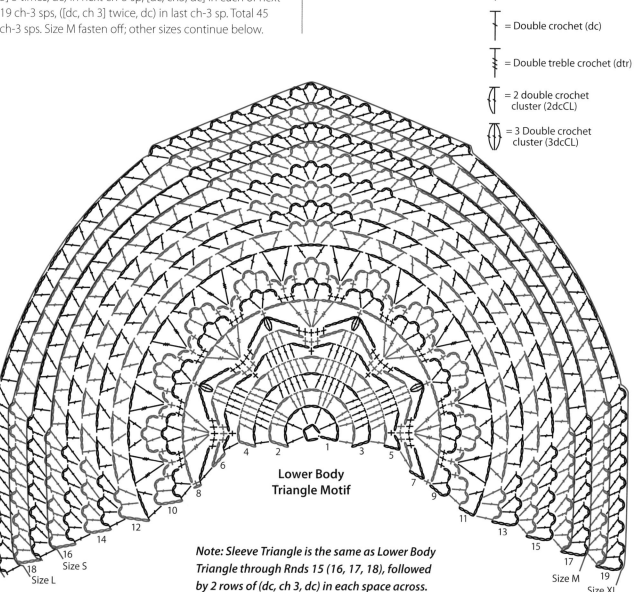

Lower Body Triangle Motif

Note: Sleeve Triangle is the same as Lower Body Triangle through Rnds 15 (16, 17, 18), followed by 2 rows of (dc, ch 3, dc) in each space across.

SLEEVE TRIANGLE (make 2)

Size S only
Rows 1–14: As for lower body triangle.

> **NOTE:** *The next 2 rows are worked in two separate sections, excluding the center point.*

Row 15: Ch 6 (counts as dc, ch 3), turn. Dc in same ch-3 sp, [dc, ch 3, dc] in each of next 14 ch-3 sps, dc in next ch-3 sp.
Row 16: Turn. Sl st into first ch-3 sp, ch 3 (counts as dc), [dc, ch 3, dc] in each of next 13 ch-3 sps, dc in last ch-3 sp. Fasten off.
Rep Rows 15–16 for opposite side of triangle. Fasten off.

Size M only
Rows 1–15: As for for lower body triangle.

> **NOTE:** *The next 2 rows are worked in two separate sections, excluding the center point.*

Row 16: Ch 6 (counts as dc, ch), dc in same ch-3 sp, [dc, ch 3, dc] in each of next 14 ch-3 sps, dc in next ch-3 sp.
Row 17: Turn. Sl st into first ch-3 sp, ch 3 (counts as dc), [dc, ch 3, dc] in each of next 13 ch-3 sps, dc in last ch-3 sp.
Rep Rows 16–17 for opposite side of triangle.

Size L only
Rows 1–16: As for lower body triangle.

> **NOTE:** *The next 2 rows are worked in two separate sections, excluding the center point.*

Row 17: Ch 6 (counts as dc, ch 3), dc in same ch-3 sp, [dc, ch 3, dc] in each of next 15 ch-3 sps, dc in next ch-3 sp.
Row 18: Turn. Sl st into first ch-3 sp, ch 3 (counts as dc), [dc, ch 3, dc] in each of next 14 ch-3 sps, dc in last ch-3 sp. Fasten off.
Rep Rows 17–18 for opposite side of triangle. Fasten off.

Size XL only
Rows 1–17: As for lower body triangle.

> **NOTE:** *The next 2 rows are worked in two separate sections, excluding the center point.*

Row 18: Ch 6 (counts as dc, ch 3), turn, dc in same ch-3 sp, [dc, ch 3, dc] in each of next 16 ch-3 sps, dc in next ch-3 sp.
Row 19: Turn. Sl st into first ch-3 sp, ch 3 (counts as dc), [dc, ch 3, dc] in each of next 15 ch-3 sps, dc in last ch-3 sp. Fasten off.
Rep Rows 18–19 for opposite side of triangle. Fasten off.

FINISHING AND ASSEMBLY

Wet block the pieces if desired.
Attach the sleeves and the lower body triangles to the diamond motifs using the join-as-you-go method or by sewing the seams (see Pattern Notes).

NECKLINE TRIM

Round 1: Sl st to any ch-2 sp, ch 1, 2 sc in each ch-2 sp around. Sl st to first st at beg of round to join. Do not turn.
Rounds 2–4: Ch 1, sc in each st around, sl st to first st at beg of round to join. Fasten off.

SLEEVE TRIM

Round 1: Sl st to any end of row, ch 1, 2 sc in each end of row around. Sl st to first st at beg of round to join.
Rounds 2–4: Ch 1, sc in each st around, sl st to first st at beg of round to join. Fasten off.

HEM TRIM

Round 1: Sl st to any end of row, ch 1, 2 sc in each end of row around. Sl st to first st at beg of round to join.
Rounds 2–8: Ch 1, sc in each st around, sl st to first st at beg of round to join. Fasten off.

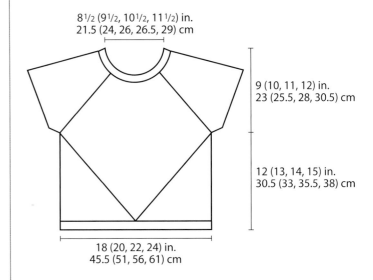

8½ (9½, 10½, 11½) in.
21.5 (24, 26, 26.5, 29) cm

9 (10, 11, 12) in.
23 (25.5, 28, 30.5) cm

12 (13, 14, 15) in.
30.5 (33, 35.5, 38) cm

18 (20, 22, 24) in.
45.5 (51, 56, 61) cm

Lacy
Sleeveless
Cardigan

Designed by Marty Miller

This all-season cardigan is made with solid-color cotton that gives the stitch patterns beautiful definition. Three panels are crocheted separately then joined together with simple crocheted seams. Use a shawl pin at the neckline if you prefer the flyaway style, or turn back the collar and pin at the waist for a more tailored silhouette.

SKILL LEVEL

EASY

MEASUREMENTS
Allowing for 4–6 in. (10.2–15.25 cm) of ease

	CHEST	**LENGTH** (including border)
X-Small	34 in. (86.4 cm)	25½ in. (64.8 cm)
Small	38 in. (96.5 cm)	25½ in. (64.8 cm)
Medium	42 in. (106.7 cm)	31½ in. (80 cm)
Large	46 in. (116.8 cm)	31½ in. (80 cm)

Instructions are for size XS, with sizes S, M, and L in parentheses.

MATERIALS

Light

Tahki Yarns Cotton Classic (100% mercerized cotton; 1.75 oz./50 g; 108 yd./100 m)
  » Leaf Green (3716): 9 (10, 13, 14) skeins

  » U.S. size H-8 (5 mm) crochet hook
  » Stitch markers (3)
  » Coilless safety pins
  » Tapestry needle
  » Blocking pins
  » Blocking board or towel

GAUGE
16 stitches and 20 rows in sc = 4 in. (10.2 cm), blocked.

Row 1 of gauge swatch can start with either foundation single crochet or a traditional chain foundation.
For fsc method:
Row 1: Work 23 fsc. Total 23 sc.

For traditional foundation chain method:
Ch 24.
Row 1: Sc in second ch from hook and in each ch across. Total 23 sc.

For both methods:
Row 2: Ch 1, turn. Sc in each sc to end.
Rep Row 2 until swatch measures at least 4½ in. (11.4 cm).

SPECIAL STITCHES
Foundation single crochet (fsc): Ch 2 (does not count as fsc). Insert hook into first ch made, yo, pull up lp, ch 1, (this will be the entry point—the foundation ch—for the next st; pinch it with your thumb and finger to make it easier to find), yo, pull through 2 loops to finish the single crochet. *Insert the hook into fch just made, yo, pull up lp, ch 1 (the entry point—the foundation ch—for the next st), yo, pull through 2 loops on hook to finish the fsc. Rep from * until you reach the target number of fsc.
Single crochet 2 together (sc2tog): Insert hook where indicated, yo, pull up lp, insert hook into next st, yo, pull up lp, yo, pull through all 3 lps.
3 double crochet cluster (CL): [Yo, insert hook as instructed, yo, pull up lp, yo, pull through 2 lps] 3 times, yo, pull through all 4 lps. In this pattern, enter the same stitch for each part of the cluster.

Cluster Pattern (CL pattern) (starts with odd number of sc):

Row 1 (RS): Ch 3 (counts as dc), sk first st at base of chs, dc in next sc, ch 1, sk next sc, CL in next sc, ch 1. *Sk next sc, CL in next sc, ch 1. Rep from * across until 2 sc remain. Dc in each of last 2 sc.

Row 2: Ch 1, turn. Sc in each of the first 2 dc, sc into ch-sp, sc into ch. *Sk cluster, sc into ch-sp, sc into ch. Rep from * until CL, ch, and 2 dcs remain. Sk CL, sc in ch-sp, sc in each of last 2 dcs.

NOTE: *Do not work into the top of the CLs. Sc stitches are worked into the ch-sp and then into the ch that creates those ch-sps.*

Row 3: Rep Row 1.
Row 4: Rep Row 2.

Filet Stitch Pattern (starts with multiple of 4 + 3 sc)

Row 1 (RS): Ch 3 (counts as dc), turn. Sk first sc, dc in next sc. *Ch 2, sk 1 sc, sc in next sc, ch 2, sk 1 sc, dc in next sc. Rep from * to last sc, dc in last sc.

Row 2: Ch 1, turn. Sc in each of first 2 dc. *Ch 2, dc in next sc, ch 2, sc in next dc. Rep from * across to last dc, sc in last dc.

Row 3: Ch 3, turn. Skip first sc, dc in next sc. *Ch 2, sc in next dc, ch 2, dc in next sc. Rep from * to last sc, dc in last sc.

Row 4: Rep Row 2.
Row 5: Rep Row 3.
Row 6: Rep Row 2.

» Most crochet patterns start with a long chain, then a row of stitches worked into those chains. Foundation crochet stitches combine these two steps. This reduces the possibility of missing a stitch or twisting the chain, makes tension more consistent throughout the garment, provides a nice finished bottom, and offers some stretch. It takes a little practice to isolate the target entry point for each stitch and to have all of the stitches on the row come out even. However, once you master foundation stitches, you may find that you prefer them to the traditional long chain!

This pattern includes both methods for the start of each panel. Whichever method you choose, the pattern instructions are the same starting on Row 2.

» Ch 3 at the beginning of a row counts as a dc.

» Because the three sections of the sweater are joined by crocheting them together around the end stitches, the sections will measure slightly larger when they are separate than when they are joined together. The edging adds approximately 1 in. (2.5 cm) to the length and 1–2 in. (2.5–5 cm) to the circumference. The width of the two front panels added together is slightly larger than the width of the back panel. This allows you to overlap the front panels a bit and pin them closed, folding back the collar for a tailored fit.

» To adjust the length, subtract or add all 6 rows of the filet stitch pattern, all 4 rows of the CL pattern, or both. If adding both, work 4 rows of sc in between. If subtracting both, also subtract the 4 rows of sc in between. Always finish with 4 rows of sc at the shoulder.

» To adjust the width of the panels, add or subtract a multiple of 4 fscs or chs.

Pattern

FRONT PANEL (make 2)

Fsc method:

Row 1 (RS): Work 31 (35, 39, 43) fsc. Place marker anywhere to indicate RS.

Traditional foundation ch method:

Ch 32 (36, 40, 44).

Row 1 (RS): Sc in second ch from hook and in each ch to end. Total 31 (35, 39, 43) sc. Place marker anywhere to indicate RS.

Both methods:

Rows 2–4: Ch 1, turn. Sc in each sc across. Total 31 (35, 39, 43) sc.

Rows 5–10: Work Rows 1-6 of Filet Stitch Pattern.

Row 11: Ch 1, turn. Sc in each of first 2 sc, sc in ch-2 sp. *Sc in next st, sc in ch-2 sp. Rep from * until 2 sts remain, sc in each of last 2 sts. Total 31 (35, 39, 43) sc.

Rows 12–14 (CL pattern): Ch 1, turn. Sc in each sc to end.

Row 15: Ch 3, turn. Sk first sc, dc in next sc, ch 1, sk next sc, CL in next sc. *Ch 1, skip next sc, CL in next sc. Rep from * across until 3 sts remain. Ch 1, sk next st, dc in each of last 2 sc. Total 13 (15, 17, 19) CL.

Row 16: Ch 1, turn. Sc in each of the first 2 dc, sc into ch-sp, sc into ch. *Sk cluster, sc into ch-sp, sc into ch. Rep from * until CL, ch, and 2 dcs remain. Sk CL, sc in ch-sp, sc in each of last 2 dcs. Total 31 (35, 39, 43) sc.

NOTE: *Do not work into the top of the CLs. Sc stitches are worked into the ch-sp and then into the ch that creates those ch-sps.*

Row 17: Rep Row 15.
Row 18: Rep Row 16.
Rows 19–22: Ch 1, turn. Sc in each sc to end.
Rows 23–76 (76, 94, 94): Rep Rows 5–22 three (3, 4, 4) times. Fasten off.

BACK

Fsc method:

Row 1 (RS): Work 59 (67, 75, 83) fsc. Place marker anywhere to indicate RS.

Traditional foundation ch method:
Ch 60 (68, 76, 84).

Row 1 (RS): Sc in second ch from hook and in each ch to end. Total 59 (67, 75, 83) sc. Place marker anywhere to indicate RS.

Both methods:

Rows 2–4: Ch 1, turn. Sc in each sc across. Total 59 (67, 75, 83) sc.

Rows 5–10: Work Rows 1–6 of Filet Stitch Pattern.

Row 11: Ch 1, turn. Sc in each of first 2 sc. *Sc in ch-2 sp, sc in next st. Rep from * until 2 sts remain, sc in each of last 2 sts. Total 59 (67, 75, 83) sc.

Rows 12–14: Ch 1, turn. Sc in each sc to end.

Key

- ⬭ = Chain (ch)
- ✕ = Single crochet (sc)
- ⊤ = Double crochet (dc)
- ⬮ = 3-double crochet cluster (CL)

Cluster Pattern (CL pattern)

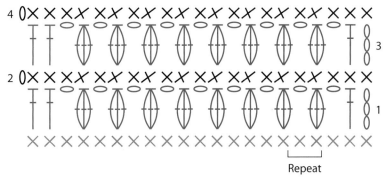

Repeat

Filet Stitch Pattern

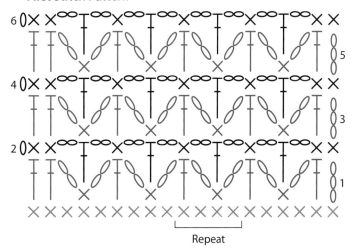

Repeat

around the post of each dc or ch-3 at the end of a row. Fasten off.

With RS facing you, join yarn to top left corner of same panel. Working down the side edge, *sc in the end of each sc row, (sc, ch 1) around the post of each dc or ch-3 at the end of a row. Fasten off.

NOTE: *The number of stitches should be the same for each edge.*

BLOCKING

Using tapestry needle, weave in ends.

Wet block each piece, pinning it gently to the correct size without overstretching. Let the pieces dry completely before unpinning them from the board or towel.

SEAMING

NOTE: *Shoulder seams are worked on the WS (inside) of the sweater. The side seams are worked on the RS of the sweater to create a feature.*

With WS together, use coilless safety pins to pin sides to back, leaving 7½ (8, 8½, 9) in. [19.1 (20.3, 21.6, 22.9) cm] for armhole. Pin shoulders and neck edge together, leaving 8½ (9, 9½, 10) in. [21.6 (22.9, 24.1, 25.4) cm] for neck opening, measured along the back. Try on the sweater to ensure you are happy with the armhole depth and the size of the neck opening; adjust as needed. Keep in mind that the finished openings will decrease approximately ½ in. (1.3 cm) for each armhole and 1 in. (2.5 cm) for the neck when the edging is complete. Remove pins as you seam the garment.

SHOULDER SEAM

With WS facing out, join yarn with a sl st at the shoulder edge of one front panel and the back panel. Working through both panels, sc in each st until 1 st before neck opening (do not go beyond the pinned part). Sl st in the last st. Fasten off.

Repeat for other shoulder seam.

LEFT SIDE SEAM

With RS facing out, join yarn with sl st through both panels at the bottom hem. Sc in each sc and ch-1 sp, working up toward the bottom of the armhole opening until 1 st before opening. Sl st in the last st. Fasten off.

RIGHT SIDE SEAM

With RS facing out, join yarn at bottom of armhole opening with sl st through both panels. Sc in each sc and ch-1 sp, working down toward the hem until 1 st remains. Sl st in the last st. Fasten off.

Row 15 (CL pattern): Ch 3, turn. Sk first sc, dc in next sc, ch 1, skip next sc, CL in next sc. *Ch 1, skip next sc, CL in next sc. Rep from * across until 3 sts remain. Ch 1, sk next st, dc in each of last 2 sc. Total 27 (31, 35, 39) clusters.

Row 16: Sc in each of the first 2 dc, sc into ch-sp, sc into ch. *Sk cluster, sc into ch-sp, sc into ch. Rep from * until CL, ch, and 2 dcs remain. Sk CL, sc in ch-sp, sc in each of last 2 dcs. Total 59 (67, 75, 83) sc.

NOTE: *Do not work into the top of the CLs. Sc stitches are worked into the ch-sp and then into the ch that creates those ch-sps.*

Row 17: Rep Row 15.
Row 18: Rep Row 16.
Rows 19–22: Ch 1, turn. Sc in each sc to end.
Rows 23–76 (76, 94, 94): Rep Rows 5–22 3 (3, 4, 4) times. Fasten off.

EDGING (for each panel)

With RS facing you, join yarn to bottom right corner. Working up the side edge, *sc in the end of each sc row, [sc, ch 1]

EDGING SEAMED GARMENT

BODY

Rnd 1: With RS facing out, join yarn to the bottom edge of the back panel, near one side seam. Sc in each sc around, working (sc, ch 1, sc) in the corner at the side of the front opening at the bottom hem of each front panel, and the corner at the top of each front panel. Sc2tog at the inner corners where the shoulder seams are. Join to first sc with sl st. Do not turn.

Rnd 2: Ch 1. Sc in each sc around, working (sc, ch 1, sc) in each ch-1 space at the four corners. Join to first sc with sl st. Fasten off.

RIGHT ARMHOLE

Rnd 1: With RS facing out, join yarn to armhole edge on back side of sweater, approximately 5 sts up from bottom of armhole. Working up toward shoulder, sc in each st around, working sc2tog around shoulder seam (1 st before, 1 st after), in the 2 sts immediately before the side seam, and in the 2 sts immediately after the side seam. Join with sl st to first sc. Do not turn.

Rnd 2: Ch 1, sc in each sc around. Join to first sc with sl st. Fasten off.

LEFT ARMHOLE

Rnd 1: With RS facing out, join yarn to armhole edge on back side of sweater, approximately 5 sts up from bottom of armhole. Working down toward the side seam, sc in each st around, working sc2tog in the 2 sts immediately before the side seam, the 2 sts immediately after the side seam, and around the shoulder seam (1 st before, 1 st after). Join to first sc with sl st. Do not turn.

Rnd 2: Ch 1. Sc in each sc around. Join to first sc with sl st. Fasten off.

FINISHING

Using tapestry needle, weave in ends.

If desired, wet block the finished garment, pinning it gently to the correct size without overstretching. Let it dry completely before unpinning it from the board or towel.

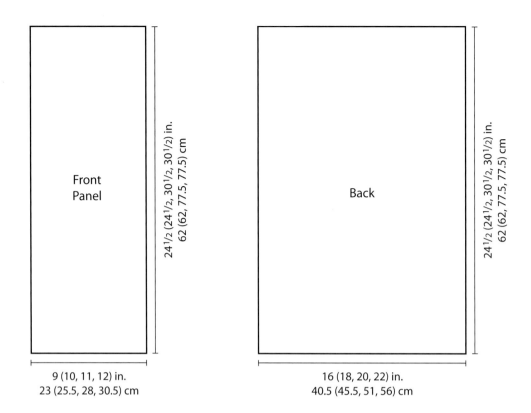

Front
Panel

24½ (24½, 30½, 30½) in.
62 (62, 77.5, 77.5) cm

Back

24½ (24½, 30½, 30½) in.
62 (62, 77.5, 77.5) cm

9 (10, 11, 12) in.
23 (25.5, 28, 30.5) cm

16 (18, 20, 22) in.
40.5 (45.5, 51, 56) cm

Note: Measurements include panel side edging, but do not include lower edging that is added after the panels are sewn together.

Lotus Wrap

Designed by Katya Novikova

*L*otus is a rectangular wrap worked in a flower stitch pattern and decorated with a picot border. The garment is created from the center back outward. After the first half is complete, yarn is rejoined into the foundation chain and the second half is worked in the other direction.

SKILL LEVEL

EASY

MEASUREMENTS

73 in. (185 cm) by 20 in. (50 cm)

MATERIALS

Super Fine

Malabrigo Sock (100% merino wool; 3.53 oz./ 100 g; 440 yd./402 m)
   » Lotus (120): 3 skeins

   » U.S. size G-6 (4 mm) crochet hook
   » Stitch marker
   » Tapestry needle
   » Blocking pins
   » Blocking board or towel

GAUGE

18 stitches and 10 rows in dc = 4 in. (10.2 cm), unblocked.
For gauge swatch, ch 20. Last 3 chs count as first dc on Row 1.
Row 1: Dc into fourth ch from hook and in each ch across. Total 18 dc.
Row 2: Ch 3 (counts as dc), turn. Sk st at base of chs. Dc in each st across, ending with final dc in top of turning ch. Total 18 dc.
Rep Row 2 until swatch measures at least 4½ in. (11.4 cm)

SPECIAL STITCHES

V-stitch (V-st): (Dc, ch 1, dc) in same st.
Fan: (4 dc, ch 2, 4 dc) in same st.
Double crochet 4 together (dc4tog): *[Yo, insert hook as

instructed, yo, pull up lp, yo, pull through 2 lps] 4 times, yo, pull through all 5 lps. In this pattern, dc4tog is worked over 4 dc stitches.
Flower: Dc4tog over 4 sts, ch 4, sc where indicated, ch 4, dc4tog over next 4 sts as indicated.
Small picot: Ch 3, sl st in sc just made (inserting hook into top front loop and front left leg of that sc).
Big picot: Ch 5, sl st in sc just made (inserting hook into top front loop and front left leg of that sc).

PATTERN NOTES

   » Wrap is worked in a multiple of 12 stitches + 5. To make the garment taller or shorter, add or subtract a multiple of 12 stitches to the starting chain. To make the garment wider, add rows on each half, ending with Row 4 and then doing the edging row.

Pattern

FIRST HALF OF WRAP

Ch 89.
Row 1 (RS): Dc in fifth ch from hook. *Ch 1, sk 5 ch, fan in next ch, ch 1, sk 5 ch, V-st in next ch. Rep from * across. Total 7 fans. Place marker anywhere on row to indicate RS.
Row 2: Ch 4 (counts as dc + ch 1 here and throughout), turn. Dc in V-st. *Ch 1, dc4tog over next 4 dc, ch 4, sc in ch-2 sp, ch 4, dc4tog over next 4 dc (flower made), ch 1, V-st in V-st. Rep from * across. Total 7 flowers.
Row 3: Ch 4 (counts as half fan), turn. 4 dc in V-st. *Ch 1, V-st in sc at center of flower, ch 1, fan in V-st. Rep from * 5 times. Ch 1, V-st in sc, ch 1, 4 dc in ch-1 sp, ch 1, dc in third

ch of beginning ch-4 (counts as half fan). Total 6 fans and 2 half fans.

Row 4: Ch 1, turn. Sc in dc, ch 4, dc4tog over next 4 dc (half flower made). *Ch 1, V-st in V-st, ch 1, dc4tog over next 4 dc, ch 4, sc in ch-2 sp, ch 4, dc4tog over next 4 dc (flower made). Rep from * 5 times. Ch 1, V-st in V-st, ch 1, dc4tog over next 4 dc, ch 4, sc in third ch of beginning ch 4 (half flower made). Total 6 flowers and 2 half flowers.

Row 5: Ch 4, turn. Dc in sc. *Ch 1, fan in V-st, ch 1, V-st in sc. Rep from * across. Total 7 fans.

Rows 6–61: Rep Rows 2–5 14 times.

Rows 62–64: Rep Rows 2–4.

Edging row: Ch 1, turn. Sc in sc, big picot, small picot. *Ch 3, sc in top of dc4tog, small picot, ch 1, sc in V-st, small picot, ch 1, sc in top of dc4tog, small picot, ch 3, sc in sc, small picot, big picot, small picot. Rep from * 5 times. Ch 3, sc in top of dc4tog, small picot, ch 1, sc in V-st, small picot, ch 1, sc in top of dc4tog, small picot, ch 3, sc in sc, small picot, big picot. Total 8 big picots. Fasten off.

SECOND HALF OF WRAP

NOTE: *This half of the pattern is not an exact mirror image of the first half. It is set up to keep the spacing consistent, to minimize the appearance of the center back seam, and to have the outer edges of the garment match. There are two fewer rows on the second half than the first half.*

With RS facing, join yarn in first foundation ch (where final dc of Row 1 was made).

Row 1: Ch 4, 4 dc in same ch (half fan made), *ch 1, sk 5 ch, V-st in next ch (opposite the fan from Row 1 of first half), ch 1, sk 5 ch, fan in next ch (opposite the V-st from Row 1 of first half). Rep from * 5 times. Ch 1, sk 5 ch, V-st in next ch, ch 1, sk 5 ch, 4 dc in last ch, ch 1, dc in same ch (half fan made). Total 6 fans and 2 half fans.

Rows 2 and 3: Rep Rows 4 and 5 from first half.

Rows 4–59: Rep Rows 2–5 from first half 14 times.

Rows 60–62: Rep Rows 2–4 from first half.

Edging row: Rep Edging Row from the first half. Fasten off.

FINISHING

Using tapestry needle, weave in ends.

Wet block the garment, pinning it gently to the correct size without overstretching. Pin the picots in place to show them off to their best advantage. Let the wrap dry completely before unpinning it from the board or towel.

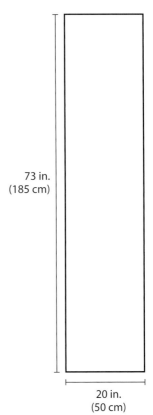

73 in.
(185 cm)

20 in.
(50 cm)

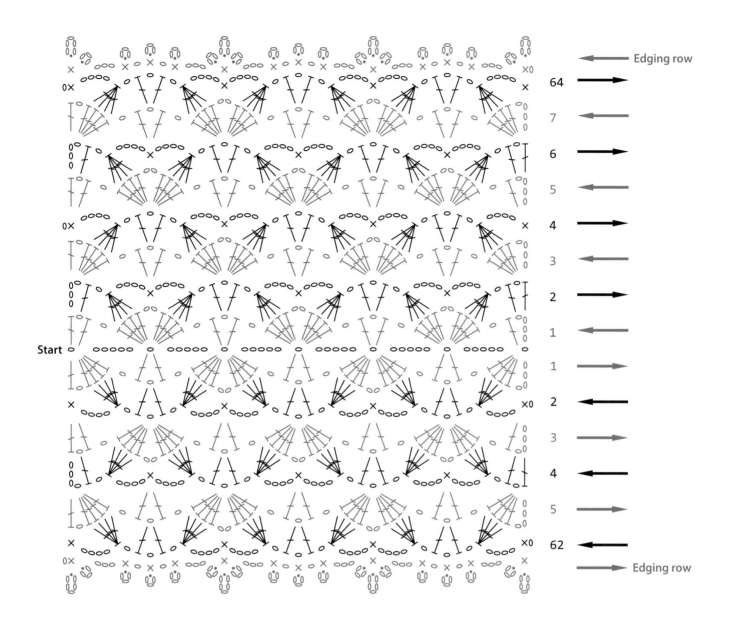

Edging row

64

7

6

5

4

3

2

1

Start

1

2

3

4

5

62

Edging row

Key

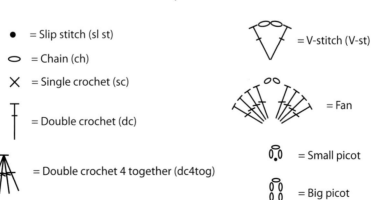

● = Slip stitch (sl st)

⬭ = Chain (ch)

✕ = Single crochet (sc)

⊤ = Double crochet (dc)

⋔ = Double crochet 4 together (dc4tog)

= V-stitch (V-st)

= Fan

= Small picot

= Big picot

Low-Back
Lace Top

Designed by Kristin Omdahl

A daringly low back framed with lace transforms this simple double crochet top into a show-stopper. The unique construction begins with the low-V back, then the rest of the garment is joined modularly.

SKILL LEVEL

INTERMEDIATE

MEASUREMENTS

Finished sizes:

	BUST	LENGTH
Small	36 in. (91.5 cm)	21 in. (53.5 cm)
Medium	40 in. (101.5 cm)	23 in. (58.5 cm)
Large	44 in. (111.5 cm)	25 in. (63.5 cm)
Extra Large	48 in. (121.5 cm)	27 in. (68.5 cm)

Instructions are for size S, with sizes M, L, and XL in parentheses.

MATERIALS

Fine

Kristin Omdahl Yarns Be So Sporty Yarn (100% bamboo; 4 oz./113 g; 325 yd./297 m)
   » Million Dollar Red: 2 (3, 3, 3) hanks

» U.S. size G-6 (4 mm) crochet hook
» Stitch markers (3)
» Tapestry needle
» Blocking pins
» Blocking board or towel

GAUGE

12 stitches and 8 rows in dc = 4 in. (10.2 cm), blocked.
For gauge swatch, ch 21. Last 3 chs count as first dc on Row 1.
Row 1: Dc into fourth ch from hook and in each ch across: 19 dc.

Row 2: Ch 3 (counts as dc), turn. Sk st at base of chs. Dc in each st across, ending with final dc in top of turning ch. Total 18 dc.
Repeat Row 2 until swatch measures at least 4½ in. (11.4 cm).

SPECIAL STITCHES

Foundation double crochet (fdc): Ch 3, yo, insert hook in third ch from hook, yo, pull up lp (3 lps on hook), yo, pull through 1 lp, [yo, pull through 2 loops] twice. Fdc made.
   *Yo, insert hook into ch just made (at bottom of just-completed fdc), yo, pull up lp (3 lps on hook), yo, pull through 1 lp, [yo, pull through 2 lps] twice. Rep from * for length of foundation.

NOTE: *When working a fdc to extend a row, yo, insert hook into bottom of previous st, yo, pull up lp (3 lps on hook), yo, pull through 1 lp, [yo, pull through 2 lps] twice.*

2-treble cluster (2trCL): *Yo twice, insert hook where indicated, yo, pull up lp, [yo, pull through 2 lps] twice. Repeat from * once (3 lps on hook), yo, pull through all 3 lps.

Pattern

V-BACK

Ch 6.
Row 1 (RS): Dc in sixth ch from hook.
Row 2: Ch 3 (counts as dc here and throughout), turn. 2 dc in same st, ch 2, sk 2 chs, 3 dc in next ch. Total 6 dc.
Row 3: Ch 3, turn. Dc in same st, dc in next dc, 2 dc in next dc, ch 2, 2 dc in next dc, dc in next dc, 2 dc in next dc. Total 10 dc.

NOTE: *Work into dc only, not into ch-sps, unless instructed otherwise. Ch-3 at beginning of row counts as dc. Final st on next row is worked into top of turning ch.*

Row 4: Ch 3, turn. Dc in same st, dc in next 3 dc, 2 dc in next dc, ch 2, 2 dc in next dc, dc in next 3 dc, 2 dc in next dc. Total 14 dc.

Row 5: Ch 3, turn. Dc in same st, dc in next 5 dc, 2 dc in next dc, ch 2, 2 dc in next dc, dc in next 5 dc, 2 dc in next dc. Total 18 dc.

Row 6: Ch 3, turn. Dc in next 3 dc, ch 3, sk dc, dc in next 4 dc, ch 2, dc in next 4 dc, ch 3, sk dc, dc in next 4 dc. Total 16 dc.

Row 7: Ch 3, turn. Dc in next 3 dc, ch 5, dc in next 4 dc, ch 2, dc in next 4 dc, ch 5, dc in next 4 dc. Total 16 dc.

Row 8: Ch 3, turn. Dc in next 3 dc, ch 7, dc in next 4 dc, ch 2, dc in next 4 dc, ch 7, dc in next 4 dc. Total 16 dc.

Row 9: Ch 3, turn. Dc in next 3 dc, ch 9, dc in next 4 dc, ch 2, dc in next 4 dc, ch 9, dc in next 4 dc. Total 16 dc.

Row 10: Ch 3, turn. Dc in next 3 dc, ch 5, sk 4 chs, dc in next ch, ch 5, sk 4 chs, dc in next 4 dc, ch 2, dc in next 4 sts, ch 5, sk 4 chs, dc in next ch, ch 5, sk 4 chs, dc in next 4 dc. Total 18 dc.

Row 11: Ch 3, turn. Dc in next 3 sts, ch 5, dc in ch-5 sp, dc in dc, dc in ch-5 sp, ch 5, dc in next 4 dc, ch 2, dc in next 4 dc, ch 5, dc in ch-5 sp, dc in dc, dc in ch-5 sp, ch 5, dc in next 4 dc. Total 22 dc.

Row 12: Ch 3, turn. Dc in next 3 dc, ch 5, dc in ch-5 sp, dc in next 3 dc, dc in ch-5 sp, ch 5, dc in next 4 dc, ch 2, dc in next 4 dc, ch 5, dc in ch-5 sp, dc in next 3 dc, dc in ch-5 sp, ch 5, dc in next 4 dc. Total 26 dc.

Row 13: Ch 3, turn. Dc in next 3 sts, ch 4, 2 dc in ch-5 sp, dc in next 2 dc, ch 3, sk dc, dc in next 2 dc, 2 dc in ch-5 sp, ch 4, dc in next 4 dc, ch 2, dc in next 4 dc, ch 4, 2 dc in ch-5 sp, dc in next 2 dc, ch 3, sk dc, dc in next 2 dc, 2 dc in ch-5 sp, ch 4, dc in next 4 sts. Total 32 dc.

Row 14: Ch 3, turn. Dc in next 3 dc, ch 6, sk ch-4 sp and 4 dc, 5 dc in ch-3 sp, ch 6, sk 4 dc and ch-4 sp, dc in next 4 dc, ch 2, dc in next 4 dc, ch 6, sk ch-4 sp and 4 dc, 5 dc in ch-3 sp, ch 6, sk 4 dc and ch-4 sp, dc in next 4 dc. Total 26 dc.

Row 15: Ch 3, turn. Dc in next 3 dc, ch 9, sk 1 dc, dc in next 3 dc, sk 1 dc, ch 9, dc in next 4 dc, ch 2, dc in next 4 dc, ch 9, sk 1 dc, dc in next 3 dc, sk 1 dc, ch 9, dc in next 4 dc. Total 22 dc.

Row 16: Ch 3, turn. Dc in next 3 dc, ch 4, sk 3 chs, dc in next 3 chs, ch 4, sk 3 chs and 1 dc, dc in next dc, ch 4, sk 1 dc and 3 chs, dc in next 3 chs, ch 4, dc in next 4 dc, ch 2, dc in next 4 dc, ch 4, sk 3 chs, dc in next 3 chs, ch 4, sk 3 chs and 1 dc, dc in next dc, ch 3, sk 1 dc and 3 chs, dc in next 3 chs, ch 4, sk 3 chs, dc in next 4 dc. Total 30 dc.

NOTE: *Separate for V back, working each side of the lace panel separately.*

Row 17: Turn. Sl st into second st from end, ch 3, dc in next 2 dc, dc in ch-4 sp, ch 9, sk 3 dc, dc in ch-4 sp, dc in dc, dc in ch-4 sp, ch 9, sk 3 dc, dc in ch-4 sp, dc in next 3 dc, leave last st unworked. Total 11 dc.

NOTE: *To work second side, sk [dc, ch 2, dc], join new ball of yarn in next dc (counts as sl st), follow instructions for Row 17 starting with the ch-3. When you start Row 18 you will continue working this side of the garment to the center, then move your hook to the other side and repeat the instructions. Continue in this fashion through Row 33.*

Alternatively, you can work the first side through Row 33, then rejoin yarn for the second side of Row 17 and complete the second side through Row 33.

Row 18: Turn. Sl st into second st from end, ch 3, dc in next 2 dc, dc in ch-9 sp, ch 4, sk 3 chs, dc in next 3 chs (the center 3 of the ch-9), ch 4, sk 3 chs and 1 dc, dc in next dc, ch 4, sk 1 dc and 3 chs, dc in next 3 chs, ch 4, dc in ch-9 sp, dc in next 3 dc, leave last st unworked. Total 15 dc.

Row 19: Turn. Sl st into second st from end, ch 3, dc in next 2 dc, dc in ch-4 sp, ch 9, sk 3 dc, dc in ch-4 sp, dc in dc, dc in ch-4 sp, ch 9, sk 3 dc, dc in ch-4 sp, dc in next 3 dc, leave last st unworked. Total 11 dc.

Row 20: Turn. Sl st into second st from end, ch 3, dc in next 2 sts, dc in ch-9 sp, ch 7, dc in same ch-9 sp, dc in next 3 dc, dc in ch-9 sp, ch 7, dc in same ch-9 sp, dc in next 3 dc, leave last st unworked. Total 13 dc.

Row 21: Turn. Sl st into second st from end, ch 3, dc in next 2 dc, dc in ch-7 sp, ch 4, 2 dc in same ch-7 sp, dc in next 2 dc, ch 3, sk dc, dc in next 2 dc, 2 dc in ch-7 sp, ch 4, dc in same ch-7 sp, dc in next 3 dc, leave last st unworked. Total 16 dc.

Row 22: Turn. Sl st into second st from end, ch 3, dc in next 2 dc, dc in ch-4 sp, ch 7, 5 dc in ch-3 sp, ch 7, dc in ch-4 sp, dc in next 3 dc, leave last st unworked. Total 13 dc.

Row 23: Turn. Sl st into second st from end, ch 3, dc in next 2 dc, dc in ch-7 sp, ch 6, sk dc, dc in next 3 dc, ch 6, sk dc, dc in ch-7 sp, dc in next 3 dc, leave last st unworked. Total 11 dc.

Row 24: Turn. Sl st into second st from end, ch 3, dc in next 2 dc, dc in ch-6 sp, ch 6, sk dc, dc in next dc, ch-6, sk dc, dc in ch-6 sp, dc in next 3 dc, leave last st unworked. Total 9 dc.

Row 25: Turn. Sl st into second st from end, ch 3, dc in next 2 dc, dc in ch-6 sp, ch 9, sk dc, dc in next ch-6 sp, dc in next 3 dc, leave last st unworked. Total 8 dc.

Row 26: Turn. Sl st into second st from end, ch 3, dc in next 2 dc, dc in ch-9 sp, ch 7, dc in same ch-9 sp, dc in next 3 dc, leave last st unworked. Total 8 dc.

Row 27: Turn. Sl st into second st from end, ch 3, dc in next 2 dc, dc in ch-7 sp, ch 5, dc in same ch-7 sp, dc in next 3 dc, leave last st unworked. Total 8 dc.

Back View

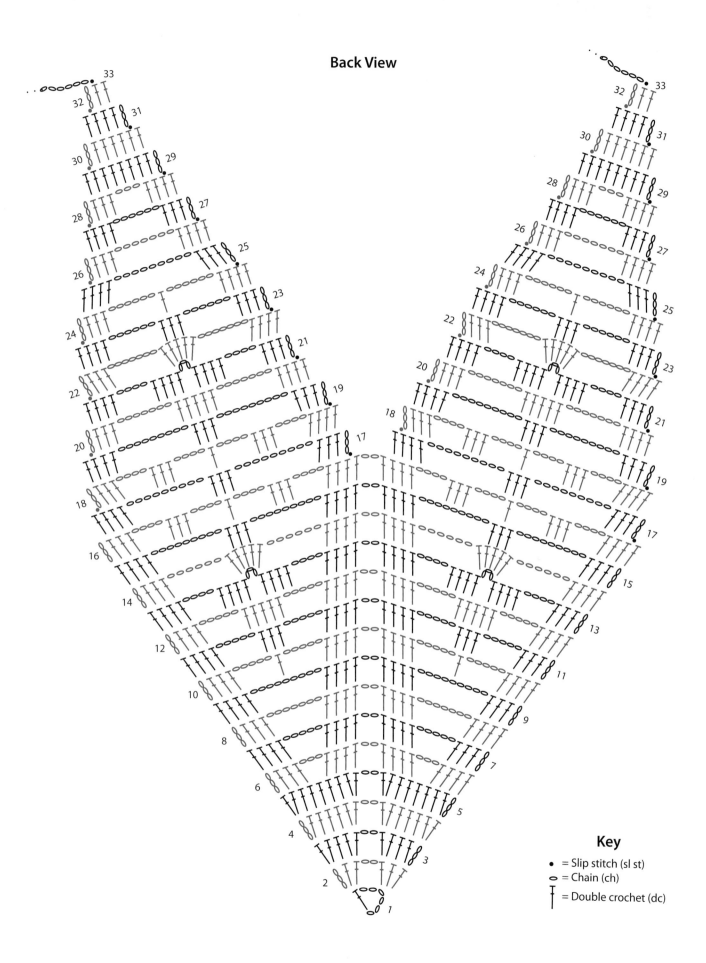

Key

- ● = Slip stitch (sl st)
- ⬯ = Chain (ch)
- † = Double crochet (dc)

Row 28: Turn. Sl st into second st from end, ch 3, dc in next 2 dc, dc in ch-5 sp, ch 3, dc in same ch-5 sp, dc in next 3 dc, leave last st unworked. Total 8 dc.

Row 29: Turn. Sl st into second st from end, ch 3, dc in next 2 dc, 3 dc in ch-3 sp, dc in next 3 dc, leave last st unworked. Total 9 dc.

Row 30: Turn. Sl st into second st from end, ch 3, dc in next 6 dc, leave last st unworked. Total 7 dc.

Row 31: Turn. Sl st into second st from end, ch 3, dc in next 4 dc, leave last st unworked. Total 5 dc.

Row 32: Turn. Sl st into second st from end, ch 3, dc in next 2 dc, leave last st unworked.

Row 33: Turn. Sl st into second st from end, ch 100 for tie. Fasten off.

UPPER BODY

> **NOTE:** *Upper body is worked and joined to either side of back panel from the bottom up, separated for sleeves/back and sleeves/front, then joined at the top of the sleeves. The lower body is then picked up and worked down to the hem. The only seams needed are along the underside of the sleeves.*

For the upper body, make sure you align the rows with the rows of the center V. Use stitch markers if necessary to make the V-rows easy to see and count. Be careful not to work 2 rows of body where there is just 1 row of V-back.

Row 1: With RS facing, sl st to center V of lowest point of lower back, ch 3, sl st to body of same dc to make the ch 3 vertical in the same fashion as the dc. Fdc 108 (120, 132, 144), sl st to join in first dc on opposite side of first row of lace panel, making sure sts are not twisted.

> **NOTE:** *With a short length of yarn, attach bottom of final fdc to bottom point at start of row.*

Row 2: Ch 3, sl st to dc on next row of lace panel, turn. Dc2tog over next 2 sts, dc in each st across until 2 sts remain. Dc2tog, sl st to dc on corresponding row at other end of lace panel. Total 106 (118, 130, 142) sts.

Rows 3–17: Rep Row 2. Each row decreases by 2 sts. Total 76 (88, 100, 112) sts at end of Row 17.

> **NOTE:** *Make sure Row 17 of the body just completed matches Row 17 of the center V of back.*

Sizes L, XL, go to Split for Sleeves.

Sizes S, M only

Rows 18–19: Ch 3, sl st to dc on next row of lace panel, turn. Dc in each st across, sl st to dc on lace panel. Total 76 (88, 100, 113) sts. Go to Split for Sleeves.

SPLIT FOR SLEEVES

BACK LEFT SLEEVE

Row 1: Ch 3, sl st to dc on next row of lace panel, turn. Dc in next 11 sts, fdc 13 sts.

Row 2: Ch 3, turn. Dc in each st across, sl st to dc on lace panel.

Row 3: Ch 3, sl st to dc on next row of lace panel, turn. Dc in each st across.

Rows 4–13: Rep Rows 2–3 five times.
Sizes S, M, fasten off.

Sizes L, XL

Rows 14–15: Rep Rows 2–3. Fasten off.

BACK RIGHT SLEEVE

Row 1: Join yarn with sl st to final dc on last complete round (next to lace panel). Ch 3, sl st to dc on next row of lace panel, turn. Dc in next 11 sts, fdc 13 sts.

Row 2: Ch 3, turn. Dc in each st across, sl st to dc on lace panel.

Row 3: Ch 3, sl st to dc on next row of lace panel, turn. Dc in each st across.

Rows 4–13: Rep Rows 2–3 five times.
Sizes S, M, fasten off.

Sizes L, XL

Rows 14–15: Rep Rows 2–3. Fasten off.

UPPER FRONT

Row 1: Fdc 13 sts, dc in each 54 (60, 66, 72) front body sts, fdc 13 sts. Total 80 (86, 92, 98) sts. Join bottom of thirteenth fdc made in first group of fdc to bottom of next st on body with short length of yarn.

Row 2: Ch 3, turn. Dc in each st across.

Rows 3–14: Rep Row 2.
Sizes S, M, skip to Join Sleeve at Shoulder.

Sizes L, XL

Rows 15–16: Rep Row 2. Go to Join Sleeve at Shoulder.

JOIN SLEEVE AT SHOULDER

Row 1: Ch 5 (counts as dtr), sl st to corresponding st on other side of sleeve. *Dtr in next st on other side of sleeve, sl st to next st on back of sleeve. Rep from * until sleeve tops are joined. Fasten off.
Repeat for other sleeve.

LOWER BODY

Rnd 1: Working in bottom of fdc of upper body, sl st to bottom of lace panel, ch 1, sc in same sp, sc in each free loop of upper body around, sl st to first st at beg of round to join. Total 109 (121, 133, 144) sc.

Rnd 2: Do not turn. Ch 3, dc in each st around, sl st to top of ch-3 to join. Total 109 (121, 133, 145) dc.

Rnds 3–9 (3–10, 3–11, 3–12): Rep Round 2.

Hem: *Ch 4, 2trCL in same st, sk 3 sts, sc in next st. Rep from * around. Fasten off.

EDGING

SLEEVE

Sew sleeve seams.

> **NOTE:** *Sleeve trim is worked around row ends. Sk 2 rows between each set of 2trCLs. The dtr sts that join the sleeve tops count as 2 rows.*

Row 1: Sl st to join at bottom seam. *Ch 4, 2trCL in same st, sk 3 sts, sc in next st. Rep from * around. Fasten off. Repeat for other sleeve.

NECK FRONT

Row 1: Sl st to front neck edge where front meets top-of-sleeve join. *Ch 4, 2trCL in same st, sk 3 sts, sc in next st. Rep from * across. Fasten off.

FINISHING

With tapestry needle, weave in ends. Block garment to size and shape.

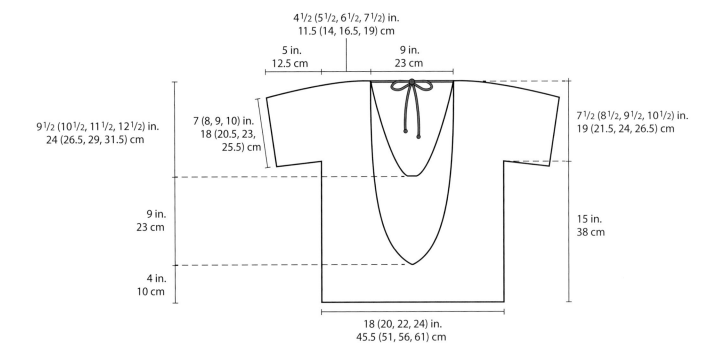

4¹⁄₂ (5¹⁄₂, 6¹⁄₂, 7¹⁄₂) in.
11.5 (14, 16.5, 19) cm

5 in.
12.5 cm

9 in.
23 cm

9¹⁄₂ (10¹⁄₂, 11¹⁄₂, 12¹⁄₂) in.
24 (26.5, 29, 31.5) cm

7 (8, 9, 10) in.
18 (20.5, 23, 25.5) cm

7¹⁄₂ (8¹⁄₂, 9¹⁄₂, 10¹⁄₂) in.
19 (21.5, 24, 26.5) cm

9 in.
23 cm

15 in.
38 cm

4 in.
10 cm

18 (20, 22, 24) in.
45.5 (51, 56, 61) cm

Muriel Lace Cardigan

Designed by Robyn Chachula

This easy-to-wear V-neck cardigan is made from openwork motifs joined together into a lacy body, finished with raglan sleeves.

SKILL LEVEL

INTERMEDIATE

MEASUREMENTS OF FINISHED GARMENT

	BUST CIRCUMFERENCE	LENGTH (shoulder to bottom edge)	SLEEVE (underarm to cuff)
Small	36 in. (91.5 cm)	22 in. (56.5 cm)	17½ in. (44.5 cm)
Medium	40 in. (101.5 cm)	22½ in. (57 cm)	17½ in. (44.5 cm)
Large	44½ in. (113 cm)	24½ in. (62.5 cm)	17½ in. (44.5 cm)
Extra Large	49½ in. (126 cm)	25 in. (63 cm)	17½ in. (44.5 cm)

Instructions are for size S, with sizes M, L, and XL in parentheses.

MATERIALS

1 Super Fine

Cascade Yarns/Heritage 150 Sock Yarn (75% merino superwash wool, 25% nylon; 5.25 oz./150 g; 492 yd./450 m)

  » Dusty Turquoise (#5704): 3 (3, 4, 4) hanks
» U.S. size F-5 (3.75 mm) crochet hook (only for sizes S and L)
» U.S. size G-6 (4.25 mm) crochet hook (for all sizes)

NOTE: *Use smaller hook and gauge for sizes Small and Large Motifs. Use larger hook and gauge for sizes Medium and X-Large Motifs. Use larger hook for sleeves on all sizes.*

» Tapestry needle
» Blocking pins
» Blocking board or towel
» ³/₈-in. (1 cm) diameter buttons

GAUGE

Sizes S and L: 4¼ in. (10.8 cm) measured on the diagonal of Muriel Motif, blocked
Sizes M and XL: 4¾ in. (12 cm) measured on the diagonal of Murial Motif, blocked
For gauge swatch, work one complete Muriel Motif.

For sleeves (all sizes), 17 tr and 10 rows in sleeve stitch pattern (alternating tr and sc rows) = 4 in. (10.2 cm), blocked.
For gauge swatch, ch 25. Last 4 chs count as tr.
Row 1 (RS): Tr in fifth ch from hook and each ch across. Total 22 tr.
Row 2: Ch 1 (does not count as st), turn. Sc in each tr and in top of turning ch. Total 22 sc.
Row 3: Ch 4 (counts as tr here and throughout), turn. Tr in each sc across. Total 22 tr.
Rep Rows 2 and 3 until swatch measures at least 4½ in. (11.4 cm).

SPECIAL STITCHES

Chain-5 join (ch-5 join): Ch 2, sl st to adjoining ch-5 sp, ch 2.
Chain-3 join (ch-3 join): Ch 1, sl st to adjoining ch-3 sp, ch 1.
Treble 2 together (tr2tog): *Yo twice, insert hook into next st, yo, pull up lp, [yo, pull through 2 lps] twice. Rep from * once (3 lps remain on hook). Yo, pull through all 3 lps.
Treble 3 together (tr3tog): *Yo twice, insert hook into next st, yo, pull up lp, [yo, pull through 2 lps] twice. Rep from * twice (4 lps remain on hook). Yo, pull through all 4 lps.
Triple treble crochet (ttr): Yo 4 times, insert hook into stitch indicated and pull up a loop, [yarn over hook and draw through 2 loops on hook] 5 times.

PATTERN NOTE

» Be sure to use the smaller hook and gauge for the motifs in the body of sizes Small and Large, and the larger hook and gauge for the motifs in the body of sizes Medium and X-Large. The combination of hook size and the number of motifs will make the sizes come out correctly. Use the larger hook for crocheting the sleeves and edging for all sizes.

Pattern

BODY

MURIEL MOTIF (make one complete motif; join 49 [49, 59, 59] motifs)

NOTE: *The RS is always facing you. Do not turn at the end of a round. See Motif Layout for your size on p. 101 for sequence of motifs.*

First (Complete) Motif:

Make an adjustable ring by starting with the tail end of the yarn and wrapping the long end around two fingers. Insert hook into the ring, pull up lp. The ch-1 on Round 1 will hold the yarn in place. Work the rest of the stitches in that round over two threads.

Rnd 1 (RS): Ch 1, [sc, ch 4] 3 times in ring, sc in ring, ch 2, hdc in first sc, pull ring closed. Total 4 sc.

Rnd 2: Ch 3 (counts as dc here and throughout), 3 dc around post of hdc. *Ch 4, [4 dc, ch 1, 4 dc] in ch-4 sp; rep from * twice, ch 4, 4 dc in first ch-sp, sc to top of beginning ch. Total 32 dc.

Rnd 3: Ch 1, sc in sc. [Ch 3, 7 dc in ch-4 sp, ch 3, sc in ch-1 sp] 3 times. Ch 3, 7 dc in ch-4 sp, dc in first sc (counts as ch-3 sp). Total 8 ch-3 sps.

Rnd 4: Ch 1, sc in dc. *Ch 5, [sc, ch 3, sc] in next dc, ch 2, sk 2 dc, [sc, ch 3, sc, ch 5, sc, ch 3, sc] in next dc, sk 2 dc, ch 2**, [sc, ch 3, sc] in next dc. Rep from * twice ; rep from * to **, sc in last dc, ch 3, sl st in first sc. Fasten off.

Subsequent Joining Motifs:

Now the first motif is complete. Subsequent square motifs are worked the same way as Muriel Motif through Round 3. On Round 4, the new motif will be joined to a finished square on one or more sides and then completed. Use the Motif Layout for your size as a guide. Substitute a ch-5 join (ch 1, sl st to adjoining ch-5 sp, ch 2) for ch-5 sps on sides and corners. Substitute a ch-3 join (ch 1, sl st to adjoining ch-3 sp, ch 1) for ch-3 sps on sides (but leave ch-3 sps in the corners—the ones that flank the ch-5 lp—alone). Make sure the RS of both motifs are facing up.

Join ch-3 lp in the middle of the side of the current motif to the corresponding ch-3 lp on the finished motif.

Return to the current motif and continue to the next join.

Make a ch-3 lp in the corner, then join the ch-5 lp to the ch-5 lp on the finished motif.

Do not work into the ch-3 lps indicated by toothpicks, just the ch-5 lp between them.

HALF MOTIF [join 8 (8, 10, 10)] motifs)

Join half motifs in similar fashion to the way full motifs are joined, working through Round 3 and then joining on Round 4, using the Motif Layout for your size as a guide. Substitute a ch-5 join (ch 2, sl st to adjoining ch-5 sp, ch 2) for ch-5 sps on sides and corners. Substitute a ch-3 (ch 1, sl st to adjoining ch-3 sp, ch 1) join for ch-3 sps on sides (but leave ch-3 sps in the corners alone). Make sure the RS of both motifs are facing up.

Make an adjustable ring as for Muriel Motif.

Row 1: Ch 1, [sc, ch 4] twice in ring, sc in ring, pull ring closed. Total 3 sc.

Row 2: Ch 8, turn. [4 dc, ch 1, 4 dc] in ch-4 sp, ch 4, [4 dc, ch 1, 4 dc] in next ch-4 sp, ch 2, ttr in last sc. Total 16 dc.

Row 3: Ch 3, turn. 3 dc in sp formed by ttr, ch 3, sc in ch-1 sp, ch 3, 7 dc in ch-4 sp, ch 3, sc in ch-1 sp, ch 3, 4 dc in beg ch-sp. Total 4 ch-3 sps.

Row 4 (if working Half Motif to completion): Ch 5, turn, [sc, ch 3, sc] in first dc, ch 2, sk 2 dc, [sc, ch 3, sc] in next dc, ch 5, [sc, ch 3, sc] in next dc, ch 2, sk 2 dc, [sc, ch 3, sc, ch 5, sc, ch 3, sc] in next dc, ch 2, sk 2 dc, [sc, ch 3, sc] in next dc, ch 5, [sc, ch 3, sc] in next dc, ch 2, sk 2 dc, [sc, ch 3, sc, ch 5, sl st] in top of tch. Fasten off.

Row 4 (if using join-as-you-go method): Ch 3, turn. Sl st to adjoining corner ch-sp, ch 2, [sc, ch 3, sc] in first dc, ch 2, sk 2 dc, [sc, ch-3 join, sc] in next dc, ch 5, [sc, ch-3 join, sc] in next dc, ch 2, sk 2 dc, [sc, ch 3, sc, ch-5 join, sc, ch 3, sc] in next dc, sk 2 dc, ch 2, [sc, ch-3 join, sc] in next dc, ch 5, [sc, ch-3 join, sc] in next dc, ch 2, [sc, ch 3, sc, ch 2, sl st to adjoining corner ch-sp, ch 3, sl st] in top of tch. Fasten off.

SLEEVE (Make 2)

Use larger hook for all sizes. Ch 41 (45, 49, 51).

Row 1 (RS): Tr in fifth ch from hook (sk ch count as tr) and each ch across. 38 (42, 46, 48) tr.

Row 2: Ch 1, turn. Sc in each tr across to tch, sc in top of tch. Sizes L/XL, skip to Increase Shaping.

(Sizes S/M only) Row 3: Ch 4 (counts as tr throughout), turn. Tr in each sc across.

(Sizes S/M only) Row 4: Rep Row 2.

INCREASE SHAPING

Row 1 (RS): Ch 4, turn. Tr in first sc, tr in each sc across, 2 tr in last sc. Total 40 (44, 48, 50) tr.

Row 2: Ch 1, turn. Sc in each tr across to tch, sc in top of tch.

Row 3: Ch 4 (counts as tr throughout), turn. (*Note: Do not tr in first sc.*) Tr in each sc across.

Row 4: Rep Row 2.

Rep Rows 1–4 of increase shaping 8 (8, 9, 8) times. Total 56 (60, 68, 66) sc.

(Sizes S/M/L only) Rep Rows 3–4 of increase shaping 2 (2, 1) more time(s).

(Size XL only) Rep Rows 1–2 of increase shaping 3 times.

CAP SHAPING SIZES S AND M ONLY

Row 1 (RS): Ch 3, turn. Sk first sc, tr2tog in next 2 sc (everything so far counts as tr3tog), tr in each sc to last 3 sc, tr3tog over last 3 sc, turn. Total 52 (56) tr.

Row 2: Ch 1, turn. Sc in each tr across.

Rows 3–4: Rep Rows 1–2 of cap shaping,

Row 5: Rep Row 1 of cap shaping. Total 44 (48) tr.

Muriel Motif

Key

● = Slip stitch (sl st)

⬭ = Chain (ch)

✕ = Single crochet (sc)

T = Half double crochet (hdc)

T = Double crochet (dc)

◯ = Adjustable ring

Sizes S and M Motif Layout

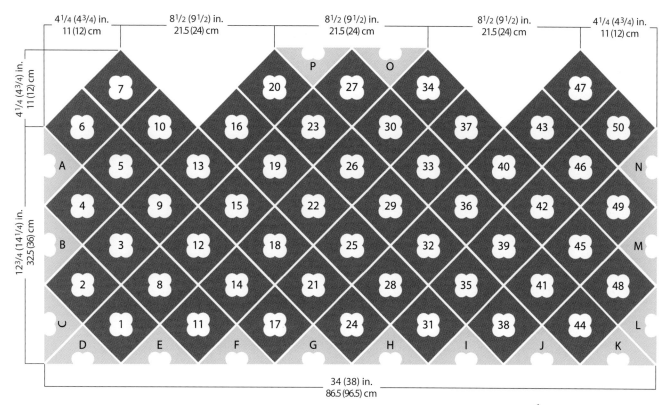

4¼ (4¾) in.
11 (12) cm

8½ (9½) in.
21.5 (24) cm

8½ (9½) in.
21.5 (24) cm

8½ (9½) in.
21.5 (24) cm

4¼ (4¾) in.
11 (12) cm

4¼ (4¾) in.
11 (12) cm

12¾ (14¼) in.
32.5 (36) cm

34 (38) in.
86.5 (96.5) cm

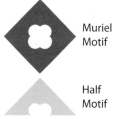

Muriel
Motif

Half
Motif

Sizes L and XL Motif Layout

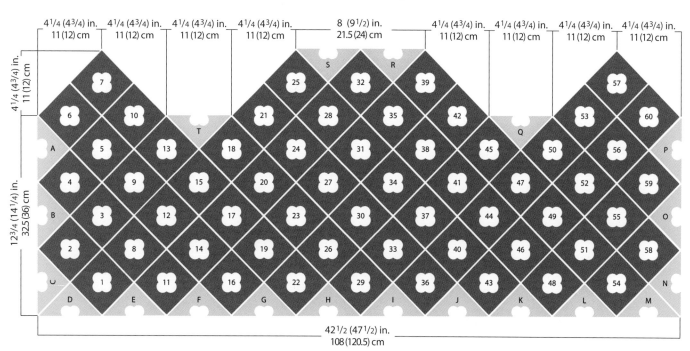

4¼ (4¾) in.
11 (12) cm

4¼ (4¾) in.
11 (12) cm

4¼ (4¾) in.
11 (12) cm

4¼ (4¾) in.
11 (12) cm

8 (9½) in.
21.5 (24) cm

4¼ (4¾) in.
11 (12) cm

4¼ (4¾) in.
11 (12) cm

4¼ (4¾) in.
11 (12) cm

4¼ (4¾) in.
11 (12) cm

4¼ (4¾) in.
11 (12) cm

12¾ (14¼) in.
32.5 (36) cm

42½ (47½) in.
108 (120.5) cm

Half Motif

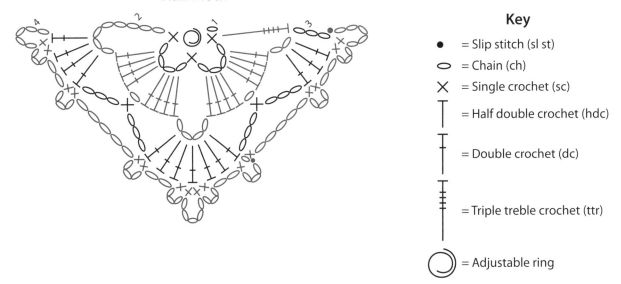

Key

- ● = Slip stitch (sl st)
- ⬭ = Chain (ch)
- ✕ = Single crochet (sc)
- | = Half double crochet (hdc)
- ╪ = Double crochet (dc)
- ╪ = Triple treble crochet (ttr)
- ◯ = Adjustable ring

Joining Motifs

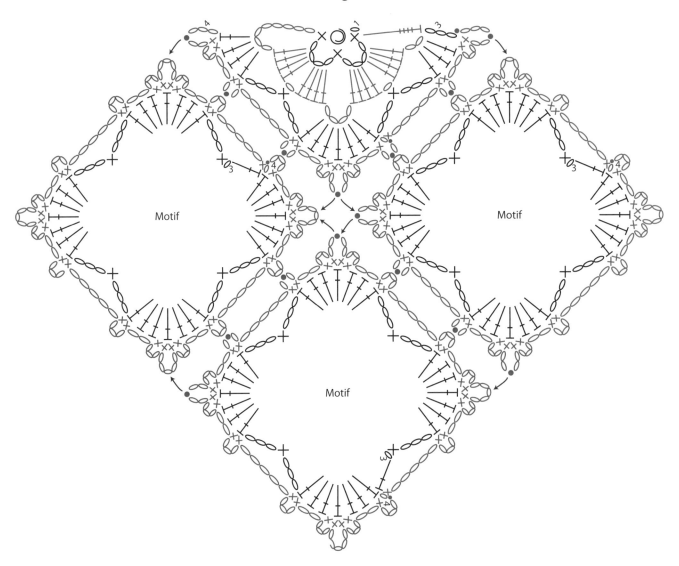

Row 6: Ch 1, turn. Sc2tog over first 2 tr, sc in each tr across to last 2 sc, sc2tog over last 2 tr. Total 42 (46) sc.

(Size S only) Rep Rows 1–2 of cap shaping. Rep Rows 5–6 of cap shaping twice. Fasten off. Total 26 sc.

(Size M only) Rep Rows 1–6 of cap shaping (32 sc). Rep Rows 1–2 of cap shaping. Fasten off. Total 28 sc.

CAP SHAPING SIZES L AND XL ONLY

Row 1 (RS): Ch 1, turn. Sl st in first 7 (8) sc, ch 3, tr2tog in next 2 sc (counts as tr3tog), tr in each sc to last 9 (10) sc, tr3tog over next 3 sc, leave remaining st unworked. Total 52 (54) tr.

Row 2: Ch 1, turn. Sc in each tr across.

Row 3: Ch 3, turn. Sk first sc, tr2tog in next 2 sc (counts as tr3tog), tr in each sc to last 3 sc, tr3tog over last 3 sc. Total 48 (50) tr.

Rows 4–5: Rep Rows 2–3 of cap shaping. Total 44 (46) tr.

Row 6: Ch 1, turn. Sc2tog over first 2 tr, sc in each tr across to last 2 sc, sc2tog over last 2 tr. Total 42 sc.

(Size L only) Rep Row 3 of cap shaping (total 38 tr), rep Rows 2–6 of cap shaping (total 28 sc), rep Rows 3–4 of cap shaping. Total 24 sc.

(Size XL only) Rep Rows 2–3 of cap shaping 5 times (total 26 tr), rep Row 2 of cap shaping.

FINISHING

With tapestry needle, weave in ends. Wet block body and sleeves to size and shape.

RAGLAN SEAMING

> **NOTE:** *The body and the sleeves are edged separately, then joined together. Wet block the pieces to size and shape after edging but before assembly.*

BODY EDGING

Join yarn with sl st to WS of body at edge of front where raglan seam begins in a ch-5 sp corner.

Row 1: *Sc in ch-5 sp corner, sk 1 ch-3 sp, ch 5, sc in next ch-3 sp, ch 2, sc in next ch-5 sp, ch 2, sc in next ch-3 sp, sk next ch-3 sp, ch 5; rep from * across Muriel motifs, sc evenly across half motifs. Rep directions across top of body to opposite edge.

Row 2: Ch 1, turn. *6 sc in each ch-5 sp, 2 sc in each ch-2 sp; rep from * across motifs to half motifs, sc in each sc across half motifs. Rep directions across body to opposite edge. Fasten off.

SLEEVE EDGING

Join yarn to RS of sleeve at cap shaping with sl st.

Row 1: Sc evenly around sleeve. Fasten off.

SEAM PIECES TOGETHER

Place WS of sleeve and body together. Join yarn to edge of raglan. Sl st in each sc up raglan seam through both fabrics at once. Fasten off. Using tapestry needle, weave in ends.

SEAM SLEEVE

Place RS of sleeve together. Whipstitch underarm seam closed. Repeat for other sleeve.

EDGE CUFF

Join yarn to RS of cuff with sl st.

Rnd 1: Sc in each st around, sl st to first sc, do not turn.

Rnd 2: Ch 1, sc in each sc around, sl st to first sc, do not turn.

Rnd 3: Sl st in each sc around, do not turn.

Rnd 4: Sl st in each sc on Rnd 1 (by inserting hook through fabric and holding yarn in back). Fasten off. With tapestry needle, weave in ends. Repeat for other cuff.

EDGE BODY

Join yarn to RS edge of body at back with sl st.

Rnd 1: Ch 1, sc evenly around entire body including up fronts and around neck. Sl st to first sc. Do not turn.

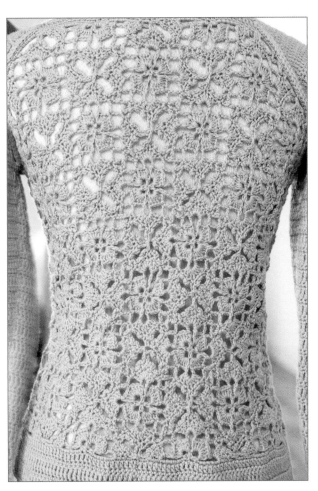

Rnd 2: Ch 3, dc in each sc across to corner of bottom and front edge, 5 dc in corner, dc in each sc up front to corner of collar, 3 dc in corner, *dc in each sc to corner of raglan, dc3tog over corner of raglan, rep from * across back neck and opposite raglan, dc in each sc to corner of opposite front, 3 dc in corner, dc in each sc to corner of bottom, 5 dc in corner, dc in each sc to tch, sl st to top of tch.

Rnd 3: Ch 1, turn. sc in each dc to corner of front, 3 sc in corner, sc in each dc to collar, 2 sc in corner, [sc in each dc to raglan corner, sc2tog over corner of raglan] rep across back neck and opposite raglan, sc in each dc to corner of opposite front, 2 sc in corner, sc in each dc to bottom corner, 3 sc in corner, sc in each sc to end, sl st to first sc, turn.

Rnd 4: Ch 4, tr in each sc to front corner, ch 3, sl st to front corner, sl st in each sc to collar corner, ch 2, [dc in each sc to raglan corner, dc3tog over raglan corner] rep across back neck and opposite raglan, dc in each sc to front corner, ch 2, sl st to front corner, sl st in each sc down front to bottom corner, ch 4, tr in each sc across bottom, sl st to top of tch, turn.

Rnd 5: Ch 1, sc in each tr across bottom edge, 3 sc in top of ch-3, 2 sc around ch-3 sp, sc in each sc on Rnd 3 up front to corner, 2 sc in corner, [sc in each dc to corner, sc2tog over corner] rep around neck, sc in each dc to front corner, 2 sc in corner, sc in each sc of Rnd 3 down front, 2 sc around ch-4 sp, 3 sc in top of ch-4 sp, sc in each tr across, sl st to first sc, turn.

Rnd 6: Ch 4, tr in each sc to front corner, ch 3, sl st to front corner, sl st in each sc up front around neck to opposite front corner, [sl st in next 4 sc, ch 3 (makes buttonhole)] 3 times, sl st in each sc down front to bottom corner, ch 4, tr in each sc across bottom, sl st to top of tch. Fasten off.

Row 7: Join yarn to WS of bottom edge with sl st. Sc in each tr across.

Row 8: Turn. Sl st in each sc across. Fasten off.

With tapestry needle, weave in ends. Wet block again if desired.

Sew buttons to front opposite buttonholes.

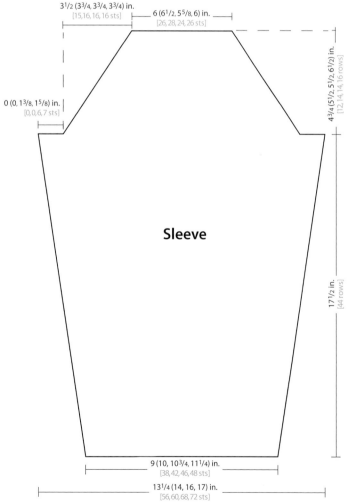

3½ (3¾, 3¾, 3¾) in.
[15, 16, 16, 16 sts]

6 (6½, 5⅝, 6) in.
[26, 28, 24, 26 sts]

0 (0, 1⅜, 1⅝) in.
[0, 0, 6, 7 sts]

4¾ (5½, 5½, 6½) in.
[12, 14, 14, 16 rows]

Sleeve

17½ in.
[44 rows]

9 (10, 10¾, 11¼) in.
[38, 42, 46, 48 sts]

13¼ (14, 16, 17) in.
[56, 60, 68, 72 sts]

New Wave Cowl

Designed by Rhonda Davis

Alternating rows of solid and striped yarns are crocheted in Tunisian knit stitch decreases and increases to create this dynamic, chevron-patterned cowl.

SKILL LEVEL

INTERMEDIATE

MEASUREMENTS
26 in. (66 cm) circumference by 11 in. (28 cm) tall

MATERIALS

Super Fine

Lang Yarns Jawoll Superwash (75% virgin wool, 25% nylon; 1.76 oz./50 g; 229 yd./210 m)
>> **A:** Black (04): 2 skeins

Super Fine

Lang Yarns Jawoll Magic Dégradé Superwash (75% virgin wool, 25% nylon; 3.5 oz./100g, 437 yd./400 m)
>> **B:** Variegated red, pink, yellow, orange, green (59): 1 skein

>> U.S. size H-8 (5.0 mm) Tunisian crochet hook or size needed to obtain gauge
>> Tapestry needle
>> Blocking pins (optional)
>> Blocking board or towel (optional)

GAUGE
22 sts and 20 rows in Tks = 4 in. (20.3 cm), blocked.
For gauge swatch, ch 30.
Row 1 forward: Insert hook in back bar of second ch from hook, yo, pull up lp. *Insert hook in back bar of next ch, yo, pull up lp. Rep from * across.
Row 1 return: Yo, pull through 1 lp. *Yo, pull through 2 lps. Rep from * until 1 lp remains on hook.
Row 2: Sk first vertical bar (at end of row). Tks in each st across, working final Tks between the vertical thread and the horizontal thread that runs behind it. Return as for Row 1.
Rep Row 2 until swatch measures at least 4½ in. (11.4 cm).

SPECIAL STITCHES
Tunisian Bar Stitch (Tbs): Insert hook under top strand of horizontal bar, yo, pull up lp.

NOTE: *In this pattern, Tunisian bar stitches are used for increasing. Work the Tbs between the stitch just completed and the vertical bar of the next st. Do not skip any vertical bars after completing the Tbs.*

PATTERN NOTES

» Cowl is worked in rows, then the beginning and end are seamed together. As you work, the chevrons are oriented up and down. When worn, the chevrons point right and left.

» The (yo, pull through 4 lps) on the return pass creates a cluster of 3 Tks. On the following row you will work into the center stitch of those 3 stitches. Do not work into the stitches on either side of that middle stitch or into the top of the cluster.

» Take care on the return pass to pull through the correct number of loops, especially when working off the Tunisian bar stitches. Spread the loops out on the hook to make it easier to see.

» To change color, drop current yarn when 2 loops remain on the hook at the end of the return pass, yo, pull through 2 lps with the new color. Do not cut the yarn, just carry it smoothly up the side; you will pick up the old color on the following row.

» Work a few rows of the pattern with a larger hook and thicker yarn if you need practice with the Tunisian chevron pattern.

Pattern

With A, ch 91.

Row 1 forward: Insert hook in back lp of second ch from hook, yo, pull up lp. *Insert hook in back lp of next ch, yo, pull up lp. Repeat from * across. Total 91 lps on hook.

Row 1 return: Yo, pull through 1 lp. [Yo, pull through 2 lps] 10 times. *Yo, pull through 4 lps, [yo, pull through 2 lps] 19 times. Rep from * twice. Yo, pull through 4 lps. [Yo, pull through 2 lps] 11 times, switching to B when 2 lps remain on the hook at the end of the return pass.

Row 2 forward: Sk first vertical bar. *Tks in next st, Tbs in horizontal bar, Tks in next 9 sts, Tks in second st of 3-Tks cluster, Tks in next 9 sts, Tbs in next horizontal bar. Rep from * 3 times. Tks in each of last 2 sts.

Row 2 return: Rep Row 1 return. Switch to A when 2 lps remain on hook at end of return pass.

Rows 3-120: Rep Row 2 forward and return, switching colors at the end of each return pass. Work the final row in B. Cut yarn approximately 24 in. (61 cm) from hook, pull through to fasten off.

FINISHING

Bring ends together with WS facing out. Thread yarn on tapestry needle and sew seam closed. Weave in ends. Wet block if desired.

The New Wave Cowl looks pretty on the wrong side, too.

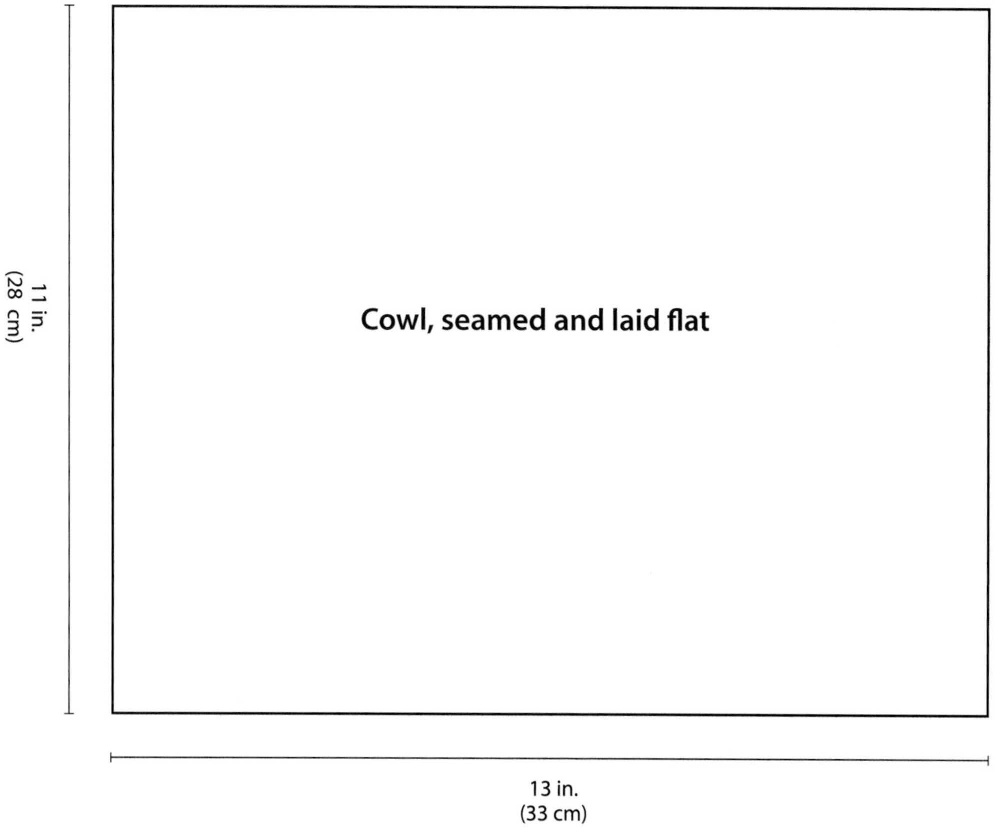
11 in.
(28 cm)
Cowl, seamed and laid flat
13 in.
(33 cm)

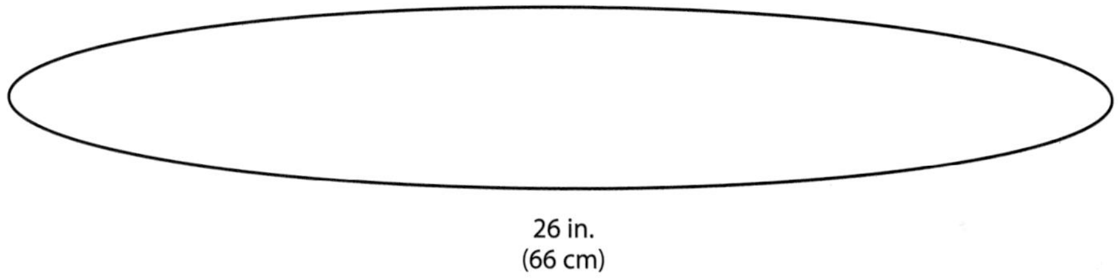
26 in.
(66 cm)

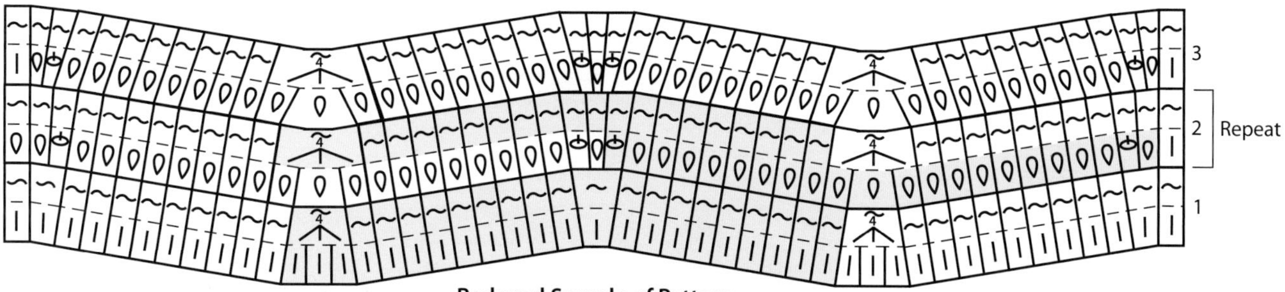
3
2
Repeat
1

Reduced Sample of Pattern

Key

FORWARD SYMBOLS

| = Tunisian Simple Stitch (Tss)

0 = Tunisian Knit Stitch (Tks)

= Tunisian Bar Stitch (Tbs)

RETURN SYMBOLS

~ = yo, draw through 1 lp for first st, yo, draw through 2 lps for each rem st

= yo, draw through 4 lps on hook

COLOR KEY

= Repeat

Optical
Illusion
Scarf

Designed by Sharon Silverman

Look at this scarf one way and you see asterisks; focus on another area and it looks like diamond shapes. No matter where your gaze lands, you'll see subtly variegated shades of purple.

SKILL LEVEL

EASY

MEASUREMENTS

57 in. (145 cm) by 4½ in. (11.4 cm)

MATERIALS

2

Fine

Blue Heron Yarns Sock Plus (80% merino wool, 20% nylon; 4 oz./113 g; 420 yd./384 m)

» Blue Violet: 1 skein

» U.S. size H-8 (5 mm) crochet hook
» Tapestry needle
» Blocking pins
» Blocking board or towel

GAUGE

14 sts and 9 rows in dc = 4 in. (10.2 cm), blocked.

For gauge swatch, ch 25. Last 3 chs count as first dc on Row 1.

Row 1: Dc in fourth ch from hook and in each ch across. Total 23 dc.

Row 2: Ch 3 (counts as dc), turn. Sk st at base of chs. Dc in each remaining st across.

Rep Row 2 until swatch measures at least 4½ in. (11.4 cm).

Pattern

Ch 21.

Row 1 (RS): Sc in second ch from hook and in next ch. *Ch 6, sk 4 chs, sc in each of next 2 chs. Rep from * across.

Row 2: Ch 3 (counts as dc), turn. Sk st at base of chs, dc into next sc. *Ch 2, sc into ch-6 arch, ch 2, dc in each of next 2 sc. Rep from * across.

Row 3: Ch 3, turn. Sk st at base of chs. Dc into next dc. *Ch 3, sl st in next sc, ch 3, dc in each of next 2 dc. Rep from * across, working last dc into top of tch.

Row 4: Ch 1, turn. Sc in each of first 2 dc. *Ch 4, sc in each of next 2 dc. Rep from * across, working last sc into top of tch.

Row 5: Ch 1, turn. Sc in each of first 2 sc. *Ch 6, sc in each of next 2 sc. Rep from * across.

Rows 6–153: Rep Rows 2–5 thirty-seven times.

Rows 154–156: Rep Rows 2–4. Do not fasten off.

BORDER

Round 1: Ch 1, turn. Sc in each of first 2 sc. *4 sc in ch-4 sp, sc in each of next 2 sc. Rep from * across. Work 2 additional sc in corner. Sc evenly down side, across bottom (4 sc in each ch-6 sp, sc in each sc on bottom), and up other side of scarf, working 3 sc in each corner. Join to ch-1 with sl st.

Round 2: Ch 1, turn. Sc down side, across bottom, up other side, and across top of scarf, working 3 sc in each corner. Join to ch-1 with sl st. Fasten off.

FINISHING

With tapestry needle, weave in ends. Wet block to size and shape.

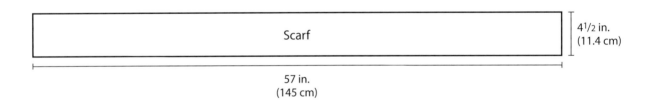

Scarf

4¹/₂ in. (11.4 cm)

57 in. (145 cm)

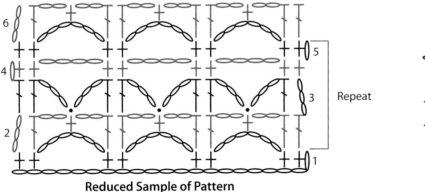

Reduced Sample of Pattern

Key

◯ = Chain (ch)

• = Slip stitch (sl st)

+ = Single crochet (sc)

┬ = Double crochet (dc)

Palmy Cardigan

Designed by Rhonda Davis

This light, airy cardigan with three-quarter sleeves has lots of swingy movement thanks to the silk yarn and short-row shaping.

SKILL LEVEL

EXPERIENCED

MEASUREMENTS

To fit 30 (34, 38, 42) in./76.2 (86.4, 96.5, 106.7) cm bust.

	CHEST	LENGTH
X-Small	34 in. (86.4 cm)	27 in. (68.6 cm)
Small	38 in. (96.5 cm)	28 in. (71.1 cm)
Medium	42 in. (106.7 cm)	30 in. (76.2 cm)
Large	46 in. (116.8 cm)	31 in. (78.4 cm)

Instructions are for size XS, with sizes S, M, and L in parentheses.

MATERIALS

Hamilton Yarns Heaven's Hand Sister Silk (100% mulberry silk; 1.7 oz./50 g; 131 yd./120 m)
» Acorn: 8 (9, 11, 12) skeins

» U.S. size G-6 (4 mm) crochet hook or size needed to obtain gauge
» Stitch markers (6)
» Tapestry needle
» Blocking pins
» Blocking board or towel

GAUGE

23 stitches and 10 rows in Pattern Stitch = 4 in. (10.1 cm), blocked.
For gauge swatch, ch 39.
Row 1: Hdc in fifth ch from hook. *Ch 1, sk ch, hdc in next ch. Rep from * across.

Row 2: Ch 2, turn. Hdc in ch-1 sp. *Ch 1, sk hdc, hdc in ch-1 sp. Rep from * across, ending with hdc in last st. (You will have 2 hdc next to each other at the end of the row.)
Row 3: Ch 3, turn. Sk hdc, hdc in ch-1 sp. *Ch 1, sk hdc, hdc in ch-1 sp. Rep from * across, working final hdc into top of turning ch.
Rep Rows 2 and 3 until swatch measures at least 5 in. (12.7 cm).

SPECIAL STITCHES

Half double crochet 2 together (hdc2tog)

Yo, insert hook where instructed, yo, pull up lp (3 lps on hook), yo, insert hook where instructed, yo, pull up lp (5 lps on hook), yo, pull through all 5 lps.

NOTE: *In this pattern, hd2tog is worked over two consecutive ch-sps, skipping over the hdc in between. This decreases the st count by 2 because you are combining 2 ch-sps and 1 hdc into one st.*

PATTERN NOTES

» The cardigan is worked from the bottom up, and begins with the border. Next, the body is worked with short row shaping. The center back is narrow because the upper bodice/sleeves are set in. The upper bodice/sleeves are worked from the top sleeve neckline border down to the cuff, then attached to the body.

» Beg ch-2 counts as hdc unless otherwise indicated.

» Beg ch-3 counts as (hdc, ch) unless otherwise indicated.

» Beg ch-5 counts as (dc, ch 2) unless otherwise indicated.

» Hdc2tog is worked over two consecutive ch-sps, skipping the hdc in between.

» When a stitch count for a row is given, it includes all stitches, including chain stitches and slip stitches.

» When working Body, remove markers when you are several rows past them.

Pattern

BORDER

Ch 338 (374, 410, 446).

Row 1: Sc in second ch from hook. *Sk next 2 chs, dc in next ch, ch 3, work 3 dc around stem of dc just made, sk 2 chs, sc in next ch. Rep from * across.

Row 2: Ch 5, turn. Sk 3 dc, sc under ch-3, ch 2, dc in sc. *Ch 2, sk 3 dc, sc under ch-3, ch 2, dc in sc. Rep from * across.

Row 3: Ch 1, turn, sc in dc. *Dc in next sc, ch 3, work 3 dc around stem of dc just made, sc in next dc. Rep from * across, working final sc in third ch of ch-5.

Row 4: Rep Row 2.

Row 5: Ch 1, turn. Sl st into each sc, ch, and dc across, working final 3 sl sts into 3 chs of ch-5. Total 337 (373, 409, 445) sl sts. Avoid making sl sts too tight since the next row will be worked into them.

Row 6: Ch 2, turn. Hdc in each of next 3 sts, ch 2, sk next 2 sts, hdc, ch 2, sk next 2 sts. *Hdc in each of next 7 sts, ch 2, sk next 2 sts, hdc, ch 2, sk next 2 sts. Rep from * across, ending with hdc in each of last 4 sts.

BODY

Row 7: Ch 3, turn. Sk next hdc, hdc in next hdc, ch 1, sk next hdc.* Hdc into ch-2 sp, ch 1, hdc into next hdc, ch 1, hdc into ch-2 sp, [ch 1, sk next hdc, hdc in next hdc] 3 times, ch 1, sk next hdc. Rep from * across until 2 ch-2 sps

Row 13: Ch 3, turn. [Hdc in next ch-sp, ch 1] 5 (7, 10, 13) times. *Hdc2tog over next 2 ch-sps, ch 1. [Hdc in next ch-sp, ch 1] 10 times. Rep from * 11 (12, 13, 14) times. Hdc2tog over next 2 ch-sps, ch 1. [Hdc in next ch-sp, ch 1] across, hdc in top of tch.

Short Row 14: Ch 2, turn. [Hdc in next ch-sp, ch 1] 45 (48, 51, 54) times, PM around ch just made. [Hdc in next ch-sp, ch 1] 55 (65, 75, 85) times, sl st in ch-sp, PM in same ch-sp.

Short Row 15: Rep Row 10.

Short Row 16: Ch 1, turn, sk (ch-1 sp, hdc). [Hdc in ch-sp, ch 1] 54 (64, 74, 84) times. The rest of the row is worked into Row 13. Hdc in same ch-sp as M, ch 1. [Hdc in ch-sp, ch 1] across until 1 ch-sp remains. Hdc in ch-sp, hdc in top of tch.

Row 17: Ch 3, turn. [Hdc in ch-sp, ch 1] 97 (110, 123, 136) times. The rest of the row is worked into Row 14. Hdc in same ch-sp as M, ch 1. [Hdc in ch-sp, ch 1] across, hdc in top of tch.

Row 18: Ch 2, turn. [Hdc in ch-sp, ch 1] 4 (7, 9, 12) times. *Hdc2tog over next 2 ch-sps, ch 1. [Hdc in next ch-sp, ch 1] 9 times. Rep from * 11 (12, 13, 14) times. Hdc2tog over next 2 ch-sps, ch 1. [Hdc in next ch-sp, ch 1] across until 1 ch-sp remains. Hdc in ch-sp, hdc in top of tch.

Short Row 19: Ch 3, turn, sk next st. [Hdc in next ch-sp, ch 1] 36 (38, 41, 43) times, PM around ch just made. [Hdc in next ch-sp, ch 1] 55 (65, 75, 85) times, sl st in ch-sp, PM in same ch-sp.

Short Row 20: Rep Row 10.

Short Row 21: Ch 1, turn, sk (sl st, ch, hdc), [Hdc in next ch-sp, ch 1] 54 (64, 74, 84) times. The rest of the row is worked into Row 18. Hdc in same sp as M, ch 1. [Hdc in next ch-sp, ch 1] across, hdc in top of tch.

Row 22: Ch 2, turn [Hdc in next ch-sp, ch 1] 93 (106, 118, 131) times. The rest of the row is worked into Row 19. Hdc in same ch-sp as M, ch 1. [Hdc in next ch-sp, ch 1] across until 1 ch-sp remains. Hdc in ch-sp, hdc in top of tch.

Row 23: Ch 3, turn. [Hdc in next ch-sp, ch 1] 4 (6, 9, 12) times. *Hdc2tog over next 2 ch-sps, ch 1. [Hdc in next ch-sp, ch 1] 8 times. Rep from * 11 (12, 13, 14) times. Hdc2tog over next 2 ch-sps, ch 1. [Hdc in next ch-sp, ch 1] across, hdc in top of tch.

Short Row 24: Ch 2, turn. [Hdc in next ch-sp, ch 1] 30 (32, 34, 36) times, hdc in ch-sp, ch 1, PM around ch just made. [Hdc in next ch-sp, ch 1] 55 (65, 75, 85) times, sl st in ch-sp, PM in same ch-sp.

Short Row 25: Rep Row 10.

Short Row 26: Ch 1, turn, sk (ch-1 sp, hdc). [Hdc in ch-sp, ch 1] 54 (64, 74, 84) times. The rest of the row is worked into Row 23. Hdc in same ch-sp as M, ch 1. [Hdc in ch-sp, ch 1] across until 1 ch-sp remains. Hdc in ch-sp, hdc in top of tch.

Row 27: Ch 3, turn, [Hdc in ch-sp, ch 1] 86 (98, 110, 122) times. The rest of the row is worked into Row 24. Hdc in same ch-sp as M, ch 1. [Hdc in ch-sp, ch 1] across, hdc in top of tch.

remain. Hdc in ch-2 sp, ch 1, hdc into next hdc, hdc in ch-2 sp, ch 1, sk hdc, dc in next hdc, sk hdc, hdc in top of tch.

Row 8: Ch 2, turn. [Hdc in next ch-sp, ch 1] 6 (8, 10, 12) times. *Hdc2tog over next 2 ch-sps, ch 1. [Hdc in next ch-sp, ch 1] 12 times. Rep from * 10 (11, 12, 13) times. Hdc2tog over next 2 ch-sps, ch 1. [Hdc in next ch-sp, ch 1] until 1 ch-sp remains. Hdc in ch-sp, hdc in top of tch.

Short Row 9: Ch 3, turn. [Hdc in next ch-sp, ch 1] 50 (53, 57, 60) times. PM around ch just made. [Hdc in next ch-sp, ch 1] 55 (65, 75, 85) times. Sl st in ch-sp, PM in same ch-sp.

Short Row 10: Ch 1, turn. Sk (sl st, ch-sp, hdc). [Hdc in next ch-sp, ch 1] 54 (64, 74, 84) times. Sl st in next ch-sp.

Short Row 11: Ch 1, turn, sk (sl st, ch 1, hdc). [Hdc in next ch-sp, ch 1] 54 (64, 74, 84) times. The rest of the row is worked into Row 8. Hdc in same ch-sp as M, ch 1. [Hdc in next ch-sp, ch 1] across, hdc in top of tch.

Row 12: Ch 2, turn. [Hdc in ch-sp, ch 1] 105 (118, 132, 145) times. The rest of the row is worked into Row 9. Hdc in same ch-sp as M, ch 1. [Hdc in ch-sp, ch 1] until 1 ch-sp remains. Hdc in ch-sp, hdc in top of tch.

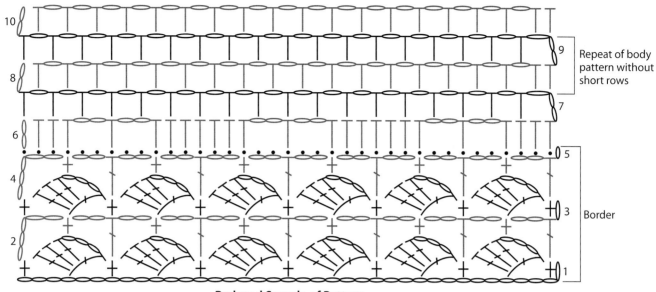

Reduced Sample of Pattern

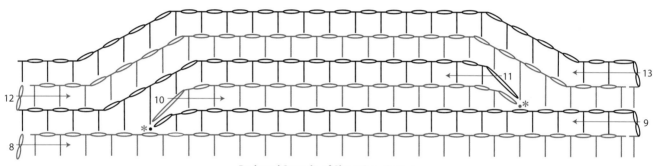

Reduced Sample of Short Row Pattern

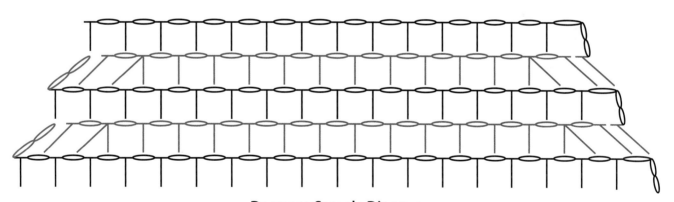

Decrease Sample Diagram

Key

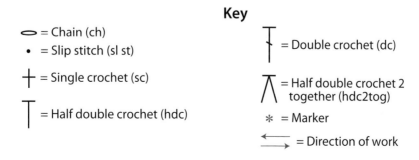

= Chain (ch)

• = Slip stitch (sl st)

╋ = Single crochet (sc)

┬ = Half double crochet (hdc)

┬ = Double crochet (dc)

⋀ = Half double crochet 2 together (hdc2tog)

＊ = Marker

⟵ = Direction of work

Row 28: Ch 2, turn. [Hdc in ch-sp, ch 1] 3 (6, 8, 11) times. *Hdc2tog over next 2 ch-sps, ch 1. [Hdc in next ch-sp, ch 1] 7 times. Rep from * 11 (12, 13, 14) times. Hdc2tog over next 2 ch-sps, ch 1. [Hdc in next ch-sp, ch 1] across until 1 ch-sp remains. Hdc in ch-sp, hdc in top of tch.

Short Row 29: Ch 3, turn, sk next st. [Hdc in next ch-sp, ch 1] 24 (25, 27, 28) times. PM around ch just made. [Hdc in next ch-sp, ch 1] 55 (65, 75, 85) times, sl st in ch-sp, PM in same ch-sp.

Short Row 30: Rep Row 10.

Short Row 31: Ch 1, turn, sk (sl st, ch, hdc), [Hdc in next ch-sp, ch 1] 54 (64, 74, 84) times. The rest of the row is worked into Row 28. Hdc in same sp as M, ch 1. [Hdc in next ch-sp, ch 1] across, hdc in top of tch.

Row 32: Ch 2, turn. [Hdc in next ch-sp, ch 1] 79 (91, 102, 114) times. The rest of the row is worked into Row 29. Hdc in same ch-sp as M, ch 1. [Hdc in next ch-sp, ch 1] across until 1 ch-sp remains. Hdc in ch-sp, hdc in top of tch.

Row 33: Ch 3, turn. [Hdc in next ch-sp, ch 1] 3 (5, 8, 11) times. *Hdc2tog over next 2 ch-sps, ch 1. [Hdc in next ch-sp, ch 1] 6 times. Rep from * 11 (12, 13, 14) times. Hdc2tog over next 2 ch-sps, ch 1. [Hdc in next ch-sp, ch 1] across, hdc in top of tch.

Short Row 34: Ch 2, turn. [Hdc in next ch-sp, ch 1] 17 (18, 19, 20) times, hdc in ch-sp, ch 1, PM around ch just made. [Hdc in next ch-sp, ch 1] 55 (65, 75, 85) times, sl st in ch-sp, PM in same ch-sp.

Short Row 35: Rep Row 10.

Short Row 36: Ch 1, turn, sk (ch-1 sp, hdc). [Hdc in ch-sp, ch 1] 54 (64, 74, 84) times. The rest of the row is worked into Row 33. Hdc in same ch-sp as M, ch 1. [Hdc in ch-sp, ch 1] across until 1 ch-sp remains. Hdc in ch-sp, hdc in top of tch.

Row 37: Ch 3, turn, [Hdc in ch-sp, ch 1] 73 (84, 95, 106) times. Return to Row 34. Hdc in same ch-sp as M, ch 1. [Hdc in ch-sp, ch 1] across, hdc in top of tch.

Row 38: Ch 2, turn. [Hdc in ch-sp, ch 1] 2 (5, 7, 10) times. *Hdc2tog over next 2 ch-sps, ch 1. [Hdc in next ch-sp, ch 1] 5 times. Rep from * 11 (12, 13, 14) times. Hdc2tog over next 2 ch-sps, ch 1. [Hdc in next ch-sp, ch 1] across until 1 ch-sp remains. Hdc in next ch-sp, hdc in top of tch.

Short Row 39: Ch 3, turn, sk next st. [Hdc in next ch-sp, ch 1] 11 (11, 12, 12) times, PM around ch just made. [Hdc in next ch-sp, ch 1] 55 (65, 75, 85) times, sl st in ch-sp, PM in same ch-sp.

Short Row 40: Rep Row 10.

Short Row 41: Ch 1, turn, sk (sl st, ch, hdc), [Hdc in next ch-sp, ch 1] 54 (64, 74, 84) times. The rest of the row is worked into Row 38. Hdc in same sp as M, ch 1. [Hdc in next ch-sp, ch 1] across, hdc in top of tch.

Row 42: Ch 2, turn. [Hdc in next ch-sp, ch 1] 66 (77, 87, 98) times. The rest of the row is worked on Row 39. Hdc in same ch-sp as M, ch 1. [Hdc in next ch-sp, ch 1] across until 1 ch-sp remains. Hdc in ch-sp, hdc in top of tch.

Row 43: Ch 3, turn. [Hdc in next ch-sp, ch 1] 2 (4, 7, 10) times. *Hdc2tog over next 2 ch-sps, ch 1. [Hdc in next ch-sp, ch

1] 4 times. Rep from * 11 (12, 13, 14) times. Hdc2tog over next 2 ch-sps, ch 1. [Hdc in next ch-sp, ch 1] across, hdc in top of tch.

Sizes M, L only

Row 44: Ch 2, turn. [Hdc in next ch-sp, ch 1] 84 (94) across until 1 ch-sp remains. Hdc in ch-sp, hdc in top of tch.

Row 45: Ch 3, turn. [Hdc in next ch-sp, ch 1] across, hdc in top of tch.

All Sizes

Row 44 (44, 46, 46): Ch 2, turn. [Hdc in ch-sp, ch 1] until 1 ch-sp remains. Hdc in ch-sp, hdc in top of tch.

Row 45 (45, 47, 47): Ch 2, turn, hdc in next 3 sts, ch 2, sk next st, hdc, ch 2, sk next st, *hdc in next 7 sts, ch 2, sk next st, hdc, ch 2, sk next st. Rep from * across, ending with hdc in last 4 sts.

Row 46 (46, 48, 48): Ch 1, turn. Sl st into each hdc and ch across. 157 (181, 205, 229) sts.

Row 47 (47, 49, 49): Ch 1, turn, sc in first st. *Sk next 2 sts, dc in next st, ch 3, work 3 dc around stem of dc just made, sk 2 sts, sc in next st. Rep from * across. Total 26 (30, 34, 38) squares.

Row 48 (48, 50, 50): Ch 5, turn. Sk 3 dc, sc under ch-3, ch 2, dc in sc. *Ch 2, sk 3 dc, sc under ch-3, ch 2, dc in sc. Rep from * across.

Row 49 (49, 51, 51): Ch 1, turn, sc in first st. *Dc in next sc, ch 3, work 3 dc around stem of dc just made, sc in next dc. Rep from * across, working final sc in third ch of ch-5.

Row 50 (50, 52, 52): Rep Row 48. Fasten off.

BACK

With the RS facing, find the exact middle of Row 50 (50, 52, 52), in the dc between 2 squares. Count 3 (4, 5, 6) dc to the right (skipping over the squares); place Marker A. Count 3 (4, 5, 6) dc to the left (skipping over the squares); place Marker B.

Row 1: With RS facing, attach yarn at A. Ch 3. [Hdc in next ch-sp, ch 1, hdc in sc, ch 1, hdc in ch-2p, ch 1, hdc in dc, ch 1] across, ending with hdc at Marker B.

Row 2: Ch 2, turn. [Hdc in ch-sp, ch 1] across until 1 ch-sp remains. Hdc in ch-sp, hdc in tch.

Row 3: Ch 3 (counts as hdc, ch 1), turn. [Hdc in next ch-1 sp, ch 1] across, ending with hdc in top of tch.

Rows 4–17 (4–19, 4–23, 4–25): Rep Rows 2 and 3. Fasten off.

SLEEVE (make 2)

NOTE: Sleeve is worked from the shoulder down.

Ch 86 (98, 110, 122).

Row 1: Hdc in third ch from hook, hdc in next 2 ch, ch 2, sk next 2 ch, hdc, ch 2, sk next 2 ch, *hdc in next 7 ch, ch 2, sk next 2 ch, hdc, ch 2, sk next 2 ch. Rep from * across, ending with hdc in last 4 chs.

Row 2: Ch 1, turn. Sl st into each hdc and ch across. Avoid making sl sts too tight. Next row will be worked into this row.

Row 3: Ch 1, turn, sc in first st. *Sk next 2 sts, dc in next st, ch 3, work 3 dc around stem of dc just made, sk 2 sts, sc in next st. Rep from * across. Total 14 (18, 22, 26) squares.

Row 4: Ch 5, turn. Sk 3 dc, sc under ch-3, ch 2, dc in sc. *Ch 2, sk 3 dc, sc under ch-3, ch 2, dc in sc. Rep from * across.

Row 5: Ch 1, turn, sc in dc. *Dc in next sc, ch 3, work 3 dc around stem of dc just made, sc in next dc. Rep from * across, working final sc in third ch of ch-5. Total 14 (18, 22, 26) squares.

Row 6: Rep Row 4.

Row 7: Ch 1, turn. Sl st into each dc, ch, and sc across, working final st into the third ch of ch-5. Avoid making sl sts too tight. Next row will be worked into this row.

Row 8: Ch 2, turn (counts as hdc), hdc in next 3 sts, ch 2, sk next 2 sts, hdc, ch 2, sk next 2 sts, *hdc in next 7 sts, ch 2, sk next 2 sts, hdc, ch 2, sk next 2 sts. Rep from * across, ending with hdc in last 4 sts.

Row 9: Ch 3, turn, sk next hdc, hdc in next hdc, ch 1, sk next hdc.*Hdc into ch-2 sp, ch 1, hdc into next hdc, ch 1, hdc into ch-2 sp, [ch 1, sk next hdc, hdc in next hdc] 3 times, ch 1, sk next hdc. Rep from * across until 1 ch-2 sp remains. Hdc in ch-2 sp, ch 1, sk hdc, hdc into next hdc, ch 1, sk hdc, hdc in top of tch.

Row 10: Ch 2, turn. [Hdc in next ch-1 sp, ch] across until 1 ch-sp remains. Hdc in ch-sp, hdc in top of tch.

Row 11: Ch 3, turn. [Hdc in next ch-1 sp, ch 1] across, ending with hdc in top of tch.

Rows 12--7 (12–19, 12–21, 12–23): Rep Rows 10 and 11. PM at beg and end of Row 17 (19, 21, 23).

Sizes XS, S, M only
Row 18 (20, 22): Ch 2, turn. [Hdc in next ch-sp, ch 1]. Hdc2tog, ch 1. [Hdc in next ch-sp, ch 1] across to last 6 sts. Hdc2tog, ch 1. Hdc in last ch-sp, hdc in top of tch.

Size L only
Row 24: Ch 2, turn, [Hdc in next ch-sp, ch 1]. [Hdc2tog, ch 1] 2 times. [Hdc in next ch-sp, ch 1] across to last 10 sts. [Hdc2tog, ch 1] twice. Hdc in last ch-sp, hdc in top of tch.

All Sizes
Rows 19–21 (21–23, 23–25, 25–27): Rep Rows 11 and 10, ending with rep of Row 11.

Row 22 (24, 26, 28): Ch 2, turn. Hdc in next ch-sp, ch 1. Hdc2tog, ch 1. [Hdc in next ch-sp, ch 1] across to last 6 sts. Hdc2tog, ch 1. Hdc in last ch-sp, hdc in top of tch.

Rows 23–25 (25–27, 27–29, 29–31): Rep Rows 11 and 10, ending with rep of Row 11.

Rows 26–41 (28–43, 30–45, 32–47): Rep Rows 22–25 (24–27, 26–29, 28–31).

Rows 42–46 (44–47, 46–51, 48–53): Rep Rows 11 and 10, ending with rep of Row 11.

Sizes S, M, L only
Row 48 (52, 54): Ch 2, turn. [Hdc in next ch-sp, ch 1] 17 (18, 22) times, hdc2tog 1 (2, 1) time(s), ch 1, [Hdc in next ch-sp, ch 1] until 1 ch-sp remains. Hdc in ch-sp, hdc in top of tch.

All Sizes

Row 47 (49, 53, 55): Ch 2, turn. Hdc in each of next 3 sts, ch 2, sk next st, hdc, ch 2, sk next st. *Hdc in each of next 7 sts, ch 2, sk next st, hdc, ch 2, sk next st. Rep from * across, ending with hdc in each of last 4 sts.

Row 48 (50, 54, 56): Rep Row 2.

Row 49 (51, 55, 57): Rep Row 3. Total 12 (14, 16, 18) squares.

Row 50 (52, 56, 58): Rep Row 4.

Row 51 (53, 57, 59): Rep Row 5. Total 12 (14, 16, 18) squares.

Row 52 (54, 58, 60): Rep Row 6. Fasten off.

SEAMING

> **NOTE:** *The sleeves encompass some of the body and back. To create the shoulder, a portion of the sleeves stick up above the front and back. (Refer to schematics.)*

ATTACH RIGHT SLEEVE TO BACK AND BODY

With RS of sleeve and back facing, position sleeve so that the corner of the sleeve meets Marker A. Count 7 (8, 9, 10) squares up the sleeve. (There will be a row of hdc and ch-sps to the left of those squares.) Attach sleeve to top of back at that position. Seam in place from WS.

From Marker A, count 6 (7, 8, 9) dc to the right (skipping over the squares). Match up Row 17 of sleeve here. Seam from A across to that point from WS.

ATTACH LEFT SLEEVE TO BACK AND BODY

With RS of sleeve and back facing, position sleeve so that the corner of the sleeve meets Marker B. Count 7 (8, 9, 10) squares up the sleeve. (There will be a row of hdc and ch-sps to the right of those squares.) Attach sleeve to top of back at that position. Seam in place from WS.

From Marker B, count 6 (7, 8, 9) dc to the left (skipping over the squares). Match up Row 17 of sleeve here. Seam from B across to that point from WS.

ATTACH RIGHT SLEEVE TO FRONT BODY

Position sweater so that the RS of the front is facing (front of sweater is folded over like it would be if you were wearing it). Join bottom corner of sleeve to top corner of front body. Join Row 17 of sleeve to match where Row 17 of the back of the sleeve attaches the body. Sew seam from WS.

ATTACH LEFT SLEEVE TO FRONT BODY

Rep as for Right Sleeve.

SEW RIGHT SLEEVE SEAM

With WS facing, sew rest of sleeve closed.

SEW LEFT SLEEVE SEAM

Rep as for Right Sleeve.

FINISHING

With tapestry needle, weave in remaining ends. Wet block to finished dimensions.

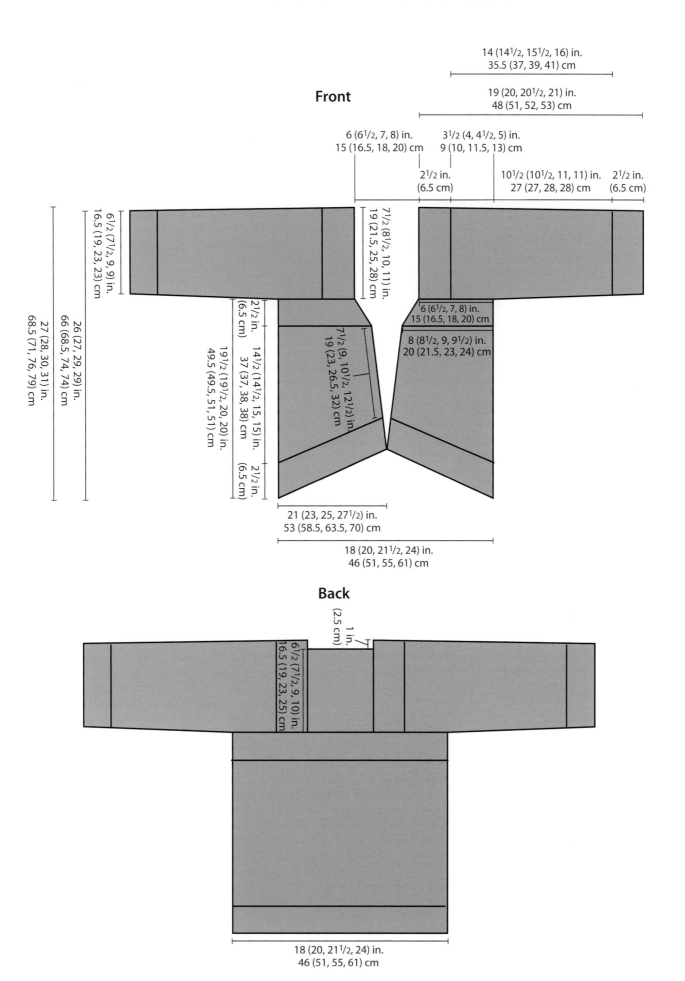

Front

14 (14½, 15½, 16) in.
35.5 (37, 39, 41) cm

19 (20, 20½, 21) in.
48 (51, 52, 53) cm

6 (6½, 7, 8) in.
15 (16.5, 18, 20) cm

3½ (4, 4½, 5) in.
9 (10, 11.5, 13) cm

2½ in.
(6.5 cm)

10½ (10½, 11, 11) in.
27 (27, 28, 28) cm

2½ in.
(6.5 cm)

7½ (8½, 10, 11) in.
19 (21.5, 25, 28) cm

6½ (7½, 9, 9) in.
16.5 (19, 23, 23) cm

27 (28, 30, 31) in.
68.5 (71, 76, 79) cm

26 (27, 29, 29) in.
66 (68.5, 74, 74) cm

6 (6½, 7, 8) in.
15 (16.5, 18, 20) cm

8 (8½, 9, 9½) in.
20 (21.5, 23, 24) cm

2½ in.
(6.5 cm)

7½ (9, 10½, 12½) in.
19 (23, 26.5, 32) cm

14½ (14½, 15, 15) in.
37 (37, 38, 38) cm

19½ (19½, 20, 20) in.
49.5 (49.5, 51, 51) cm

2½ in.
(6.5 cm)

21 (23, 25, 27½) in.
53 (58.5, 63.5, 70) cm

18 (20, 21½, 24) in.
46 (51, 55, 61) cm

Back

1 in.
(2.5 cm)

6½ (7½, 9, 10) in.
16.5 (19, 23, 25) cm

18 (20, 21½, 24) in.
46 (51, 55, 61) cm

*Peacock
Lace Shawl*

Designed by Sharon Silverman

This top-down shawl worked in broomstick lace has openwork areas that look like the "eyes" on peacock feathers.

SKILL LEVEL

EASY

MEASUREMENTS

80 in. (203 cm) across the top, 18 in. (46 cm) across the bottom, by 10 in. (25.5 cm).

MATERIALS

Manos del Uruguay Fino (70% extrafine merino wool, 30% silk; 3.5 oz./100 g; 490 yd./450 m)
» Watered Silk (404): 1 skein

» U.S. size H-8 (5 mm) crochet hook
» Size 19 knitting needle (15 mm)
» Tapestry needle
» Blocking pins
» Blocking board or towel

GAUGE

16 st and 10 rows in dc = 4 in. (10.2 cm), blocked.
For gauge swatch, ch 27. Last 3 chs count as first dc on Row 1.
Row 1: Dc in fourth ch from hook and in each ch across.
Row 2: Ch 3 (counts as dc), turn. Sk st at base of chs. Dc in each st across.
Rep Row 2 until swatch measures at least 4½ in. (11.4 cm).

SPECIAL STITCHES

Broomstick Lace: Broomstick lace is a 2-row pattern, the loop row and the stitch row, created with a crochet hook and a knitting needle. The RS of the work always faces you. (This pattern turns the work at the end of the stitch row to allow you to sl st into position; the work is then turned again so the RS is facing you for the loop row.)

Moving one direction, loops are pulled up and added onto the knitting needle. This is the loop row. At the end of the row, the loops are slipped off the needle.

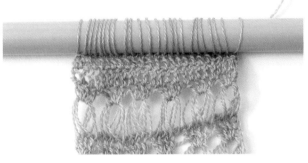

Moving back the other direction, groups of loops are gathered with crochet stitches. This is the stitch row. You can use any crochet stitch on the stitch row; this pattern uses dc.

PATTERN NOTES

» Shawl is worked from the top down.
» You may find it easier to hold the knitting needle in place by sticking it under your arm or leg.
» Loops are live when you slip them off the knitting needle. Be careful not to snag one or it will pull the adjacent loops.
» Only the first st of the first group on the stitch row needs to be anchored with a ch.

Pattern

Ch 301.

Row 1 (RS): Sc in second ch from hook and in each ch across. Total 300 sc.

Row 2 (loop row): Pull up the loop that's on the hook so it is big enough to slip on to the knitting needle. Do not twist the lp. Slip it onto the knitting needle, remove crochet hook, and tighten the lp. *Insert hook in the next sc. Yo, pull up lp, slip lp onto knitting needle, remove crochet hook from lp. Repeat from * across. Total 300 lps on knitting needle.

Row 3 (stitch row): Slip all of the lps off the knitting needle. Insert crochet hook through first 4 lps, yo, pull up lp, ch 1 to lock stitch. Ch 3 (counts as dc). Work 3 more dc into the same place. *4 dc into next group of 4 lps. Repeat from * across. Total 75 broomstick clusters.

Row 4: Ch 1, turn. Sl st loosely in each of the first 21 sts. Turn again so RS is facing you. Ch 1, pull up that lp, slip it onto the knitting needle. Pull up lp in each st across, leaving final 20 dc unworked.

Row 5: Rep Row 3. Total 65 broomstick clusters.
Row 6: Rep Row 4.
Row 7: Rep Row 3. Total 55 broomstick clusters.
Row 8: Rep Row 4.
Row 9: Rep Row 3. Total 45 broomstick clusters.
Row 10: Rep Row 4.
Row 11: Rep Row 3. Total 35 broomstick clusters.
Row 12: Rep Row 4.
Row 13: Rep Row 3. Total 25 broomstick clusters.
Row 14: Rep Row 4.
Row 15: Rep Row 3. Total 15 broomstick clusters. Fasten off.

FINISHING

With tapestry needle, weave in ends. Wet block to size and shape.

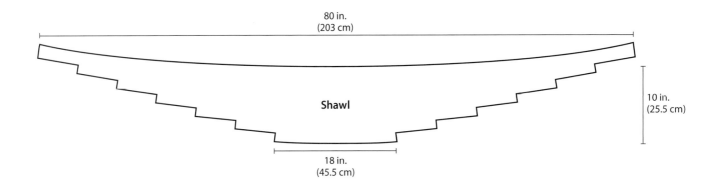

Shawl

80 in.
(203 cm)

10 in.
(25.5 cm)

18 in.
(45.5 cm)

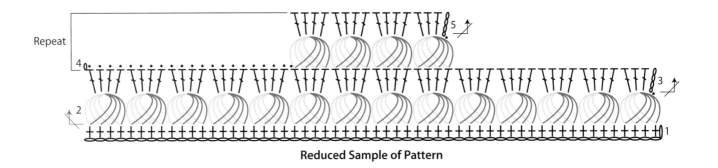

Repeat

Reduced Sample of Pattern

Key

 = Chain (ch)

• = Slip stitch (sl st)

+ = Single crochet (sc)

T = Double crochet (dc)

= 4 broomstick lace loops

= Do not turn

Sea and Shells Poncho

Designed by Karen McKenna

This Tunisian crochet garment uses several stitch patterns worked in a comfortable cotton blend yarn. Aquatic colors alternate with crisp white to make this poncho just the thing for cool summer evenings.

SKILL LEVEL

INTERMEDIATE

MEASUREMENTS

48 in. wide (122 cm) by 22 in. (56 cm) from shoulder to hem. Neck opening is 10 in. (25.5 cm).

MATERIALS

2 Fine

Premier Yarns Cotton Fair (52% cotton, 48% acrylic; 3.5 oz./100 g; 317 yd./290 m)
» **A:** White (27-01): 3 balls
» **B:** Cloud Gazing (32-04): 4 balls
» U.S. size H-8 (5 mm) Tunisian crochet hook (or size needed to obtain gauge)
» Stitch markers (4)
» Tapestry needle
» Blocking pins
» Blocking board or towel

GAUGE

16 sts and 8 rows in Tdc = 4 in. (10.2 cm), blocked.
For gauge swatch: With A, ch 27.
Row 1 (RS): Insert hook in back bump of second ch from hook, yo, pull up lp. *Insert hook in back bump of next ch, yo, pull up lp. Rep from * across. Total 27 lps on hook. Return.
Row 2: Ch 1. *Tdc in next vertical bar. Rep from * across. Return.
Rep Row 2 until swatch measures at least 4½ in. (11.4 cm).

SPECIAL STITCHES

Tunisian double crochet (Tdc): Yo, insert hook as for Tss, yo, pull up lp, yo, pull through 2 lps. Each st adds 1 lp to the hook.

PATTERN NOTES

» Skip vertical bar (at starting edge of work) on each row unless instructed otherwise.
» Always work the last stitch on the forward pass into the final vertical bar and the horizontal bar behind it for stability.
» The standard return pass is as follows: Yo, pull through 1 lp. *Yo, pull through 2 lps. Rep from * until 1 lp remains on hook. Work a standard return unless instructed to do otherwise. Nonstandard returns are explained in the pattern instructions.
» To change colors, work return pass until just before final pull-through. Drop first color, yo with new color, complete final pull-through with new color. Cut first color, leaving a 4-in. (10.2 cm) tail. Continue working with the new color.
» Poncho is made in two panels then seamed at shoulders.

Pattern

PONCHO PANEL (make 2)

With A, ch 197.
Row 1: Insert hook in back bump of second ch from hook, yo, pull up lp. *Insert hook in back bump of next ch, yo, pull up lp. Rep from * across. Total 197 lps on hook. Return.
Row 2 forward: Ch 3. *[Tss, yo, Tss] in next st, yo, pull through 3 lps, ch 1, sk 1 st. Rep from * across until 2 sts remain. [Tss, yo, Tss] in next st, yo, pull through 3 lps, ch 1. Tss in last st, ch 2. Total 100 lps on hook.

Row 2 Return: Yo, pull through 1 lp. *Yo, pull through 2 lps, ch 1. Rep from * until 3 lps remain on hook. [Yo, pull through 2 lps] twice.

Row 3: *Tss in next st (in the lp above the cluster), insert hook under top lp of next ch, yo, pull up lp. Rep from * across, working final st into the top of the ch-2 from Row 2. Total 197 lps on hook. Return.

Rows 4–5: Rep Rows 2 and 3. Change to B when 2 lps remain on hook at end of Row 5 return.

Row 6: Ch 1. *Tdc in next st. Rep from * across. Total 197 lps on hook. Return.

Rows 7–9: Rep Row 6. Change to A when 2 lps remain on hook at end of Row 9 return.

Row 10 forward: Ch 1. *Tdc in next st. Rep from * across. Total 197 lps on hook.

Row 10 Return: Ch 1, yo, pull through 4 lps, ch 3, yo, pull through 6 lps. *Ch 4, yo, pull through 6 lps. Rep from * until 4 lps remain on hook. Ch 3, yo, pull through 4 lps.

***NOTE:** Row 10 has a partial cluster along the right-hand edge, then 38 full clusters, then a partial cluster, ch, and Tdc at the left-hand edge.*

The first ch to the left of each full or partial cluster can be tight. Stretch your stitches gently on Row 11 forward to make sure you do not inadvertently skip over those chs.

Row 11 forward: Ch 1, Tdc in top of PCL, Tdc in each of next 3 chs (5 lps on hook so far). *Tdc in top of next CL, Tdc in each of next 4 chs. Rep from * until 1 full CL and 1 PCL remain. Tdc in top of CL, Tdc in each of next 3 chs, Tdc in top of PCL, Tdc in next ch and in final Tdc. Total 197 lps on hook.

Row 11 Return: Ch 1, yo, pull through 4 lps, ch 3, yo, pull through 6 lps. *Ch 4, yo, pull through 6 lps. Rep from * until 4 lps remain on hook. Ch 3, yo, pull through 4 lps. Change to B before last pull-through on return pass.

Row 12: Ch 1. Tdc in top of PCL, Tdc in each of next 3 chs (5 lps on hook so far). *Tdc in top of next CL, Tdc in each of next 4 chs. Rep from * until 1 full CL and 1 PCL remain. Tdc in top of CL, Tdc in each of next 3 chs, Tdc in top of PCL, Tdc in next ch and in final Tdc. Total 197 lps on hook. Return.

Rows 13-15: Rep Rows 7–9. Change to A when 2 lps remain on hook at end of Row 15 return.

Row 16: Sk first vertical bar. *Tss in next st. Repeat from * across. Return.

Rows 17–20: Rep Rows 2–5. Change to B when 2 lps remain on hook at end of Row 20 return.

Rows 21–24: Rep Rows 6–9. Change to A when 2 lps remain on hook at end of Row 24 return.

Rows 25–26: Rep Rows 10–11. Change to B before last pull-through on return pass.

Rows 27–30: Rep Row 12–15. Change to A when 2 lps remain on hook at end of Row 30 return.

Row 31: Rep Row 16.

Rows 32–35: Repeat Rows 2–5. Change to B when 2 lps remain on hook at end of Row 35 return.

Rows 36–39: Rep Rows 6–9. Change to A when 2 lps remain on hook at end of Row 39 return.

Row 40: Sk first vertical bar. *Tss in next st. Rep from * across. Return. Fasten off.

FINISHING

With tapestry needle, weave in ends. Wet block each piece, pinning it to the correct size. Let dry completely before unpinning it from the board or towel.

PM in the 78th and 119th sts along the top row of each panel to mark the edges of the neck opening. With RS together, use A to whipstitch the first shoulder seam, starting at marker and working toward the edge of the garment. Repeat for other side. Weave in ends.

EDGING

With RS facing, join B at bottom corner. Sc evenly along row ends up the side, over the seam, and down the other side. Fasten off.

NOTE: Because not all rows are the same height, you will not have the same number of sc along each row-end. Try to keep the stitches approximately the same distance apart. If the edging starts to ruffle, you have too many sts; if it puckers, too few. The suggested number of sc from hem to shoulder seam is 63 to keep the edging flat.

Rep for other side of poncho. Weave in ends. Gently block if desired.

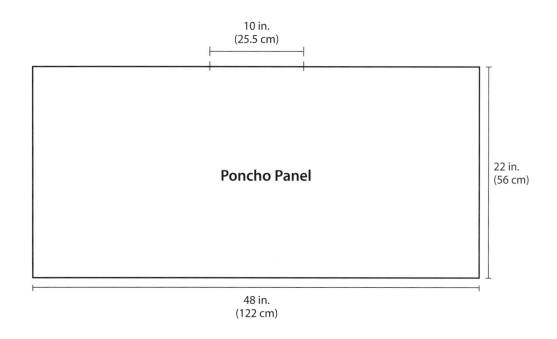

Poncho Panel

10 in.
(25.5 cm)

22 in.
(56 cm)

48 in.
(122 cm)

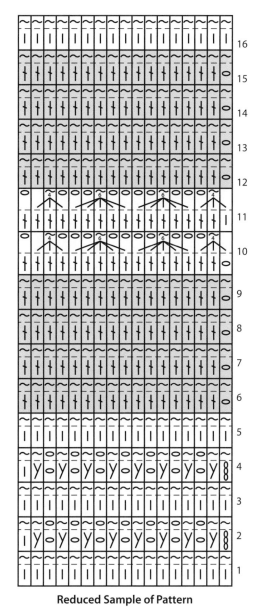

Reduced Sample of Pattern

Key

FORWARD SYMBOLS

| = Tunisian Simple Stitch (Tss)

† = Tunisian double crochet (Tdc)

○ = ch 1

Y = Tss, ch 1, Tss

⁸ = ch 3

RETURN SYMBOLS

~ = yo, draw through 1 lp for first st, yo, draw through 2 lps for each rem st

○ = ch 1

= yo, draw through 4 lps on hook

= yo, draw through 6 lps on hook

COLOR KEY

☐ = A

▨ = B

Yveline Wrap

Designed by Vashti Braha

A simple Tunisian crochet mesh in offset rows gives this wrap its interesting angles, while airy bubble-like frills of miniature love knots add textural highlights to its dynamic drape.

SKILL LEVEL

INTERMEDIATE

MEASUREMENTS

20 in. (51 cm) by 55 in. (140 cm)

MATERIALS

2 Fine — DesigningVashti.com Lotus (52% cotton, 48% rayon; 3.5 oz./100 g; 256 yd./235 m)
  » **A:** Carbonite #0006: 512 yds, or 2 balls

2 Fine — DesigningVashti.com Lotus Snack (52% cotton, 48% rayon; 1.16 oz./33 g; 85 yd./77.7 m)
  » **B:** Pearly Pearl #0001: 1 ball
  » **C:** Lustrous Tan #0007: 1 ball
  » **D:** Satin Grey #0003: 1 ball
  » **E:** Carbonite #0006: 1 ball
» U.S. size J-10 (6 mm) Tunisian crochet hook, either rigid or with a flexible plastic extension, that totals at least 12 in. (30.5 cm) long
» U.S. size G-7 (4.5 mm) regular crochet hook for edging
» U.S. size I-9 (5.5 mm) regular crochet hook for edging
» Stitch marker (4)
» Tapestry needle
» Blocking pins
» Blocking board or towel

GAUGE

14 sts (3.5 st reps) and 6 rows in Tunisian offset mesh pattern = 4 in. (10.2 cm), blocked.

For gauge swatch, with Tunisian crochet hook ch 23.

Row 1 (RS): Tss into second ch from hook and in each ch across, inserting hook under 2 lps of each ch. Total 23 lps on hook. Return.

Row 2: Ch 1 (counts as first Tes), Tes in first st (along edge), Tss in next Tss. *2 Tyo, sk next 2 Tss, Tss in each of next 2 Tss, rep from * until 5 Tss remain. 2 Tyo, sk next 2 Tss, Tss in next Tss, Tss2tog in the vertical bars of the last 2 Tss, ch 1. Total 23 lps on hook. PM in last loop on hook. Return.

Row 3: Ch 1, Tes in first st (along edge), Tss in next Tes. *2 Tyo, sk next Tss and Tyo, Tss in diagonal strand of next Tyo, Tss in next Tss. Rep from * until 5 sts remain (1 Tss, a 2-Tyo sp, and 2 Tss). 2 Tyo, sk next Tss and Tyo, Tss in next Tyo, Tss-2tog in next Tss and marked loop of last st, ch 1. Total 23 lps on hook. MM to last loop on hook. Return.

Rep Row 3 until swatch measures at least 4½ in. (11.4 cm).

***NOTE:** Each row runs diagonally, so it is longer than the distance from side to side of swatch (i.e., the wearable width of wrap).*

SPECIAL STITCHES

Love Knot (LK), also known as Solomon's Knot:

1. Pull up the lp on your hook to just under ½ in. (1.2 cm) long.

2. Pinch the bottom of the stitch so the lp does not move. Yo, pull through lp on hook to make a loose ch.

3. Sc in the sp between the yarn coming from the skein and the lp (into the bump of the ch just made).

Tunisian Decrease/Tunisian Simple Stitch 2 Together (Tss-2tog): Insert hook under the vertical bar of next st and in the designated loop of the following st, yo, pull up a loop.

Tunisian Extended Stitch (Tes): Insert hook under front vertical bar of a Tunisian st, yo, pull up a lp, ch 1.

Tunisian Yarn Over (Tyo): Yo, leave the lp on hook as a st. After the return pass is completed, the front vertical bar of the Tyo looks like a diagonal strand wrapping around the front of the return pass ch sts.

PATTERN NOTES

» Wrap is crocheted of Tunisian crochet rows in the main color, starting at one short end. Each row is offset by one stitch, resulting in a parallelogram. Ruffle-like love knots in contrasting colors are then surface-crocheted along selected stitch columns.

» In this project you will work into the stitch along the leading edge. This is different than in most Tunisian crochet items. You will also join two stitches together at the far end. This balanced increase at the beginning and decrease at the end creates the parallelogram.

» Standard return is worked as follows: Yo, pull through 1 lp, *yo, pull through 2 lps. Rep from * until 1 lp remains on hook.

» Make sure the lps do not overlap and get out of order on the return. Stretch them out on the hook as needed to keep them in the proper order.

Pattern

With A and Tunisian crochet hook, ch 87.

Row 1 (RS): Tss into second ch from hook and in each ch across, inserting hook under 2 lps of each ch. Total 87 lps on hook. Return.

Row 2: Ch 1 (counts as first Tes), Tes in first st (along edge), Tss in next Tss. *2 Tyo, sk next 2 Tss, Tss in each of next 2 Tss. Rep from * until 5 Tss remain. 2 Tyo, sk next 2 Tss, Tss in next Tss, Tss2tog in the vertical bars of the last 2 Tss, ch 1. PM in last loop on hook. Return.

2 yo

The 2 yo are followed by sk 2 Tss, Tss in each of next 2 Tss

End of Row 2 return

Row 3: Ch 1, Tes in first st (along edge), Tss in next Tes, *2 Tyo, sk next Tss and Tyo, Tss in diagonal strand of next Tyo, Tss in next Tss. Rep from * until 5 sts remain (a Tss, a 2-Tyo sp, a Tss, and a Tes2tog). 2 Tyo, sk next Tss and Tyo, Tss in next Tyo, Tss2tog in next Tss and marked loop of last st, ch 1. Total 87 lps on hook. MM to last lp of row. Return.

Work into this diagonal strand of the second Tyo

End of Row 3 forward

End of Row 3 return

Rows 4–82: Rep Row 3.

Row 83: Switch to regular crochet hook size I-9 (5.5 mm). Ch 1, sc in front vertical bar of first Tss, sc in front vertical bar of next Tss, *[sc in front "vertical" bar of next Tyo] twice, [sc in front vertical bar of next Tss] twice. Repeat from * across, placing last sc in 2 lps of the last Tss. Fasten off.

EDGING AND EMBELLISHMENTS
EDGE FIRST ROW (RS)

With regular crochet hook size I-9 (5.5 mm), attach A with sl st in the free lp of first foundation ch to crochet along the opposite edge of Row 1. Ch 1, sl st in the free lp of each remaining foundation ch. Fasten off.

With tapestry needle, weave in ends. Block to finished dimensions. Let dry completely before adding the surface frills.

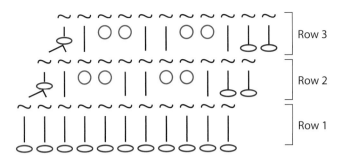

Key

$\varnothing$ = Chain (ch)

$|$ = Tunisian simple stitch (Tss)

$\sim$ = Return pass

$\bigcirc$ = Tunisian yarn over (Tyo)

$\underline{|}$ = Tunisian extended stitch (Tes)

$\underset{\times}{\underline{|}}$ = Tunisian decrease/Tunisian simple stitch 2 together (Tss2tog)

SURFACE FRILLS

NOTE: *The first four frills are crocheted into return pass sts (the yo "openwork" areas, not the Tss) along a column from Row 1 to Row 82, across the top to the next return pass column, down that column in the return pass sts to Row 1, and then across the bottom to where you started. The other four are worked the same way but start at Row 82 and work down to Row 1, then across and back up. All work is done on the RS of the garment.*

Switch to regular crochet hook size G. Position the wrap so the RS of Row 1 is facing you. Count over to the fourth st from the leading edge (leading edge counts as 1) and attach B. *Ch 1 tightly, LK, ch 1 tightly, sl st in the equivalent st of the next row above. Rep from * in each remaining row up to and including Row 82.

Now work across 2 sts along the top of Row 82 (these are both Tss). (Ch 1 tightly, LK, ch 1 tightly, sl st) in each of those 2 sts. Rotate your work so you can move down the next column. (Ch 1 tightly, LK, ch 1 tightly, sl st) in the return pass of the next row below until you reach Row 1. Work across back toward where you started. (Ch 1 tightly, LK, ch 1 tightly) in each of next 2 sts, sl st to beginning sl st to join. Fasten off.

Rep the frills with colors C, D, and E. C starts in st 12, D starts in st 20, E starts in st 28.

Rotate garment so RS of final row is facing you. Attaching yarn in Row 82 (not the sc sts of Row 83), rep frills to mirror the completed ones. B starts in the fourth st from the leading edge, C starts in st 12, D starts in st 20, E starts in st 28

FINISHING

With tapestry needle, weave in ends. Mist lightly and block gently to avoid crushing the frills.

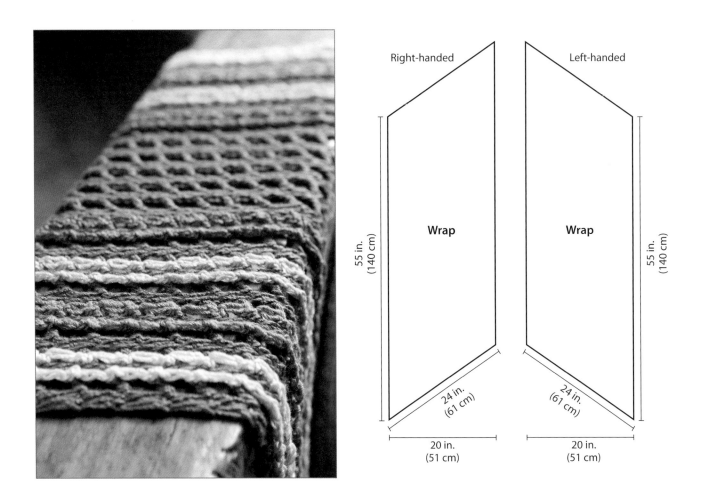

Right-handed

Left-handed

Wrap

Wrap

55 in.
(140 cm)

55 in.
(140 cm)

24 in.
(61 cm)

24 in.
(61 cm)

20 in.
(51 cm)

20 in.
(51 cm)

Ziggy Vest

Designed by Vashti Braha

Turn a simple rectangle of Tunisian lace into a fashionable vest by opening the armholes *after* you've finished crocheting it. This airy ripple stitch pattern takes advantage of how easy it is to "steek" (open a hole by cutting) it. Don't be scared! Everyone who tries this technique loves how easy and liberating it is.

SKILL LEVEL

EXPERIENCED

MEASUREMENTS (BLOCKED)

	BUST	LENGTH
X-Small	31 in. (78.5 cm)	20 in. (51 cm)
Small	35 in. (89 cm)	20½ in. (52 cm)
Medium	38¾ in. (98.5 cm)	20½ in. (52 cm)
Large	42½ in. (108 cm)	22 in. (56 cm)

Instructions are for size XS, with sizes S, M, and L in parentheses.

MATERIALS

2 Fine

DesigningVashti.com Lotus (52% cotton, 48% rayon; 3.5 oz./ 100 g; 256 yd./ 235 m)
  » Teal Glimmer #023: 630 (710, 790, 920) yds., or 3 (3, 4, 4) balls
» U.S. size J-10 (6 mm) Tunisian crochet hook, either rigid or with a flexible plastic extension, that totals at least 12 in. (30.5 cm) long
» U.S. size H-8 (5 mm) regular crochet hook for edging
» Stitch markers (4)
» Small sharp scissors
» Tapestry needle
» Spray bottle for misting
» Blocking pins
» Blocking board or towel

GAUGE

16 Return pass sts and 6.25 rows in Tunisian ripple lace pattern = 4 in. (10.2 cm), blocked.
For gauge swatch, ch 26. Last 2 chs count as first Teks.

NOTE: *Row 1 sts won't resemble Teks until the next row is begun. See Special Stitches.*

Row 1: With Tunisian crochet hook, Teks in second ch from hook. [Sk next ch, Teks in next ch] 3 times. *Sk next ch, 3 Teks in next ch, [sk next ch, Teks in next ch] 3 times. Rep from * until 2 chs remain. Sk next ch, 2 Teks in last ch, ch 1 for edge. PM in ch just made. Total 19 loops on hook. Lacy Return (see Special Stitches).

Row 2: Ch 1, Teks in first (edge) Teks, Teks in next Teks, Teks in center Teks of the Teks3tog, Teks in next Teks. *3 Teks in next Teks, Teks in next Teks, Teks in center Teks of Teks3tog, Teks in next Teks. Rep from * until last Teks remains, 2 Teks in outermost 2 lps of marked ch of Teks, ch 1 for edge, MM. Total 19 lps on hook. Lacy Return.

NOTE: *Only work into the center Teks of the Teks3tog; do not work in the sts on either side of the center one.*

MM up to the ch 1 on the edge as you go.
Repeat Row 2 until swatch measures at least 4½ in. (11.4 cm).

SPECIAL STITCHES

Double Crochet Decrease/Double crochet 3 together (dc3tog): [Yo, insert hook in next st, yo, pull up lp, yo, pull through 2 lps] 3 times. Yo, pull through all 4 lps on hook for a net dec of 2 sts. Used for edging vest.

Lacy Return: Yo, pull through 1 lp (this third ch at the edge counts as first ch-space), yo, pull through 2 lps, yo, pull through 1 lp, yo, pull through 4 lps. *[Yo, pull through 1 lp, yo, pull through 2 lps] 3 times, yo, pull through 1 lp, yo, pull through 4 lps. Rep from * until 3 lps remain on hook, [yo, pull through 1 lp, yo, pull through 2 lps] twice.

Slip Stitch in Back Loop Only (sl st blo): Insert hook in thread of st that is farthest away from you, yo, pull through both lps.

Split Double Crochet Cluster (split-dc): Yo, insert hook in same st, yo, pull up lp, yo, pull through 2 lps on hook, yo, insert hook in next st, yo, pull up a lp, yo, pull through 2 lps on hook, yo, pull through all 3 lps on hook. Used for edging vest.

Split Half Double Crochet Cluster (split-hdc): Yo, insert hook in same st, yo, pull up a lp, yo, insert hook in next st, yo, pull up a lp, yo, pull through all 5 lps on hook. Used for edging vest armholes.

Tunisian Extended Knit Stitch (Teks): Insert hook between the front and back vertical bars of st as for Tks, yo, pull up lp, ch 1 and leave lp on hook. For Row 1, insert hook under 2 lps of a foundation ch, yo, pull up lp, ch 1 and leave lp on hook.

Tunisian Decrease/3 Tunisian Extended Knit Stitches Together (Teks3tog): Created during the Lacy Return when a group of 3 Teks is worked off the hook as 1: Yo, pull through 4 lps.

PATTERN NOTES

» Vest is worked side to side in one piece with no armholes.

» Armholes are added at the finishing stage by cutting one forward pass stitch lp. Teks sts are then slowly unraveled one at a time until armhole is desired size.

» The lacy ripple effect is created on the return pass by adding a ch-sp between some of the Teks and grouping other Teks together in threes.

» It is helpful to mist or lightly steam block your work every 15 rows or so as you go along to double-check your gauge and open up the Tunisian extended stitches. Leave the 2–3 rows closest to where you are currently working unblocked.

Pattern

VEST

Ch 122 (122, 122, 130).

Row 1: With Tunisian crochet hook, Teks in second ch from hook. [Sk next ch, Teks in next ch] 3 times. *Sk next ch, 3 Teks in next ch, [sk next ch, Teks in next ch] 3 times. Rep from * until 2 chs remain. Sk next ch, 2 Teks in last ch, ch 1 for edge and PM. Total 91 (91, 91, 97) loops on hook. Lacy Return.

Row 2: Ch 1, Teks in first (edge) Teks, Teks in next Teks, Teks in center Teks of the Teks3tog, Teks in next Teks. *3 Teks in next Teks, Teks in next Teks, Teks in center Teks of Teks3tog, Teks in next Teks. Rep from * until last Teks remains, 2 Teks in outermost 2 lps of marked ch of Teks, ch 1 for edge and PM. Total 91 (91, 91, 97) lps on hook. Lacy Return.

MM up to the ch 1 on the edge as you go.

> **NOTE:** *Only work into the center Teks of the Teks3tog; do not work in the sts on either side of the center one.*

The toothpick shows the center stitch, where you insert the hook

Here is that stitch after it is worked

End of forward pass

End of return pass

Rows 3–47 (3–51, 3–59, 3–61): Rep Row 2. Do not fasten off. Remove st marker. Switch to regular crochet hook and continue with edging.

EDGING

Rnd 1 (RS): With regular crochet hook, ch 3 (counts as first dc of round), dc between two vertical bars of first Teks (crochet into all Teks this way), dc in next ch-space (between same and next Teks), dc in next Teks, dc3tog over [next ch-space, next teks3tog, next ch-space], dc in next Teks. *Dc in next ch-space, 3 dc in next Teks, dc in next ch-space, dc in next Teks, dc3tog over [next ch-space, next teks3tog, next ch-space], dc in next Teks. Rep from * until last ch-space and Teks remain. Dc in ch-space, 2 dc in marked ch.

Edge second side (crochet all stitches around the post of each row-end st). Ch 2, dc around post of last dc. *Split-dc around same post and around post of edge Teks of next row, dc in same st. Rep from * for remaining rows, end with split-dc in Teks of last row and in first corner foundation ch, dc in same ch.

Edge third side (crochet all stitches in each ch-space and between the Teks base lps that wrap around a ch). Ch 2, 2 dc around post of last dc, dc in next ch-space. *Dc in base of next Teks, dc in next ch-space, 3 dc in base of next Teks, dc in next ch-space, dc in base of next Teks, dc3tog over [next ch-space, base of next teks3tog, next ch-space]. Rep from * until 5 Teks remain. Dc in base of next Teks, dc in next ch-space, 3 dc in base of next Teks, dc in next ch-space, dc in base of next Teks, dc in next ch-space, dc in last foundation ch at corner.

Edge fourth side: Ch 2, 2 dc around post of last dc. *Split-dc around same post and around post of edge Teks of next row, dc in same st. Rep from * across. In last corner, end with split-dc around Teks of last row and around starting ch-3 of round, dc around same ch-3, dc in top of same ch-3.

Round 2 (WS): Ch 1, turn. Sl st in each dc to corner.

***NOTE:** If your sts are much tighter than Round 1, switch to a larger hook until gauge matches.*

Edge second side: Ch 1, sl st in each ch of the ch-2, sl st in each of next 4 dc, ch 1. *Sl st in each of next 4 dc, sl st in next split-dc, sl st in each of next 3 dc, ch 1. Rep from * until 7 dc remain. Sl st in each dc.

Edge third side: Ch 1, sl st in each ch of the ch-2, ch 1, sl st in each dc to next corner.

Edge fourth side: Ch 1, sl st in each ch of the ch-2, sl st in each of next 4 dc, ch 1. *Sl st in each of next 4 dc, sl st in next split-dc, sl st in each of next 3 dc, ch 1, rep from * until 7 dc remain. Sl st in each dc. Ch 1, sl st to first sl st of round, fasten off. Spread out the base lps of the dc evenly.

FINISHING

BLOCK

Wet block to the finished dimensions. With RS facing you, the last Teks row is the scalloped Left Front edge of the vest, and the scalloped foundation row is the Right Front edge. One straight edge of your rectangle forms the top neck (collar) edge, and the other is the bottom hem of the vest. When the garment is finished, the collar will fold back and drape over the shoulders.

When blocking, stretch the return passes firmly from the top to bottom edge of the rectangle so that their length matches the finished vest Length measurement. Stretch the Teks sts to their full height so that the rectangle's width matches the finished Bust measurement. Let dry completely and leave fabric in the same position for creating the armholes.

OPEN ARMHOLES

Mark the position for the armholes: In the 15th (17th, 19th, 21st) Teks row, place Marker A in the Teks that is 10 (9½, 9½, 10) in. (25.4, 24.1, 24.1, 25.4 cm) down from the straight Neck edge. Along the same row (toward the hem), place Marker B in the Teks that is 8 (8½, 9, 9½) in. (20.3, 21.6, 22.9, 24.1 cm) from Marker A.

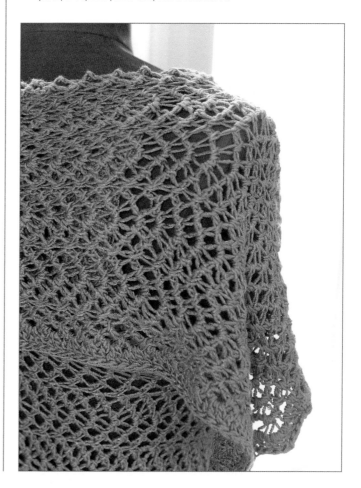

For the second armhole, place two markers—C and D—in the 15th (17th, 19th, 21st) Teks row from the last (47th, 53rd, 59th, 65th) Teks row. Marker C should be level with Marker A, in the Teks that is the same number of sts down from the Neck edge. Marker D should be level with Marker B, in the Teks that is the same number of sts down from Marker C.

NOTE: *Make sure Markers A and B are on the same row, and Markers C and D are on the same row. Markers A and C should be the same number of sts from the neck edge and the same number of rows from each scalloped edge of the rectangle; Markers B and D should be the same number of stitches away from A and C. Refer to schematic. Also make sure that the position of the armholes will give you the right size across your back. Check this again, because now is the moment of truth: time to steek!*

Keep the rectangle in its flat blocked position; do not lift it up. For the first armhole, cut one vertical bar of the Teks that is centered between Markers A and B. Unravel one Teks at a time between the markers. The stitches will not unravel on their own; use a tapestry needle to help pick out each stitch. Stop unraveling when you get to each marked Teks. Leave the ends long enough to weave in later. Do not remove markers.

Repeat for the armhole between Markers C and D.

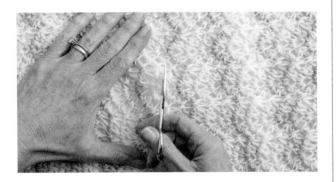

How to Steek a Teks

Snip that red X. Snip it.

EDGE ARMHOLES

Rnd 1 (RS): Using regular crochet hook, attach yarn with a sl st at Marker A, ch 2. [Split-hdc over the same st and the next st] evenly down the long side of the armhole, work additional 2 hdc around post of marked st, [split-hdc over the same st and the next st] evenly up other side of armhole, work additional 2 hdc around post of marked st. Sl st in top of ch-2 to join.

Rnd 2 (RS): Ch 1, do not turn. Sl st in blo of each split-hdc and hdc of round, sl st to join round. Fasten off.

Repeat Rounds 1 and 2 for second armhole, starting at Marker C.

With tapestry needle, weave in ends. Wet block to size and shape as necessary.

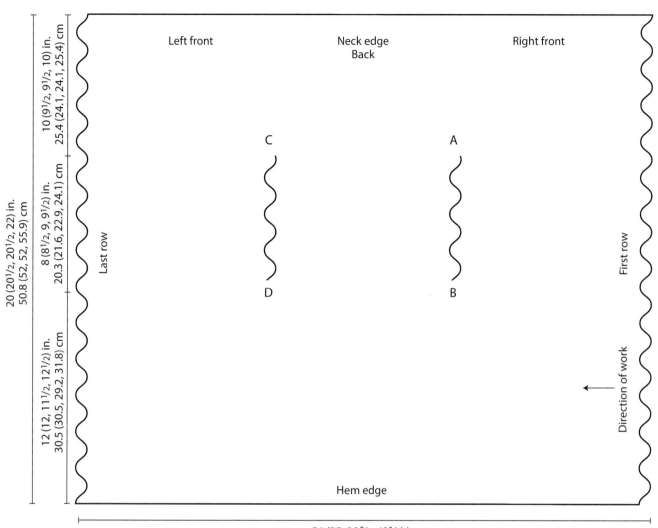

9¼ (10¾, 12, 13½) in.
23.5 (27.3, 30.5, 34.3) cm

12½ (13½, 14¾, 15½) in.
31.8 (34.3, 37.5, 39.4) cm

9¼ (10¾, 12, 13½) in.
23.5 (27.3, 30.5, 34.3) cm

Left front

Neck edge
Back

Right front

10 (9½, 9½, 10) in.
25.4 (24.1, 24.1, 25.4) cm

C

A

8 (8½, 9, 9½) in.
20.3 (21.6, 22.9, 24.1) cm

20 (20½, 20½, 22) in.
50.8 (52, 52, 55.9) cm

Last row

First row

D

B

12 (12, 11½, 12½) in.
30.5 (30.5, 29.2, 31.8) cm

Direction of work

Hem edge

31 (35, 38¾, 42½) in.
78.7 (88.9, 98.4, 108) cm

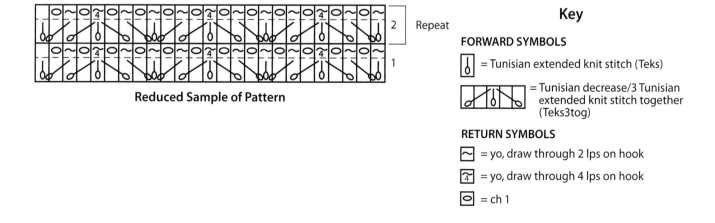

2   Repeat

1

Reduced Sample of Pattern

Key

FORWARD SYMBOLS

= Tunisian extended knit stitch (Teks)

= Tunisian decrease/3 Tunisian
extended knit stitch together
(Teks3tog)

RETURN SYMBOLS

= yo, draw through 2 lps on hook

= yo, draw through 4 lps on hook

= ch 1

TECHNIQUES

Traditional Crochet

In traditional crochet—the style most people are familiar with—only one stitch at a time is active. Each is worked to completion before the next stitch is begun. Stitch heights progress from the low-profile slip stitch through single crochet, half double crochet, double crochet, treble crochet, and beyond, based on how many times the yarn is wrapped around the hook and how the loops are pulled through other loops. Hooks for traditional crochet are usually 5 to 8 inches long and can be made of metal, plastic, bamboo, wood, or other materials.

CHAIN STITCH

1. Attach yarn to hook with slip knot. Yarn over, pull through.

FOUNDATION SINGLE CROCHET (FSC)

1. Ch 2 (does not count as fsc).
2. Insert hook into first ch made.

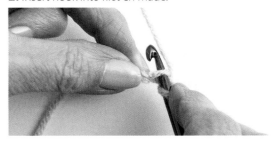

3. Yo, pull up lp.

4. Ch 1 (this will be the entry point—the foundation ch—for the next st; pinch it with your thumb and finger to make it easier to find), yo, pull through 2 loops to finish the single crochet.

5. Insert the hook into fch just made, yo, pull up lp.

6. Ch 1 (the entry point—the foundation ch—for the next st), yo, pull through 2 loops on hook to finish the fsc.

7. Rep from * until you reach the target number of fsc. The photo shows the entry point for the next fsc.

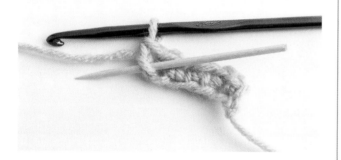

SLIP STITCH

1. Insert hook into work where instructed. (This stitch is often used to close a ring.)

2. Yarn over, pull through both loops.

SINGLE CROCHET

1. Insert hook into work where instructed. If you are working into the foundation chain, this will be the second chain from the hook.

2. Yarn over, pull up a loop.

3. Yarn over, pull through both loops.

HALF DOUBLE CROCHET

1. Yarn over.

2. Insert hook into work where instructed. If you are working into the foundation chain, this will be the third chain from the hook.

3. Yarn over, pull up a loop.

4. Yarn over, pull through all three loops.

DOUBLE CROCHET

1. Yarn over.

2. Insert hook into the work where instructed. If you are working into the foundation chain, this will be the fourth chain from the hook.

3. Yarn over, pull up a loop.

4. Yarn over, pull through two loops.

5. Yarn over, pull through remaining two loops.

TREBLE CROCHET

1. Yarn over twice.

2. Insert hook into the work where instructed. If you are working into the foundation chain, this will be the fifth chain from the hook. Yarn over, pull up a loop.

3. Yarn over, pull through two loops.

4. Yarn over, pull through two loops.

5. Yarn over, pull through remaining two loops.

CHANGE COLORS OR START A NEW YARN

1. Work in pattern as indicated. The photo shows double crochet fabric.

2. Work the next stitch until two loops remain on hook, no matter what type of stitch it is.

3. Drop the current yarn to the back. Yarn over with the new color and complete the stitch.

4. Continue to work with new yarn.

Tunisian Crochet

Tunisian crochet, also known as the "afghan stitch," combines aspects of crocheting and knitting. Like crocheting, it uses a hook and the same hand motions used in traditional crochet; as in knitting, loops are added to the hook so there are many active stitches at once. Tunisian crochet uses either a long hook with a stopper on the end or a shorter hook with a plastic extension to accommodate the many loops that will be on the hook at one time. Tunisian fabric can look knitted, woven, or textured and lacks the "loopy" appearance of traditional crochet.

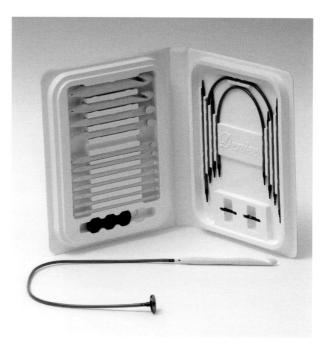

Here is a set of versatile Denise Interchangeable Crochet Hooks. Different size hooks can be attached to different lengths of plastic cord.

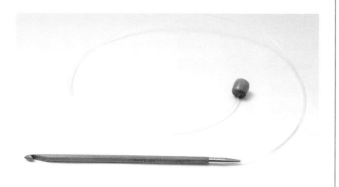
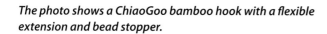

The photo shows a ChiaoGoo bamboo hook with a flexible extension and bead stopper.

Helpful Hints for Tunisian Crochet

- Never turn your work. The right side is always facing you.

- Always skip the first vertical bar.

- Pull the yarn snug at the start of each row to keep the edge from getting baggy.

- The final stitch on every forward pass should be a Tunisian simple stitch, regardless of the other stitches on that row.

- Work the final stitch on the forward pass into the vertical bar and the horizontal bar behind it for stability. If you turn that edge toward you, those two threads should look like a backwards 6 for right-handers and a regular 6 for lefties.

- Make sure you count the last stitch of the forward pass and the first stitch of the return pass separately.

- You can work any stitch into any other type of stitch (for example, Tunisian purl stitch into Tunisian knit stitch, or Tunisian simple stitch into Tunisian purl stitch, and so on).

- Count! Check your stitch count regularly to make sure you did not miss picking up a stitch on a forward pass or mistakenly pull through the wrong number of loops on a return pass.

- To reduce the curl in Tunisian crochet, work the foundation row into the back bumps of the starting chains. Working a border around the piece helps, too. To eliminate any remaining curl, gently steam block your finished pieces.

NOTE: *All Tunisian fabrics start with this basic row.*

Foundation Row Forward

1. Make the number of chain stitches indicated in the pattern.

NOTE: *The number of Tunisian stitches on subsequent rows will be the same as the number of chains you start with.*

2. Insert hook in second chain from hook. Yarn over, pull up loop. There will be two loops on the hook.

NOTE: *To minimize the curl in Tunisian crochet, you could work into the back bump of the chain. I usually put the stitches in the regular place, not the back bump, and rely on steam blocking to eliminate the curl.*

3. Insert hook in the next chain. Yarn over, pull up loop. Each stitch adds another loop to the hook.

4. Continue in this fashion all the way across.

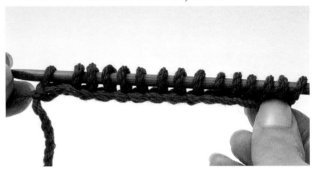

5. Count the loops. You should have the same number of loops on the hook as the number of foundation chains.

Foundation Row Return

1. Yarn over, pull through one loop.

2. Yarn over, pull through two loops.

3. Repeat Step 2 all the way across until one loop remains on the hook.

NOTE: This return method is referred to as the "standard return." Follow this procedure for the return pass unless instructed otherwise.

TUNISIAN SIMPLE STITCH

Work foundation row forward and return. Look at the finished stitches. You will see a vertical bar for each stitch. These bars are what you will work behind as you make the Tunisian simple stitch forward pass.

1. Skip the first vertical bar that is on the far right side, directly below the hook.

2. Put the hook from right to left through the next vertical bar. Keep the hook to the front of the work. Yarn over, pull up a loop. There will be two loops on the hook.

3. Repeat Step 2 in each stitch across (except for the far left bar), adding a loop to the hook with each stitch.
4. To work the final stitch, identify the final vertical bar and the horizontal thread that runs behind it. Insert the hook so it is behind both of these threads. When viewed from the side, the two threads look like a backwards 6 for right-handers and a regular 6 for lefties.

Yarn over, pull up a loop. Count the loops. You should have the same number as you did on the foundation row.
5. Work standard return.

The photo below shows Tunisian simple stitch fabric.

TUNISIAN KNIT STITCH

Work foundation row forward and return. Look at the finished stitches. Each stitch has two "legs" in an upside-down V shape. Instead of keeping the hook to the front like you did in Tunisian simple stitch, for Tunisian knit stitch you will poke the hook from front to back through the center of each stitch.

Forward Pass

1. Skip the first vertical bar that is on the far right side, directly below the hook.
2. Put the hook from front to back through the next stitch. (Stretch the stitch out slightly to see where the two vertical legs are; go right between them, not between two stitches.) Yarn over. Pull up a loop. There will be two loops on the hook.

The photo below shows the hook poking out the back.

3. Repeat Step 2 in each stitch across (except for the far left bar), adding a loop to the hook with each stitch.

4. To work the final stitch, identify the final vertical bar and the horizontal thread that runs behind it. Insert the hook so it is behind both of these threads. When viewed from the side, the two threads look like a backwards 6 for right-handers and a regular 6 for lefties.

NOTE: *Even though you are working in Tunisian knit stitch, the final stitch is a Tunisian simple stitch. This creates stability along the left side.*

Yarn over, pull up a loop. Count the loops. You should have the same number as you did on the foundation row.
5. Work standard return.
The photo shows Tunisian knit stitch fabric.

Here is what it looks like on the back.

CHANGE COLORS OR START A NEW YARN

Sometimes you will need to change colors for a stripe pattern. You will also need to start a new ball of yarn when the previous one runs out. The method is the same in both cases.

The ideal place to start a new yarn is at the end of a return pass.
1. Work return pass until two loops remain on hook. Drop first yarn to the back. Yarn over with new yarn.

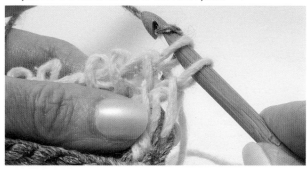

Pull through both loops.

Pull old and new tails firmly to hold stitches in place.
2. Continue working with the new yarn, making sure you are using the working end of the yarn and not the short tail.

NOTE: *You can also change colors at the beginning of a return pass. Simply lay the new yarn over the hook, leaving approximately a 3-inch tail, and begin the return pass with the new yarn.*

FINAL ROW

The top row of Tunisian crochet looks looser than the previous rows because nothing is worked into it. One way to end the piece neatly is to work single crochet stitches across the top of that row.

1. Insert your hook as you would for whatever stitch pattern you're using. In the example, this is Tunisian simple stitch.

2. Yarn over, pull up loop, yarn over, pull through two loops. This creates a single crochet.

3. Repeat Step 2 across.

Blocking Your Work

Blocking is an essential tool in giving your garments a professional finish. The technique uses water or steam to relax the fibers and set them to the desired size and shape.

Start by blocking your swatch to obtain an accurate gauge. This often-overlooked step can make the difference between a garment that fits and one that never gets worn.

The general recommendation is to block natural fibers with heat and steam, and to use cool water for synthetics, mohair, and novelty yarn. However, I have found that I can successfully use steam on any fiber as long as I hover the iron over the fabric without touching it. Steaming has the added advantages of softening most fibers and helping to ease the curl that some crocheted fabrics, especially Tunisian crochet, can suffer from.

To wet block your crochet work without using steam, spray it with cool water or soak it in cool water. Do not wring, just squeeze out the moisture gently. Place the pieces right-side down on a towel or blocking board. Pin to the appropriate size and shape using non-rusting pins. You can also use blocking wires to hold the edges of a garment in place while it dries. This is especially helpful with lace or picots. Leave in place until garment is completely dry, then remove the pins.

To steam block, place the pieces right-side down on a towel or blocking board. Pin as for wet blocking. Hover the steam iron above the fabric, allowing the steam to penetrate the fibers without touching them. (Put a thin cloth on top of the fabric if you are concerned that you might accidentally touch the fabric.) Allow to dry completely, then remove the pins.

Reading a Pattern

Before you begin working from a pattern, read through it thoroughly, paying particular attention to the information at the beginning such as yarn, gauge, special stitches or stitch patterns, and notes. There is a wealth of information here that will aid you throughout the project. Note and practice any unfamiliar stitches, and crochet a gauge swatch using the stitches indicated in the gauge section. Adjust your hook size if necessary to meet gauge; this will put you on your way toward a successful garment in the size you intend. (Gauge is fairly flexible for the projects in this book, but it's best to get as close as possible.)

Make sure that you are familiar with the abbreviations used in the pattern. Most crochet patterns use standard abbreviations, but there may be some that are particular to a pattern; these will be noted. Read the master list in the back of this book (page 163) to familiarize yourself with the standard abbreviations, then refer to it as necessary when working the projects.

Patterns use parentheses ( ) or brackets [ ] to enclose a sequence of instructions meant to be repeated, either into a stitch or in a series of stitches. After the closing parenthesis or bracket, you'll be told how many times to repeat the instructions. For example, "[2 dc in next dc, 1 ch] twice" means to work 2 double crochet stitches in the next double crochet (from the row below), then 1 chain stitch, then 2 double crochet stitches in the next double crochet, then 1 chain stitch. Sometimes parentheses are just for explanatory information. For example, "(the center of three double crochet stitches in the corner)" clarifies the position of the stitch the pattern is referring to.

An asterisk * means to work the instructions following it as many more times as indicated. Sometimes the instructions will say, for example, "*2 dc in next st, sc in next st. Repeat from * to end of row." You would do the [2 double crochet, 1 single crochet] pattern until you got to the end of the row.

Reading a Symbol Chart

Crochet instructions can be given in text or charts. A visual representation of a pattern can be very useful in understanding how the item is made.

Here are some guidelines when reading charts:

First, look at the key to see which symbols represent which stitches. Make sure you know how to make the specified stitches.

When you are crocheting in rows for regular or Tunisian crochet, the pattern is charted row by row from the bottom up, starting with the foundation chain. Read the chart starting at bottom left for the chain.

For regular crochet, turn your work at the end of each row, following the chart. Read Row 1 right to left, Row 2 left to right, and so on.

In general, the only time you will actually work into a chain stitch is on Row 1, when you work into the foundation chain. On subsequent rows, if the symbol for the stitch you are supposed to make appears above one or more chains, work that stitch into the chain space rather than the chain stitch itself (unless the pattern or chart specifically says otherwise).

For Tunisian crochet, each row is worked in two passes: the forward pass (indicated by moving right to left in the chart) and the return pass (indicated by moving left to right in the chart). Patterns are charted in pairs of rows, starting after the foundation is complete. The bottom row in each pair represents the forward pass; the top row in each pair indicates the return pass. Read the bottom row right to left; read the top row left to right. Do not turn your work. The loop on the hook at the beginning of every forward pass, called the first vertical bar, counts as a stitch and is represented in charts by a Tunisian simple stitch symbol. Do not work an additional stitch in that spot, unless you are instructed to do so.

When the final part of a Tunisian crochet project is worked in regular crochet stitches, treat that part of the chart as if it were for a regular crochet pattern.

When part of the pattern is repeated, that portion of the chart may be printed just once to save space.

Regular Crochet Sample Chart

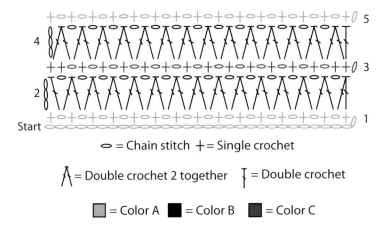

○ = Chain stitch   + = Single crochet

⋀ = Double crochet 2 together   ⊺ = Double crochet

■ = Color A   ■ = Color B   ■ = Color C

Tunisian Crochet Sample Chart

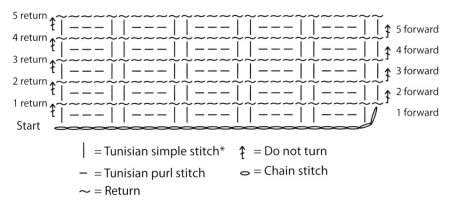

| = Tunisian simple stitch*   ↕ = Do not turn

– = Tunisian purl stitch   ○ = Chain stitch

∼ = Return

When this symbol is the first stitch in the row, it represents the loop already on the hook.

bch	beaded chain		patt	pattern
beg	beginning		PM	place marker
bet	between		rep	repeat
blo	back loop only		RS	right side
blp	beaded loop		sc	single crochet
ch(s)	chain(s)		sc2tog	single crochet 2 together
ch sp	chain space		sk	skip
CL	cluster		sl st(s)	slip stitch(es)
dc	double crochet		sp	space
dc2tog	double crochet 2 together		st(s)	stitch(es)
dc3tog	double crochet 3 together		tch	turning chain
dc4tog	double crochet 4 together		Tbs	Tunisian bar stitch
dec	decrease		Tes	Tunisian extended stitch
dtr	double treble crochet		Tks	Tunisian knit stitch
fsc	foundation single crochet		tog	together
hdc	half double crochet		tr	treble crochet
hdc3tog	half double crochet 3 sts together		tr2tog	treble 2 together
lp(s)	loop(s)		tr3tog	treble 3 together
M	marker		Tss	Tunisian simple stitch
MM	move marker		WS	wrong side
PCL	partial cluster		yo	yarn over

Resources

Crochet Hook Sizes

Millimeter Size	U.S. Size Range
2.25 mm	B-1
2.50 mm	
2.75 mm	C-2
3.125 mm	D
3.25 mm	D-3
3.50 mm	E-4
3.75 mm	F-5
4 mm	G-6
4.25 mm	G
4.50 mm	7
5 mm	H-8
5.25 mm	I
5.50 mm	I-9
5.75 mm	J
6 mm	J-10
6.50 mm	K-10½
7 mm	
8 mm	L-11
9 mm	M/N-13
10 mm	N/P-15
11.50 mm	P-16
12 mm	
15 mm	P/Q
15.75 mm	Q
16 mm	Q
19 mm	S
25 mm	T/U/X
30 mm	T/X

Skill Levels for Crochet

SKILL LEVELS FOR CROCHET

1	⬛⬜⬜⬜	**Beginner**	Projects for first-time crocheters using basic stitches. Minimal shaping.
2	⬛⬛⬜⬜	**Easy**	Projects using yarn with basic stitches, repetitive stitch patterns, simple color changes, and simple shaping and finishing.
3	⬛⬛⬛⬜	**Intermediate**	Projects using a variety of techniques, such as basic lace patterns or color patterns, mid-level shaping and finishing.
4	⬛⬛⬛⬛	**Experienced**	Projects with intricate stitch patterns, techniques, and dimension, such as non-repeating patterns, multicolor techniques, fine threads, small hooks, detailed shaping and refined finishing.

Standard Yarn Weight System

Yarn Weight Symbol & Category Names	0 LACE	1 SUPER FINE	2 FINE	3 LIGHT	4 MEDIUM	5 BULKY	6 SUPER BULKY	7 JUMBO
Type of Yarns in Category	Fingering, 10-Count Crochet Thread	Sock, Fingering, Baby	Sport, Baby	DK, Light Worsted	Worsted, Afghan, Aran	Chunky, Craft, Rug	Bulky, Roving	Jumbo, Roving

Books

Barnden, Betty. *The Crochet Stitch Bible*. Iola, WI: Krause Publications, 2004.

Chin, Lily. *Couture Crochet Workshop: Mastering Fit, Fashion, and Finesse*. Loveland, CO: Interweave Press, 2006.

Guzman, Kim. *Tunisian Crochet Stitch Guide*. Little Rock, AR: Leisure Arts, Inc., 2013.

Matthews, Anne. *Vogue Dictionary of Crochet Stitches*. Newton, UK: David & Charles, 1987.

Paden, Shirley. *Knitwear Design Workshop: A Comprehensive Guide to Handknits*. Loveland, CO: Interweave Press, 2009.

Reader's Digest. *The Ultimate Sourcebook of Knitting and Crochet Stitches*. Pleasantville, NY: Reader's Digest, 2003.

Silverman, Sharon Hernes. *Crochet Cowls*. Mechanicsburg, PA: Stackpole Books, 2016.

———. *Crochet Scarves*. Mechanicsburg, PA: Stackpole Books, 2012.

———. *Tunisian Crochet*. Mechanicsburg, PA: Stackpole Books, 2009.

Yarn

Blue Heron Yarns
www.blueheronyarns.com

Cascade Yarns
www.cascadeyarns.com

Debbie Bliss Ltd.
www.debbieblissonline.com

Designing Vashti
https://designingvashti.com

Hamilton Yarns LLC
www.hamiltonyarns.com

Knit Picks
www.knitpicks.com

Kristin Omdahl Yarn
www.kristinomdahl.com

Lang & Co. AG
www.langyarns.com

Make It Coats
www.makeitcoats.com/us

Malabrigo Yarn
www.malabrigoyarn.com

Manos del Uruguay
www.manosyarns.com

Plymouth Yarn Company, Inc.
www.plymouthyarn.com

Premier Yarns
www.premieryarns.com

SpaceCadet Creations
www.spacecadetyarn.com

Spinrite LP
www.yarnspirations.com

Tahki Stacy Charles, Inc.
www.tahkistacycharles.com

Hooks

ChiaoGoo/Westing Bridge LLC
www.chiaogoo.com

Denise Interchangeable Knitting and Crochet
www.knitdenise.com

Other Resources for Crocheters

Craft Yarn Council of America (CYCA)
The craft yarn industry's trade association has educational links and free projects.
www.craftyarncouncil.com

Crochet Guild of America (CGOA)
The national association for crocheters, CGOA sponsors conventions, offers correspondence courses, and maintains a membership directory.
www.crochet.org

Ravelry
This free online community for knitters, crocheters, and other fiber fans is *the* place to exchange information, manage projects, get advice on techniques, and keep up with everything yarn-related.
www.ravelry.com

VASHTI BRAHA

"I love to promote crochet as many things: an art, hobby, learning tool, and practical medium," says Vashti. "I do this with designs, classes, and my website. For my crochet newsletter I try to highlight what I don't see others writing about."

Vashti's information-rich newsletters enjoy a loyal readership, and her crochet classes consistently sell out. Vashti created DesigningVashti.com in 2010, and gave it a major makeover in 2017 to include her new crochet how-to videos and Lotus yarn shop.

Magazine editors have described Vashti's design style as "breezy," probably thanks to her sunny Florida studio. She started designing professionally in 2004 after attending a Crochet Guild of America conference. Her home page is https://designingvashti.com. Visit her Lotus yarn shop at https://designingvashti.com/product-category/yarns-kits/designingvashti-lotus-yarn/. You can find information about her classes at https://designingvashti.com/learn/vashti-crochet-classes/. Subscribe to Vashti's newsletter at https://designingvashti.com/newsletter/.

JUDITH BUTTERWORTH

Jude learned to crochet in her late teens. While in university in Canada, she often crocheted intead of doing readings and writing essays, putting off these school tasks to the last minute to pursue yet another stitch pattern. In spite of this, she obtained her master's degree in Philosophy with a special interest in deviant logic systems. She brings this same way of looking at things sideways to her work in crochet.

Jude's designs can be found on Ravelry (www.ravelry.com/designers/jude-butterworth) and Etsy (www.etsy.com/shop/IrreplaceableYou). She infrequently posts to her blog (www.randomthoughtsbyjude.blogspot.ca).

ROBYN CHACHULA

Robyn Chachula is the author of *Modern Vintage Crochet*, *Blueprint Crochet Sweaters*, *Unexpected Afghans*, *Crochet Stitches Visual Encyclopedia*, and more. Her work has been featured in several magazines, including *Interweave Crochet*, *Crochet!*, *Love of Crochet*, and *Vogue Crochet*.

Robyn is one of the crochet experts on the PBS show *Knit and Crochet Now!* She is an online crochet instructor at Annie's Craft Store and Interweave; her latest classes are "Learn Reversible Crochet" and "Irish Crochet Made Modern and Easy." All of Robyn's crochet inspiration comes from her little "office assistants" while out and about in Pittsburgh, Pennsylvania. Stop by crochetbyfaye.com to see what she has cooked up recently.

VICKY CHAN

A self-taught designer, Vicky is a left-brain thinker who craves right-brain activities. She lives with her wonderful husband in their cozy empty nest in Ontario, Canada.

Vicky learned to crochet and knit as a kid from her grandmother and her aunt one summer when she was bored and rowdy. Many summers later, in 2013, she unleashed her creativity and has been designing and publishing patterns independently ever since. Sadly, her husband still cannot tell the difference between crocheting and knitting. To Vicky's consolation, however, her delightful kids report that they enjoy their mother's work.

Drawn to beautiful flowers and plants (edible or not), Vicky often likes to incorporate botanical themes into her work. The lace elements in her designs disclose that she is secretly a romantic at heart, though her family and friends are likely to say otherwise.

You can find Vicky Chan at ravelry.com, loveknitting.com, lovecrochet.com, and https://vickychandesigns.wordpress.com.

RHONDA DAVIS

Rhonda "TurquoizBlue" Davis is a crochet designer, fiber artist, and instructor in Atlanta, Georgia. Her work has been featured in various publications, including *Interweave Crochet*, *Crochet World*, and *First Light* (Knit Picks). Rhonda also self-publishes her unique designs on her website at www.thisiscrochet.com. She is a professional member of the Crochet Guild of America, and she loves to use traditional techniques to create contemporary crochet fashion, accessories, and home decor.

In addition to her design work, Rhonda serves as a director on the board of the Southeast Fiber Arts Alliance (SEFAA), an organization that promotes fiber arts awareness and artists through education, events, and exhibitions. She has an MFA in digital media design and enjoys her career as a professional web designer/developer.

KAREN MCKENNA

Karen grew up in New Jersey, where she learned to crochet at age 9 from her grandmother. Many years later, Karen inherited her grandmother's books and hooks, which renewed her interest in crocheting.

Since then, Karen has designed for several yarn companies, including Cascade Yarns, Red Heart US and UK, Windy Valley Muskox, and Kraemer Yarns. Her designs have been published in *Crochet!*, *Crochet World,* and *Love of Crochet*. Karen's books include *Elegant Fashionable Chic Accessories to Crochet* and *In A Weekend Baby Blankets*, both from Annie's Publishing, and *Formal Jewelry to Crochet* and *Hand Picked—Design Your Own Gloves and Mittens,* published by Leisure Arts.

Karen and her husband have traveled extensively and now live in Florida.

When not on her bicycle or traveling, she can be found as I Hook Design on Ravelry, Instagram, and Facebook. Her website is IHookDesign.com.

MARTY MILLER

Marty (aka The Crochet Doctor) learned to crochet when she was 5 years old. Her teacher, Grandma Tillie, didn't read English, so instead of reading patterns, Mary learned how to look at objects and figure out how to design and crochet them. When her eighth-grade teacher taught the class to crochet granny squares, Marty came home and taught her mother how to make and assemble them—her mother was her very first student!

Marty had learned from her grandma that she loved crocheting and designing, and from her mother that she loved teaching. Now she does both: She teaches crochet everywhere from her local yarn shop to national venues, including the Crochet Guild of America's Chain Link conferences. Her Mastering Foundation Crochet Stitches is on Craftsy.com.

Marty is a nationally recognized crochet designer whose work has been published in magazines, books, and yarn company publication. She is the author of a Leisure Arts book, *Totes for all Reasons*. In addition, Marty is an editor and a technical editor. She writes articles on crochet techniques for various magazines. Marty served on the board of the Crochet Guild of America for four years, and is a past president.

When she has time, Marty posts on her two blogs: thecrochetdoctor.blogspot.com and notyourgrannys crochet-marty.blogspot.com. You can also catch her on Facebook: Marty Miller.

KATYA NOVIKOVA

Katya lives in Moscow, Russian Federation. "I started to crochet for my daughter when she was about 6 months old," she says. "Very soon it turned into an obsession." Now Katya never goes a day without crocheting. She primarily designs accessories and recently started to make crochet jewelry.

"My best inspiration is fiber," Katya says. "I always start out by choosing a yarn and letting it tell me what it wants to become."

Find out more about Katya on Ravelry (Katyanovikova). And, if you are too busy or lazy to crochet yourself, you can purchase her finished works at her Etsy shop, KatyaCrochetNest.

KRISTIN OMDAHL

Kristin Omdahl is a powerhouse in the yarn industry. Inspired by the beauty of the Florida coast that surrounds her, along with her love of mathematics, Kristin is both a crochet and knit designer. She's the author of fourteen books and hundreds of published patterns. Her award-winning YouTube channel (www.youtube .com/user/KristinOmdahl) provides in-depth tutorials and video resources for knitters and crocheters at all levels.

The Kristin Omdahl brand, which includes yarn and accessories, is all sustainable and thoughtfully sourced. Ever mindful of those in need, Project Kristin Cares donates a portion of every sale to benefit survivors of domestic violence.

Visit www.KristinOmdahl.com to learn more about how Kristin chooses to *create—share—inspire* every day.

AMY SOLOVAY

Amy is a freelance writer, pattern designer, and cat lover whose background is in textile design. She writes about crochet and other crafts for a variety of websites, including knittingandcrochet.net and crochet-books.com. Amy invites you to subscribe to her free crochet and knitting newsletter by visiting knitting andcrochet.net/newsletter/.

Amy began her textile design career as a print colorist for a manufacturer that supplied fabrics to the USA's major retailers. She was later promoted to knit designer and then design department stylist. Amy says, "I enjoyed learning how to forecast color and fashion trends. I still draw on my textile industry experience as I design new crochet patterns." You can keep up with Amy's latest projects, travel adventures and cute cat photos by visiting amysolovay .com/blog/.

Acknowledgments

"Many hands make light work," the saying goes, and in this case, many hands also made *Delicate Crochet*!

I am indebted to the ten amazing designers who agreed to submit original patterns for this book. Their creativity and hook skills are unparalleled. I also appreciate their patience with me (for whom "demanding" is an adjective that falls laughably short). Each one of them taught me new things about crocheting and about collaborating. Hats off to Vashti Braha, Judith Butterworth, Robyn Chachula, Vicky Chan, Rhonda Davis, Karen McKenna, Marty Miller, Katya Novikova, Kristin Omdahl, and Amy Solovay.

Symbol charts are helpful adjuncts to written instructions, but they are not easy to make. Kj Hay and Karen Manthey were indispensable in creating diagrams and schematics to supplement the ones submitted by the designers. I would never have met my manuscript deadline if I had tried to do those on my own.

For yarn support, thanks are due to Demian Savits of Blue Heron Yarns; Carly Waterman of Cascade Yarns; Bobbie Matela of Coats & Clark; Cornelia Tuttle Hamilton of Hamilton Yarns LLC; Stacey Winklepleck of Knit Picks; Katja Läuppi of Lang & Co. AG; Vanessa Ewing and Kaelin Hearn of Plymouth Yarn Company, Inc.; Sandra Rosner of Premier Yarns; Stephanie Alford of SpaceCadet Creations; Emily Stewart of Spinrite LP; Stacy Charles of Tahki Stacy Charles, Inc.; and Amy Gunderson of Universal Yarn. It has been a wonderful opportunity to work with their fine products.

The Stackpole Books team did a stellar job shepherding this book through the editorial and production process. Thanks to Candice Derr, editor, and Judith M. Schnell, publisher for Stackpole Books. The book's design and cover are due to the time and meticulous effort of Tessa Sweigert and Sally Rinehart. Thanks also to Caroline Stover for art preparation and Kristen Mellitt for guiding the book through the production process.

Daniel Shanken's photographs are works of art. I am deeply grateful for his participation in this project, and for his expertise in staging and taking pictures of the garments. Thanks also to the women who modeled the garments: Alexis Lebo, Nina Magnani, Aron Rook, and Shay Strawser. As is the case with all of my Stackpole crochet titles, I am indebted to photographer Alan Wycheck, whose technique photos are an essential part of the pattern instructions.

I am grateful to the Craft Yarn Council of America (CYCA) for permission to reprint standards, to the Crochet Guild of America (CGOA) for industry information and news, and to The National NeedleArts Association (TNNA) for its support of yarn industry professionals.

I could not have completed this project without the support and encouragement of my family and friends, especially my husband, Alan, and our sons, Jason and Steven. Not a day goes by without my thinking how much you mean to me. Thank you for everything.

Berrywine Wrap   2

Blox Shawl   7

Cyndi Floral Lace   12
Skirt

Damask Rose Wrap   19

Diamond Dreams   25
Scarf

Elegant Trios   30
Beaded Necklace

Filet Crochet Pullover 35

Fingerless Gloves   41

Flirt Cardigan   46

Gentle Whisper   58
Shawl

Hourglass Scarf   66

Iced Silver Fox   70
Sweater